GLOBAL

FINANCE AT

RISK

GLOBAL FINANCE AT RISK

The Case for International Regulation

JOHN EATWELL
LANCE TAYLOR

THE NEW PRESS   NEW YORK

© 2000 by John Eatwell and Lance Taylor

Library of Congress Cataloging-in-Publication Data

Eatwell, John.
    Global finance at risk : the case for international regulation /
John Eatwell, Lance Taylor.
            p.   cm.
    Includes bibliographical references and index.
        1. International finance—Law and legislation.   I. Taylor, Lance.
II. Title.
K3820.E18   2000
332′.042—dc21   99-35706

Published in the United States by The New Press, New York
Distributed by W. W. Norton & Company, Inc., New York

The New Press was established in 1990 as a not-for-profit alternative to the large,
commercial publishing houses currently dominating the book publishing industry. The New Press operates in the public interest rather than for private gain,
and is committed to publishing, in innovative ways, works of educational, cul-
tural, and community value that are often deemed insufficiently profitable.

www.thenewpress.com

Printed in the United States of America

9 8 7 6 5 4 3 2 1

Contents

GLOBAL

FINANCE AT

RISK

Preface

The Asian currency crisis of 1997 precipitated a world-wide reappraisal of the performance of international financial arrangements. It is being conducted in academia, in international financial institutions (the International Monetary Fund, the World Bank, the Bank for International Settlements), and in political gatherings (most notably the Group of Seven major industrial countries). This debate has been labeled "Reform of the International Financial Architecture." The presumption, widely held before 1997, that financial liberalization is invariably beneficial has now been abandoned by almost all serious commentators. But there is as yet no consensus either about the appropriate analysis of the impact of financial liberalization or about what should be done.

Our analysis of the results of liberalization is based on a research project sponsored by the Ford Foundation that began in mid-1997. For that project, we gathered together a number of colleagues to evaluate the effects of liberalization on the performance of real economies throughout the world. Our synthesis of their insights was contained in our report entitled *International Capital Markets and the Future of Economic Policy*, presented to the Ford Foundation in August 1998. The report considers the effects of liberalization, evaluated both over many years (trend performance) and in the light of the recurrent financial crises that have, over the past thirty years, periodically disrupted both developed and developing economies. We argued that while international liberalization has brought some benefits, they have been tarnished by considerable costs. Those costs could have been substantially mitigated if a key lesson had been drawn from the development of domestic financial markets—liberal markets are efficient only if they are efficiently regulated. The task of financial regulation is to manage the risks that follow in the wake of liberalization. Without regulation, the risks and associated costs can become unbearable. We proposed the establishment of a World Financial Authority (WFA) to perform in the domain of world financial markets what national regulators do in domestic markets. A natural place to build the WFA is on the foundations of global financial surveillance and regulation that have already been laid at the Bank for International Settlements in Basel.

Ideas similar to ours have come from several prominent sources. In the United States for example, the February 1999 *Economic Report of the President* argued that "financial liberalization and innovation have rendered national boundaries irrelevant. If regulation was necessary within national boundaries, then it is now (at least) equally necessary in the international market." In the United Kingdom in late September 1998, one of us (John Eatwell) received a telephone call from a *Financial Times* reporter asking him to comment on a speech British prime minister Tony Blair had given the day before. The speech had covered aspects of international financial reform, and, declared the journalist, "we know you wrote it." Eatwell protested that he had done no such thing. His objections were cut short by the journalist: "The prime minister's press officer is telling us that you did." In fact, Eatwell had not written Blair's speech. But he had sent Blair's office a copy of our Ford Foundation report, and parts of the speech were based on some of our proposals.

Despite the similarities between our analysis and arguments emanating from the White House and Downing Street, our specific recommendation for the creation of a WFA has been dismissed by some (including a few people generally sympathetic to our analysis) as "utopian" and "lacking political feasibility."

To us, these criticisms seem misconceived.

First, even if the WFA as a specific institution is not created, it is still important to identify the *WFA function*, i.e. the tasks that need to be done by somebody. In this respect the WFA is a template upon which we have developed an analysis of markets and policies that would enhance the efficiency of international finance. In this book we stress that financial markets are not automatically self-regulating, and illustrate the point in four key areas:

- A breakdown of national regulatory capacities has occurred as liberalization has spread worldwide over the past four decades. Consequences have included high and variable real interest rates, increased volatility of asset prices, poor national economic performances, and the contagious spread of market instabilities worldwide.
- Such developments create the possibility for massive upheavals even in the large and integrated financial markets of the industrialized economies. Past examples are presented and potential risks to the American economy are pointed out.
- The recent wave of currency crises in developing and transitional economies has clearly been associated with rapid capital market liberalization and the absence both internationally and at the country level of appropriate regulatory procedures to deal with the financial flows unleashed.
- There is a complete absence of "fundamentals" in determining exchange rates; changes in rates are driven exclusively by shifting speculative "conventions" in the markets. Exchange rate volatility exacerbates all the deficiencies of unregulated markets.

In all four areas, intelligent international regulation is essential to help markets perform more effectively and reduce the danger of massive market failures. A major component of the WFA function is the provision for the surveillance, enforcement, and policy development that lie at the heart of efficient regulation.

Second, if the experience of policy changes in international finance over the past few years has taught us anything, it is that what is utopian one day is conventional wisdom the next. In finance, innovation happens at breakneck speed. That includes institutional and political innovation. In the nine months following the Russian default on August 17, 1998, an event that sent shock waves around the financial world, the G7 took the initiative to establish the Financial Stability Forum (FSF), a nascent international regulatory institution. Whether the FSF develops to perform the WFA function only time will tell. After the Brazilian crisis of early 1999 waned, a period of relative calm in financial markets slowed the pace of institutional reform. Further storms will quicken the pace again. There are no absolute standards of what is and is not politically feasible. What does matter is the balance of powers and interests, and the fear of the consequences of doing nothing. In the face of another severe crisis a WFA may become politically feasible, and if that should happen it is important to have thought through in advance how it would actually work.

Another aspect of the Ford Foundation report that led to some misunderstanding is our insistence that financial regulation is not only a problem of seeking microeconomic efficiency through the use of rules and procedures to reduce the risks to the public implicit in any financial transaction. Taking on market risk is what financial enterprises do. But they do not price into their activities the costs that their losses under adverse circumstances impose on the economy as a whole—the familiar consequences of financial failures. The blowup of one house can create a conflagration as loss of confidence sweeps away the entire street.

In the new international economy, regulation has to transcend national financial "streets." Unavoidably, it has vaulted to the macroeconomic plane. Regulation plays a vital role in determining the transmission mechanisms of monetary policy. Prudential supervision not only seeks to manage risk, it also defines relationships between liquidity and credit. Without prudential supervision there is likely to be less prudence, i.e. the erection of ever higher towers of financial risk on a given liquid base. This is particularly clear in periods of deregulation when authorities lose all control of credit and a speculative financial bubble first inflates and then bursts. This is what happened in the late 1980s in the Japanese "bubble economy" and the British house price boom, in the early 1990s in the Swedish bank crisis, and, of course, to the US savings and loan industry. Without regulatory structures in place, democratic authorities lose all control of the financial side of the economy; there is no traction for monetary and financial policy. That is why regulation, the prudential management of risk, and macroeconomic policy need to be considered together. It is the "package" that establishes democratic control and accountability, and which can secure the efficient operation of markets. That is another essential component of the WFA function.

The challenge today is to secure efficiency in a financial marketplace that is truly "global," meaning by that term "outside the jurisdiction of any one nation state." But it is not outside the jurisdiction of the collectivity of nations. Over the past twenty-five years, increasing attempts to forge cooperative relationships have been made among financial regulators appropriate to the global task they face. As the task has grown with the ever greater integration of global financial markets, so cooperation has ripened into coordination, and, with the establishment of the Financial Stability Forum, into potential new structures of political control. This book charts that process, explains the economic dynamics at work in today's financial markets, and constructs a framework within which a coherent international policy can be worked out and implemented.

John Eatwell
Lance Taylor
June 17, 1999

1—The Privatization of Risk

On August 15, 1971, the world of international finance was changed forever.

On that day President Richard Nixon instructed the US Secretary of the Treasury to suspend all sales and purchases of gold. The gold window was closed. It has never reopened, and the international economy has never been the same.

President Nixon's decision marked the beginning of the end for the Bretton Woods system then used to manage global finance and trade. It took its name from a founding conference held at Bretton Woods, New Hampshire, in 1944. A fundamental aspect of the system was that exchange rates between major currencies were fixed in terms of the dollar, and the value of the dollar was tied to gold at a US guaranteed price of thirty-five dollars per ounce. The fixed exchange rates did not long survive the closing of the gold window. After three months of confusion, new fixed rates were agreed by the major economies at a meeting at the Smithsonian Institution in Washington. But soon this system fell apart too. The pound sterling was allowed to float against the dollar in July 1972. A further attempt by the US to negotiate new fixed rates in early 1973 also failed. Japan allowed the yen to float in February, and in March the then six members of the European Community[1] agreed to a joint float against the dollar. The Bretton Woods system was finished.

PRIVATIZING RISK

For twenty-five years the system had maintained remarkable stability in exchange rates. They were changed only at lengthy intervals (the exchange rate of sterling against the dollar was lowered in 1949 and then again in 1966). For long periods everyone could be confident about the rate at which they could exchange one currency for another. The fixed rates were protected by powerful controls on the flows of capital between countries. Domestic financial markets were tightly managed, too.

The fact that governments maintained fixed exchange rates meant that the private sector was freed from foreign exchange risk. In the face of such stability there was no need for the large-scale currency dealing facilities (the rooms full of computer screens and young men in striped shirts and red suspenders shouting into, at least, three telephones at once) so familiar today—even if regulatory structures had not placed significant barriers in the path of capital flows. In 1971 only eleven Wall Street banks traded in the foreign exchange markets. Today nearly two hundred major foreign exchange trading institutions do business on Wall Street.

Nonetheless, in the 1960s growing speculative capital flows and the consequent pressure on fixed parities, notably the dollar price of gold, played a large part in the demise of the Bretton Woods system. Once Bretton Woods collapsed and significant fluctuations in exchange rates became commonplace, opportunities for profit proliferated, regulatory structures inhibiting flows of capital were challenged as "inefficient" and "against the national interest," and the modern machinery of speculation was constructed.

The incentive to deregulate international capital flows was driven by the overwhelming need to hedge against the costs that fluctuating exchange rates imposed upon the private sector. To reduce risk, those who traded in foreign markets needed to be able to diversify their portfolios at will, changing the mix of currencies and financial assets both at present and in the future in line with the changing perception of foreign exchange risk. Under the Bretton Woods system, foreign exchange risk was borne by the public sector. When that system collapsed, risk was privatized.

Privatization imposed substantial strains on both domestic and international financial systems. It demanded the creation of new financial instruments, which in turn required removing many of the regulatory barriers that had previously limited the possibilities of laying off risk. A major restructuring of financial institutions was also needed to ensure that they could balance foreign exchange and other risks created by increasing volatility in all financial markets. Combined with other domestic pressures to remove financial controls, the collapse of Bretton Woods was a significant factor driving the worldwide deregulation of financial systems. Exchange controls were abolished. Domestic restrictions on cross-market access for financial institutions were scrapped. Quantitative controls on the growth of credit were eliminated, and monetary policy was now conducted predominantly through the management of short-term interest rates. A global market in monetary instruments was created.

On New Year's Day, 1974, the United States abolished all restrictions on international capital movements, following the same move by Canada, Germany, and Switzerland during 1973. Britain scrapped all controls in 1979, Japan in 1980, France and Italy in 1990, and Spain and Portugal in 1992.

Following the privatization of risk and the consequent abolition of controls, the volume of international capital flows has grown exponentially. It is no accident that the growth of international capital flows coincided with the demise of fixed exchange rates. Apart from comparatively rare realignments, fixed rates offered only the profits of limited arbitrage. The fluctuating rate system that took its place stimulated capital flows with a powerful cocktail of the carrot of speculative profit and the stick of financial risk, laced with the proceeds of extensive arbitrage.

In 1973 daily foreign exchange trading around the world varied between $10 billion and $20 billion per day. The ratio of foreign exchange trading to world trade did not exceed 2/1. By 1980, according to the Bank for International Settlements, foreign exchange trading had reached a daily average of $80 billion, and the ratio of foreign exchange trading to world trade was about 10/1. By 1992 daily trading averaged $880 billion, a ratio to world trade of 50/1. In 1995 the amount was $1260 billion, a ratio to world trade of nearly 70/1, equal to the entire world's official gold and foreign exchange reserves. These figures are for an *average* day's trading and are greatly exceeded on days of high activity, such as in September 1992 when the pound sterling was forced out of the European exchange rate mechanism (ERM) and the French franc was under sustained speculative attack.

By far the greatest part of currency trades are very short run. Since they are not undertaken for the finance of trade in goods or services or long-term investment, these short-term trades must be based on expectations of the gains or fear of the losses that may result from changes in the value of financial assets. In the broadest sense, they are speculative, made in hope of capital gain, or to hedge against potential capital loss, or to seek the gains of arbitrage.

International bond markets began to build up steam in the 1980s. Between 1983 and 1993 total cross-border (cross-currency) sales and purchases of United States Treasury bonds rose from $30 billion to $500 billion. Sales and purchases of bonds and equities between foreigners and United States residents rose from 3 percent of United States gross domestic product (GDP) in 1970 to 9 percent in 1980, to 135 percent in 1993. Over the same period, cross-border securities transactions in the United Kingdom rose from "virtually nothing" to more than 1000 percent of GDP.

By the mid-1990s cross-border ownership of tradable securities was of the order of $2.5 trillion, with the US net supply accounting for around 40 percent of the total. The expansion of the Treasury bond market in particular permitted the United States to finance its escalating trade deficits during the 1980s, with implications for global macro stability to be taken up in later chapters.

Following bonds, foreign equity ownership became a major factor in the 1990s. By mid-decade, capitalization of "emerging" (or developing and transition economy) stock markets amounted to around 13 percent of the world total, up from a negligible proportion a decade earlier. International bank lending expanded from $265 billion in 1975 to $4.2 trillion in 1994. These currency flows helped fuel massive capital gains in emerging market share values. But in 1997, the East Asian stock market collapse and a $100 billion reversal of bank lending to the region showed how profoundly speculative many of these financial placements were.

The new international financial system, created by liberalization, is characterized by highly liquid capital being traded in huge volumes in an ever-expanding complex of markets for an evolving portfolio of instruments. The sheer scale and speed of these flows have produced a succession of major financial crises, which seem to be occurring with disturbing frequency: Latin America's Southern Cone crisis of 1979-81, the developing country debt crisis of 1982, the Mexican crisis of 1994-95, the Asian crisis of 1997-98, the Russian crisis of 1998, and the Brazilian crisis of 1999. And not only developing countries and emerging markets have been hit. The deregulation of Swedish financial markets in the 1980s was followed by a severe financial crisis in 1992 that saw overnight interest rates exceed 200 percent. This was followed by a long recession. In the fall of 1992 the whole of Europe was convulsed by the financial crisis which hit the ERM.

These crises in developed and developing countries have revealed two important characteristics of the new international financial system:

First, the new international financial system is highly volatile, with exchange rates, interest rates, and asset prices subject to both large short-term fluctuations and longer-term swings.

Second, the new system is susceptible to contagion when financial tremors spread from their epicenter to countries and markets that have seemingly little connection with the initial problem.

These characteristics are, of course, the outcome of the scale and speed of liquid flows, and of the deregulation that has resulted in the global integration of financial markets.

A WORLD FINANCIAL AUTHORITY

The sheer scale and liquidity of capital flows in the new international financial order have destroyed the boundaries that used to exist between national capital markets and the international capital market. The result has been a far less stable world increasingly haunted by the threat of financial crises. A crucial question to be addressed in this book is whether some of the stability achieved in former national capital markets can be achieved in the new international financial order.

The story of the new order is about financial risk. All financial assets embody some risk. The new international rules of the game have changed the character, the incidence, and the scale of risk. In turn, this has brought about radical changes in the operations of the private sector, both households and corporations. The public sector has changed too, both because the financial risks it faces have changed, and because it has the responsibility of managing the dangers that the new risks can pose for the national economy—for growth and employment and for the standard of living. The privatization of foreign exchange risk in 1973 disrupted the structure of financial risk management established after World War II. Not only did the scale of risk increase, but also the new liberalization of financial markets took financial risk outside the jurisdiction of national management. Today, financial markets know no borders. Yet regulatory power remains trapped within increasingly irrelevant national boundaries.

That is why the new international order needs a World Financial Authority.

The existing strands of international cooperation in financial management and regulation must be focused in a single authority with clearly defined powers to act in international markets. It is because some of the groundwork has been laid at the Bank for International Settlements located in Basel and in other organizations such as the International Organization of Securities Commissions (IOSCO) and the International Association of Insurance Supervisors (IAIS), that this proposal is *realistic*. It is because of the characteristics of today's international financial markets, that it is *necessary*.

The development of international institutions is fraught with political difficulties, none more so than in the case of an international *economic* institution which, to be effective, should be endowed by treaty with supranational powers. Even after being launched, such an organization is likely to founder on the rocks of national political interests. Experience suggests that only in the face of clear and present danger, and when the power to act is highly concentrated, does something actually get done. This was the case with the original Bretton Woods agreement to create the IMF and the World Bank. Both institutions grew out of a powerful desire shared by all Allied nations to ensure that the conditions that created the Great Depression of the 1930s would not be repeated after the war. And it was forced through by a powerful alliance of the major governments, led by the United States. Even so, despite the powers given them by treaty, the ability of the Bretton Woods institutions to exercise authority over national governments has been typically confined to those desperate for financial support.

The recent financial crises and the severe damage they have inflicted on economies throughout the world have created a desire to act. Moreover, that desire, although widespread among developing countries, has been focused in the exclusive, powerful arena of the world's leading industrial countries, the Group of Seven,[2] or G7.

For example, from the White House it was argued in the 1999 *Economic Report of the President* that:

> Traditionally, supervision and regulation of financial systems have been domestically based. But the increased global

integration of financial markets and the proliferation of institutions doing cross-border transactions suggest the desirability of enhanced *international* financial supervision and surveillance. (emphasis in original).

Similarly, in a speech at Harvard in December 1998, British Chancellor of the Exchequer Gordon Brown argued that, "In the international economy the era of absentee government is over."

These statements raise the questions of just how the powers of "supervision and regulation" employed by "domestically based" authorities could be exercised in new international financial arrangements, and indeed, what powers would be needed to end "absentee government" in the international economy. Will it be sufficient to increase cooperation and coordination between national authorities? Or should international regulatory powers be deployed by a World Financial Authority operating in the international markets in a manner akin to domestic regulators?

DOMESTIC FINANCIAL REGULATION

Few issues concentrate the economic policymaker's mind quite so wonderfully as a financial panic. The scale of the losses, the speed with which panic spreads from bank to corporation to household to government, the shuddering impact on real jobs in real factories, all cry out for "something to be done."

The US banking panic of 1907 brought with it a sharp decline in output from the nation's factories and farms as well as a major stock market crash. The fragile state of the US financial system and its potentially terrifying consequences were clear for all to see. But something could be done. Congress agreed that a method had to be found "to furnish an elastic currency, to afford a means of rediscounting commercial paper [and] to establish a more effective system of banking in the United States."

These words are taken from the Federal Reserve Act of 1913. They set out the three tasks which the new Federal Reserve System, established by that Act, was expected to perform: to conduct monetary policy, to act as a lender of last resort, and to regulate and supervise the banking sector. All this needed to be done if the benefits of a free financial market, a fundamental component in the working of a market economy, were to be enjoyed without suffering unbearable costs. Congress had recognized that effective regulation is necessary for the operation of an efficient market. All prosperous market economies have similar histories — financial crises followed by the development of institutions through which the authorities can exercise powers of financial management.

Over the past two hundred years the creative power of the market economy has resulted in a massive expansion in the output of goods and services. The material causes of human misery have been reduced to a greater extent than ever before in human history. For many millions of people life is no longer nasty, brutish, and short. Today the possibilities seem endless.

But this powerful engine for good also displays serious flaws that from time to time appear to be fatal.

Most relevant for the argument of this book is the ominous contradiction between the fact that a market economy must be a monetary economy, and the equally potent fact that the institution of money, and of monetary instruments, inevitably introduces a pernicious fragility which may have damaging consequences for the economy and for the society in which it is embedded.

MONEY AND FINANCE

The very essence of a market economy is that it operates by a generalized process of exchange. All means of production and all goods and services produced can be, and are, bought and sold, including the services of labor. Economic life is driven by individual and corporate calculation of profit and loss. The market economy fosters a complex division of labor, in which each individual's well-being is linked by a myriad of sales and purchases to thousands of individuals throughout the world. In such an economy money is a necessity. Without money the organization of this multidimensional interactive system would be impossible. Imagine trying to barter for all the goods and services a household needs, or for the flows of materials into and out of a factory. Imagine trying to compare prices without a monetary standard in which to express them.

In a market economy, flows of money determine the flows of inputs and outputs. Possession of money defines power in the marketplace. Accordingly, with the development of the market system the monetary system that supports it has become ever more elaborate. Money doesn't simply facilitate exchange, it sets the wheels of commerce in motion.

But money is not, in itself, worth anything. You can't eat it, or wear it, or live in it. Even when commodities like gold are used as money, they are worthless if there is nothing to eat. Money acquires its value from the fact that it is accepted as a payment. Acceptance of money discharges a debt.

This acceptance is enforced by the government. That is why inscribed on every dollar bill are the words "This note is legal tender for all debts, public and private." Refusal to accept dollars in payment is a federal offense. So pieces of paper printed with green ink are accepted for our labor, or our property, because we are confident that the government will ensure that we, in turn, can obtain labor or property in exchange for those pieces of paper. When people lose confidence in the powers of their government, they lose confidence in their money too. When a government collapses, the monetary system collapses with it. After the defeat of Nazi Germany, the paper money it had issued became worthless. Instead, nylon stockings and cigarettes were used as money. People could be reasonably confident that someone was always willing to sell them bread for a few cigarettes!

Government collapses are rare. Bank collapses are not. Hence deposits in bank accounts are equivalent to money only to the extent there is confidence that checks drawn on those deposits will be accepted in payments of debt, *or* that the bank deposit can be withdrawn as cash. Any loss of confidence in the bank will result in a run as everybody tries to take their money out. But it is impossible for banks to transform all their assets into instant cash. Many of those assets are loans to families or corporations who cannot pay their loans back on demand. So in the face of a run the bank is forced to close its doors. The money in the bank is lost, and the losses spread in destructive contagion as those who lost money in turn default on their debts.

As the market economy develops, ever more elaborate monetary instruments are also developed. The economy is bound together by an interlocking structure of financial assets and liabilities. The value of each and every one of those assets depends upon the confident belief that they will be redeemed. Any loss of that confidence and they become worthless bits of paper (or worthless entries in computer files). This is particularly true when financial assets are just claims on money, like bank deposits or bonds. But it can also be the case when financial assets are claims on real property, like shares in a corporation. A loss of confidence in the holder's ability to transform those shares into cash can render them worthless.

Moreover, confidence in money and other financial assets does not depend on their own intrinsic qualities. Confidence may be affected by changes in confidence in other assets which are similar, or that are believed to be similar. Typically, those who hold financial assets don't know too much about the institution to which they have lent their money. So even if a bank that fails doesn't hold someone's deposit, that person may nonetheless believe it to be prudent to withdraw funds from her or his own bank just in case there is something wrong with banks in general. So failure of confidence becomes contagious, and even the best-run institutions can be swept up in the general panic. Confidence can also be affected by changes in the economy as a whole, or changes in "macro prices" such as the interest rate or the exchange rate, which may be totally divorced from the characteristics of a particular firm or a particular asset.

Because money and financial assets are so central to the operation of a market system, monetary failures can have very severe consequences for the economy as a whole. Bankruptcy and default lead to plant closures, unemployment, and sharp falls in living standards. Of course, much the same could be said of markets for automobiles or corn. A major failure or an unexpected downturn in a large market can reverberate throughout the economy. But money and financial instruments are different. Not only are they at the core of every single transaction in a market economy, but also, having no intrinsic value, they are peculiarly susceptible to swings in confidence.

THE OPERATION OF FINANCIAL MARKETS

The economist John Maynard Keynes, writing in the depths of the Depression of the 1930s, likened the operations of financial markets to a "beauty contest." He was not referring to a 1930s equivalent of Miss World, in which "expert" judges decide the winner. He had in mind a competition that was at the time very popular in down-market British Sunday newspapers. Readers were asked to rank pictures of young women in the order they believed would correspond to the average preferences of the other respondents as a whole. So in order to win, the player should not express his or her own preferences, nor even try to estimate the genuine preferences of average opinion. Instead the successful player should anticipate "what average opinion expects average opinion to be." In the same way, the key to success in the financial markets is not what the individual investor considers to be the virtues or otherwise of any particular financial asset, nor even what the mass of investors actually believe are virtues of that financial asset. The successful investor is concerned to establish what everyone else in the market will believe everyone believes.

Since the markets are driven by average opinion about what average opinion will be, an enormous premium is placed on any information or signals that might provide a guide to the swings in average opinion and to how average opinion will react to changing events. These signals must be simple and clear-cut. Sophisticated interpretations of the economic data would not provide a clear lead. Hence the money markets and foreign exchange markets become dominated by simple slogans—larger fiscal deficits lead to higher interest rates, an increased money supply results in higher inflation, public expenditure is bad, falling unemployment always leads to accelerating inflation, and so on. For substantial periods of time markets may be stabilized by convention—everyone believes that everyone else believes that the economy is sound and financial markets are fundamentally stable. But if convention is questioned or, worst of all, shattered by a significant change in beliefs, then the values of financial assets may soar to great heights or collapse to nothing.

To some extent it doesn't matter whether the simplistic slogans of the conventional wisdom that dominate financial markets are true or false. What matters is that average opinion believes them to be true. Average opinion is reinforced by labeling these beliefs "fundamentals," as if they were revealed truths. For many years it was believed that the UK balance of payments was a "fundamental." Any deficit in the current account would result in selling pressure on the pound sterling, as the markets followed their beliefs. In the past decade opinion has changed, the current account is no longer a "fundamental," so deficits no longer produce the reaction they once did. A "fundamental" is what average opinion believes to be fundamental. Of course, this is not to say that some characteristics of the real economy will not eventually overwhelm even the most stubborn beliefs. Belief in the profitability of the stock of a nonexistent silver mine will eventually be punctured by the evident lack of any silver. Belief in the sustainability of a large and persistent current account deficit may eventually be punctured by the accumulation of debt and debt interest which that deficit entails. The reversal of average opinion can then be frighteningly sudden.

So long as the market follows what average opinion believes average opinion to be, then anyone who bucks the trend will lose money. Anyone who invests for the long term against conventional short-term wisdom will require extraordinary confidence in his or her predictions as short-term losses pile up.

But convention doesn't come out of thin air. It is formed from experience. So if experience showed that the simple economic propositions embedded in the market's beliefs were consistently wrong, then convention would change. Profits could be earned by those who ignored the slogans. "Average opinion" would tend to change, and a newfound stability of convention would underpin stable money and finance. What is impossible to predict with certainty is whether this stability will be the stability of high levels of growth and economic success or the stability of stagnation and despair. It is impossible because "average opinion" can be self-fulfilling. If the markets believe that a bank is about fail, then it will. If the markets believe that a particular currency is about to fall sharply in value, then typically it will.

Average opinion has its own history. It is heavily influenced by fashionable theories and the exercise of the financial powers of national governments, particularly the more economically powerful ones. The recent history of capital market liberalization has coincided with a swing in the balance of intellectual influence from a postwar theory of economic policy that urged national governments to limit international capital movements to the present-day theory that encourages free capital movements and the abdication of national regulatory powers. And that theory is itself the product of changing historical circumstances. The abandonment of the Bretton Woods system was not necessarily the preferred choice of most governments, but resulted from international financial developments they could not fully recognize, let alone control.

So financial stability is largely a matter of convention. Convention may be stable for long periods. But even stable conventions may contain the seeds of their own destruction. When stock markets are rising rapidly it quickly becomes the convention that they will rise forever. When convention breaks down, financial markets will be very unstable. Convention is peculiarly vulnerable when there is a shift in the balance of risk. Just such a shift took place in the early 1970s, when foreign exchange risk was privatized.

The dangers of high-risk financial investments are reduced if those investments can be readily sold or switched into a predictable amount of cash, i.e. if they are highly liquid. A market that operates as a beauty contest is likely to be highly unstable and prone to occasional severe loss of liquidity as all opinion shifts in the same direction. Everyone wants to sell at the same time and nobody wants to buy. The operation of the beauty contest destroys the liquidity that would encourage risk-taking. Increased instability may therefore result in systematic changes in the behavior of both public and private sectors, as decision-makers become ever more risk-averse. Although these changes may succeed in reducing instability, they do so only at the cost of less risk-taking, less investment, and medium-term deterioration in overall economic performance.

The potential instability of financial markets is based on the possibility of switching funds into and out of investments. Swings of convention translate into sharp fluctuations in asset prices that in turn reinforce the swings in confidence. In these circumstances it might be thought desirable to limit the ease with which investors can make the switch. If investors were locked into long-term investments, then markets would not be plagued by boom and bust waves of buying and selling. But here lies an important paradox. Without liquidity, without the ability to sell and recover cash invested, many investors would be simply unwilling to take risks at all. Although it is true that when the opinion of the whole market swings one way, liquidity vanishes, nonetheless individual investors tend to believe that their investments are liquid and that they will sell out in time. The ability to exit from an investment by selling a financial asset is, at one and the same time, a necessary foundation for investment in a market economy, *and* the source of the instability that can undermine investment and wreck the market.

So a fundamental task of the monetary authorities is to ensure that convention is stable and stabilizing, and to sustain confidence in the liquidity of financial markets. That task is made all the more difficult due to some built-in limitations of those markets.

First, financial markets tend to suffer from asymmetric information—many people trading in financial assets know very little about them. Shareholders typically know little about the companies whose shares they hold. Investors in mutual funds know little about the projects their money is invested in. Bondholders know little about the companies or even the governments issuing the bonds. Pensioners typically have only a very vague knowledge of the financial terms of their pensions, and know nothing of the investment policies of their pension fund. Some investment professionals are well aware of the underlying characteristics of particular financial assets. But sophisticated knowledge is the exception rather than the rule. And even the knowledgeable professional is often more concerned with judging how swings in conventional opinion might change market valuation rather than with the long-term returns on investments.

Second, attempts by the monetary authorities to sustain confidence in the liquidity of financial markets can have the perverse effect of encouraging investors to take excessive risks. If, for example, bank officials know that the authorities will always bail them out because a bank failure will inflict intolerable damage on the economy, then bankers may take risks they would never contemplate if bail-outs were unknown. This problem, the problem of moral hazard, poses another contradiction at the very core of financial policy—the policies needed to maintain confidence themselves encourage the excessive risk-taking which undermines confidence.

Third, even without the problem of moral hazard, financial investors systematically underestimate the true cost society as a whole pays for the risks they take. They fail to take proper account of "systemic risk."

SYSTEMIC RISK

"Systemic risk" is to financial markets what dirty smoke is to the environment. In reckoning cost of production, the factory owner fails to take into account the cost his smoking chimney imposes on the community. The dirty smoke is an *externality*. Its production has an impact on the welfare of society, but that impact is external, it is not priced through the market. The factory owner doesn't pay for the extra cost of laundry or for the medical bills the smoke precipitates. This failure introduces a fundamental inefficiency into workings of the market—cost to the firm does not reflect cost to society. The result is pollution. The factory owner produces more smoke than would be the case if all society's bills were reckoned into the factory's profit and loss account.

In the same way, financial firms do not price into their activities the costs their losses might impose on society as a whole. Yet those costs are a familiar consequence of financial failures. Not only do many financial dealings resemble the cliché house of cards, but one house going up in flames can spark a financial firestorm as loss of confidence sweeps away the entire street. Taking risks is what financial institutions are for. But markets reflect the private calculation of risk, and so tend to under-price the risk faced by society as a whole. The consequence is that from the point of view of society, investors take excessive risks. Totally free financial markets induce risks that pose a threat to the economy.

This is why the authorities responded to domestic financial liberalization by creating powerful national regulators. It is the responsibility of the regulator to ensure that investors take into account the risks their activities impose on society. This is done by requiring firms to recognize the full costs of such risks, either by enforcing the provision of adequate capital and instituting powerful risk management standards, or by the direct regulation of activities. Capital adequacy standards require banks and other financial institutions to hold liquid capital equal to a certain proportion of their entire assets. These holdings yield a negligible return, and involve giving up potentially profitable investments. They are a cost. So higher capital adequacy standards impose higher costs. Risk management procedures involve the detailed calculation of the risk involved in all a firm's activities, and the provision of liquid capital in proportion to those risks. The more stringent the risk management, the higher the costs will be. By forcing businesses to behave *as if* they took systemic risk into account, the regulators hope the financial system will be able to weather normal storms.

Regulatory authorities also take steps to correct distortions created by asymmetric information. These take the form of consumer information and protection, together with compulsory compensation for consumers who have been misled.

Regulation also seeks to reduce moral hazard. The regulator attempts to monitor investment policies and enforce adequate risk management procedures in firms. When a firm is about to fail because excessive risks have been taken, it *may* be rescued by the authorities, but the regulator will impose severe penalties upon the individuals who ran the firm.

As well as dealing with these market distortions, regulators also play an important role in the prevention of economic crime—by taking measures against money laundering, for example. They also seek to prevent any manipulation of financial markets, use of insider information, and other forms of what is labeled "market abuse."

In broad terms, the regulators' tasks can be summed up under two headings:

> *First*, to ensure that markets work efficiently by managing systemic risk and by preventing market abuse and economic crime.
>
> *Second*, protecting the consumer.

Of course, regulation is not always effective. Typically the regulator is running several steps behind market practitioners, trying to understand the implications of their new innovations for risk and for the consumer. And regulation can be expensive and oppressive or even downright wrongheaded. Overly fastidious regulation may result in risks being *over*priced, and hence will stifle enterprise. Or the regulator may bombard consumers with information they neither desire nor can use.

A balance needs to be struck, and, unsurprisingly, there is considerable dispute over precisely where that balance should be. Typically, those being regulated see regulation as onerous and commend the advantages of reducing regulation, at least as it applies to them if not to others. The authorities on the other hand are understandably nervous about the damage that can be done by excessive risk-taking or by exploiting consumers. Anxiety and calls to increase regulation follow closely behind financial crises or consumer scandals.

The balance of the argument shifts back and forth. The dividing line between the activities of the authorities and the unregulated activities of the market is not a fixed point, it is a pendulum. After a period in which the authorities fall behind developments in financial markets, the need to regulate becomes more pressing. But when fears subside, arguments promoting the advantages of financial innovation in a liberal environment become more persuasive. Moreover, the interrelationship between the financial markets and the authorities is always changing as the integration of markets proceeds domestically and internationally, and as technical innovation changes the speed at which markets operate and the product mix traded. Not only does the swing of the pendulum change, but the point from which the pendulum is suspended changes too. Technological changes transform the economy from local to global. Institutional changes have largely eliminated the traditional distinction between banks, investment firms, mutual funds, pension funds, and insurance companies—all now do similar business in similar ways. Nonetheless, the problem remains the same—how to harness the creative power of markets while curbing their tendency to self-destruct.

In the management of systemic risk, the regulator seeks to ensure that the market can weather normal storms. No private sector financial institution can weather abnormal storms. If for some reason there is a complete loss of confidence in the banking system, or in the bond market, or even in sophisticated finance houses, then even the most prudent and secure institutions will be sunk. In the face of a total loss of confidence, no amount of regulation is enough. A lender of last resort is required.

The role of the lender of last resort is to provide liquidity to the market that the failure of confidence has drained away. In the face of a severe loss of confidence only the government can do this, for the simple reason that in such circumstances, only the government can issue money. Every modern economy has a lender of last resort in the form of a central bank that will carry out the government's wishes to shore up confidence. The very existence of central banks that fulfill this role is a clear indication of the need for intervention by government institutions to ensure that the market operates efficiently. Deposit insurance offered by the authorities plays a similar "last resort" role for consumers. As an insurer, the government will not be overwhelmed by even the wildest financial panic. It can always print the cash.

INTERNATIONAL REGULATION

The argument in the *Economic Report of the President* makes a powerful case for international regulation:

> Financial liberalization and innovation have rendered national boundaries irrelevant. If regulation was necessary within national boundaries, then it is now (at least) equally necessary in the international market.

International regulation began to develop in the mid-1970s in response to the liberalization of financial markets. Clearly there was a need to promote sound banking standards throughout the new open markets, and to prevent respectable banks from being undermined or out-competed by the cut-price activities of the less respectable.

International financial regulation was pioneered by the central bank Governors of the Group of Ten countries.[3] In late 1974 they agreed to establish a Committee on Banking Regulations and Supervisory Practices (now called the Basle Committee on Banking Supervision). The Committee, that first met in early 1975, is based at the Bank for International Settlements (BIS) in Basle. It reports to the committee of central bank governors of the Group of Ten countries, which also meets at the BIS. The BIS provides a secretariat and research support. In the 1980s the Committee on Banking Supervision formulated capital adequacy requirements for banks. The then thirteen BIS members agreed to adhere to these standards and to use them as a tool to keep foreign banks not adhering out of their markets. The result was that more and more countries voluntarily signed on to BIS requirements in order to achieve market access and financial credibility. The BIS is also home to a tripartite committee of banking, securities and insurance regulators whose task is to propose regulatory standards for financial conglomerates. In addition, the IOSCO is the forum where national securities regulators are creating common standards and developing techniques of cross-border regulation. The

International Association of Insurance Supervisors (IAIS) does a similar job in the insurance industry. These developments have all been a response to liberalization and to the new risks it created.

The risks faced by financial firms can be divided into two broad categories (though, as will become clear later, the distinction between them is not as clear-cut as has often been assumed).

First are the risks peculiar to the activities of the firm itself. For example, counter-party risk arises from the reliability of the counter-party in a transaction—what is the risk that the counter-party will default? Similarly, credit risk arises from the risk of debtors defaulting, or of creditors failing to provide promised credit and so disrupting an investment program.

Second are the risks that derive from changes in the market in general, changes that may have little or nothing to do with the behavior of the individual firm. For example, there is the risk of changes in monetary policy that will alter interest rates and not only impose unexpected charges, but also change the market valuation of financial assets. Changes in market sentiment pose similar widespread risks.

This neat distinction between "firm specific" and "market" risks does not survive any significant shift in the characteristics of markets.[4] A counter-party who is thoroughly honest, whose business is conducted with the utmost care and prudence, and hence may be judged a good credit risk, may be totally undermined by a shift in general market sentiment and so transformed into a bad risk. The evaluation of the credit risk will be completely changed. In these circumstances the distinction between credit risk and market risk loses much of its meaning. What in normal circumstances may be judged as sound investments may, in a recession, become nonperforming loans.

The scale of market risk is enormously increased in an open international capital market spanning many financial authorities and currencies. The open market permits financial innovations in a particular currency outside the supervision and control of the monetary authority to which the currency "belongs." In London, banks operating in the Eurodollar market create credit in US dollars outside the supervisory powers of US authorities. Over time the major financial centers have co-operated in an attempt to bring such activities under supervisory control, but their efforts have been limited by the growth of "offshore" havens such as the Cayman Islands, where investors are attracted by low taxes and "light" regulatory regimes. A "light" regime reduces the cost to the firm by permitting it to operate without taking account of the systemic risk it creates. The low cost, low regulation regime leads to firms taking excessive risks, and so threatens the economic stability and efficient operation of financial markets far beyond the "offshore" center.

The existence of different currencies creates an entirely new set of risks. Changes in exchange rates can lead to a dramatic redistribution of the values of assets and liabilities. Currency mismatch can create severe imbalance on balance sheets. The rate of return implicit in exchange rate changes can completely disrupt the structure of interest rates throughout the economy. And the lender of last resort function is severely compromised for the simple reason that printing another country's money is just not allowed!

Foreign exchange risk is, of course, a market risk. But it readily translates into counter-party and credit risk as the redistribution of wealth that accompanies a change in the exchange rate transforms the circumstances of individual debtors and creditors. And the failure of an individual institution can lead to a general loss of confidence in a currency, transforming individual risk into market risk.

The privatization of foreign exchange risk in 1973 was followed necessarily by the liberalization of international financial markets. The need for financial institutions to spread their risks over many assets and activities in turn led to the liberalization of domestic markets. This was particularly important in the US, where a wide range of controls and regulations governing domestic markets were rapidly eroded in the late 1970s and 1980s. Many of these regulations, such as those governing private savings accounts and money market funds, were extensively ignored even before they were repealed. The consequent integration of domestic and international financial markets into a "seamless" whole has imported foreign exchange risk into Middle America. Volatility of exchange rates translates into volatility in interest rates, in domestic bond prices, in mortgages, and in the cost of car loans. Privatization of foreign exchange risks has imported new risks into domestic financial markets. Their regulation is therefore inadequate without regulation of the external risks. International regulation is now a domestic issue.

Regulating foreign exchange risk and its reverberations will pose entirely new problems for the World Financial Authority, problems which go beyond any characterization of the WFA as a domestic regulator writ large. The WFA will need to develop measures to diminish foreign exchange risk and reduce the contagion which spreads from crises in the foreign exchange market. It must also supervise national measures taken to reduce foreign exchange risk by reducing capital flows. Since the Asian crisis there has been renewed interest in controls on short-term, highly liquid capital flows, but there is no forum where the significance of such controls and their interrelationship one with another can be evaluated. Yet capital controls are measures for dealing with systemic risk, and are in principle no different from regulations limiting domestic financial placements.

THE ROLE OF
THE WORLD FINANCIAL AUTHORITY

The fundamental role of the WFA will be the regulation of systemic risk, together with the coordination of national action against market abuse and international financial crime. The task of consumer protection is predominantly the remit of national authorities. The success of the WFA will be measured not only in terms of financial stability but also by its contribution to economic growth and employment. After all, as Alan Greenspan, chairman of the Federal Reserve, has argued, "A global financial system, of course, is not an end in itself. It is the institutional structure that has been developed over the centuries to facilitate the production of goods and services."

The WFA will be a regulator, not a lender of last resort. But effective regulation is a necessary condition for the development of a successful lender of last resort. Without requiring that capital is adequate, that risks are carefully managed, and that management is responsible to the regulator for proper conduct, the authorities are exposed to excessive moral hazard. The development of the WFA will therefore be a precondition for the successful development of the lender of last resort function of the IMF, or of such collaborative arrangements between national central banks as may be put in place to emulate the role of a lender of last resort on an international scale. Today, IMF "conditionality" attached to its credits prevents the development of a successful lender of last resort function. Money with strings, and money much delayed, is not liquidity. Effective regulation replaces some of the conditionality strings.

It will be the task of the WFA to develop rules that would ensure the international adoption of the best regulatory practices and effective risk management procedures, and to lay the foundations for the development of a credible lender of last resort function. But the WFA should not simply be a body that develops and imposes regulatory procedures. It should also be a forum where the rules of international financial cooperation are developed and implemented. Many goals of an efficient international financial policy can be achieved by effective coordination of the activities of national authorities. The problem is that the means of achieving that coordination are, at the moment, and despite the valiant efforts of the Basel committees, very limited.

This coordinating role will also include acting as a forum for considering different national policies to manage exchange rates and limit capital flows. Without such a forum, increases in internationally generated systemic risk will be accompanied by a growing number of capital controls, such as those imposed by Malaysia following its financial crisis. The usual requirement of regulatory capital and reserve ratios imposed on firms will tend to be supplemented with quantitative or tax-based obstacles to cross-border flows of funds. Instead of the random and cumulative growth of capital controls, any such measures should be determined in consultations with the WFA. The WFA could ensure that controls are indeed an effective means of managing systemic risk and that they do not impose beggar-my-neighbor risks on other countries.

Recognition by the G7 that the coordinating and policy roles of the BIS committees do not go far enough led, in February 1999, to the proposal to establish the Financial Stability Forum (FSF). This new forum, which is based at the BIS, will seek to coordinate the activities of national financial regulators and enhance the flow of financial information upon which public and private sector decisions are based. It will bring together major international institutions such as the IMF and the World Bank, and national regulators and central bankers of the G7 economies together with the BIS and other international bodies. The objective of the FSF will be, in the words of the proposal drafted by Hans Tietmeyer, governor of the Bundesbank, to attain "a better understanding of the sources of systemic risk . . . ensure that international rules and standards of best practice are developed . . . ensure consistent international rules . . . and a continuous flow of information amongst authorities having responsibility for financial stability."

All this is worthy. But the recent crisis in Asia and its contagious spread to Russia, South Africa, and Latin America has demonstrated beyond all reasonable doubt that information and coordination are not enough. It doesn't matter how many numbers are available or how transparent financial institutions might be, the market still underprices risk and is still systemically inefficient. It doesn't matter how many national regulators sign up to common standards if there is no enforcement procedure to ensure that those standards are met. And it doesn't matter how effective national financial authorities might be, if, when global financial crises demand concerted action, they cannot provide a swift, unified response.

Powers to act and enforce are badly needed, and they are what the FSF conspicuously lacks. This is understandable. National governments, especially G7 governments, do not look kindly on the idea of surrendering any part of their financial regulation to an international body. But the die is already cast. In a world of open financial markets, national governments cannot effectively regulate the financial risks to which their societies are exposed. *That can only be done by an international body with policymaking and policy-enforcing powers.* And certainly not by an FSF that plans to meet only twice a year.

The creation of a World Financial Authority that has appropriate powers of surveillance, enforcement, policymaking, and action is the logical conclusion of the process that the establishment of the Financial Stability Forum has begun. This process will have to be extended in several dimensions, not least by listening to voices beyond those of the financial authorities of the G7. Representatives of developing and transition economies and nongovernmental organizations (NGOs) will have to be brought prominently into the governing structure of the WFA if it is to attain political credibility.

But the essential point to be recognized is that without a WFA, the risks imposed on the world economy by the volatility and contagion now characteristic of international financial markets will be translated into serious losses of real output, declines in living standards, and rising unemployment. The Asian crisis, the most severe of a regular series of financial crises since 1970, has demonstrated beyond all reasonable doubt that the international financial system as currently constituted is not working. It is not playing its historical role of stimulating real activity, funding real investment, and underpinning growth and employment. Instead, market volatility and contagion have resulted not only in huge negative shocks to the real economy, but have also been accompanied by a general slowdown in growth and employment throughout the world. Governments are often constrained to deflationary policies, while companies are deterred by the additional costs and risk of committing resources to investment.

Something must be done.

NOTES

1. At that time they were Belgium, France, Italy, Luxembourg, the Netherlands, and West Germany. The EC members attempted a collective float against the dollar, but this disintegrated in 1975. In 1979 these six European states plus Ireland inaugurated the European Monetary System (EMS). The exchange rate mechanism (ERM) of the EMS attempted to maintain a fixed rate system in Europe. But until the advent of European monetary union on January 1, 1999, the Europeans never achieved the stability of rates they had enjoyed under the Bretton Woods system.
2. The members of the G7 are Canada, France, Germany, Italy, Japan, the UK, and the US.
3. The Group of Ten is actually twelve. The member countries are Belgium, Canada, France, Germany, Italy, Japan, Luxembourg, the Netherlands, Sweden, Switzerland, the UK and the US.
4. Other risks exist which do not fit neatly under the two headings and which are attributable to institutional or technical operations necessary for the smooth running of the market. For example, settlement risk refers to the technical possibility of settlement procedures taking an unexpectedly long time or breaking down altogether.

2—Liberalized Capital Markets and Global Economic Performance

Comparisons of trend growth rates of GDP in the 1980s and 1990s with growth rates achieved in the 1960s pose an economic policy question of supreme importance. In all of the Group of Seven (or G7) large, rich industrial countries, output growth slowed in the 1990s to around two-thirds of the rate in the 1960s, and unemployment rose. In developing countries taken as a whole, the average growth rate also fell to roughly the same extent. Even in East and Southeast Asia, trend growth per capita declined in four of seven of the major economies, and that was before the onset of the region-wide economic crisis in mid-1997.

This growth slowdown has been accompanied by a worldwide fall in capital formation. Between the 1960s and 1990s, the share of investment in GDP declined in all G7 countries except Canada (where it was particularly low to begin with), in sixteen out of twenty Organization for Economic Cooperation and Development (OECD) economies, and in all Latin American economies. Only in Asia, prior to the crisis, were investment ratios higher in the 1980s and 1990s than they were in the 1960s.

The fact that growth rates decelerated worldwide demands an explanation. Some countries bucked the trend, but the overwhelmingly common experience was of slower output growth typically accompanied by slower growth of real wages and output per person-hour (or labor productivity). It is possible that the common experience was just a fluke, that the slowdowns were due to special local factors that just happened by chance to reduce growth rates throughout the world at the same time. It is surely more likely however that some common factor has been at work. And there is one all-pervasive factor that has affected all countries over the past twenty years. *All have been affected by the liberalization of the international financial regime that began with the development of the Eurocurrency markets in the 1950s and has been hastened by the explosive growth of capital markets since the early 1970s.*

Many expected liberalization of international financial markets to deliver improved resource allocation and lower costs of capital, and hence more rapid growth of productivity and output.

In fact, most countries have experienced a decline in overall economic performance. But in addition to the growth of jobs and incomes in the financial industries, the massive increase in financial flows undoubtedly brought benefits to some countries some of the time. In the early 1990s, flows of investment toward emerging markets in Asia and in Latin America were a welcome replacement for official development finance. Relaxation of external capital constraints led to increases in growth and reductions in inflation. But these successes have been followed by financial turbulence leading to either stagnation or severe declines in real output. The key questions suggested by this experience are:

First, has capital market liberalization led to systemic failures that create problems for all?

Second, in particular, has it helped cause the decline in trend growth rates and investment ratios observed in advanced countries and the developing world?

Third, what framework of international financial institutions and regulations, if any, would produce the most efficient outcomes in terms of growth, employment, and rising living standards?

THE GOLD STANDARDS

The possibility of systemic failure is intimately related to the "stability" of financial and other markets, that is, their resistance to big fluctuations in prices, asset rates of return, and in volumes of claims or commodities lent, borrowed, and sold.

These fluctuations destroy confidence, and hit investment and growth. Both macroeconomic and microeconomic market stability can be of concern. To think about the effects of capital market liberalization, it helps to consider what has happened before. Much can be learned from the experiences of the world economy when it operated within a liberal financial framework over the past century or so.

Since around 1870, there have been three periods during which cross-border movements of financial capital were substantially unregulated: first, under the "high" gold standard before World War I; second, during the gold exchange standard between the wars; and third, the new liberal financial order existing today. Was global macroeconomic stability assured during the two gold standard episodes? In the first it was, after a fashion. In the second it most clearly was not.

The high gold standard was the linchpin of the late Victorian world economic order. Under its rules, most countries fixed their currencies in terms of gold (thus maintaining fixed exchange rates among themselves), held gold reserves to settle their international accounts, and often used gold coins as well. Between 1870, when gold triumphed over silver as the monetary standard, and the outbreak of World War I, international macro adjustment pivoted on the Bank of England, often acting in cooperation with other central banks. Capital flows stabilized the system because they tended to move out of the UK when it was at the bottom of its business cycle and the London interest rate was low. Import demand was down in the UK, but the low interest rate stimulated real investment in borrower countries of European settlement and the colonies. In time the British economy would recover or the Bank of England would raise the discount rate to counter reserve losses. Capital would move back toward London and high rates would force raw materials exporters to sell off stocks on unfavorable terms, improving the British terms of trade and trade balance as well. The system operated counter-cyclically, stimulating demand outside Britain when UK demand was low, and reducing demand outside Britain when UK demand was high.

This overall stability did *not* rule out national crises. When their capital inflows dried up, capital-importing countries could not in many cases raise exports sufficiently to avoid suspending debt payments or abandoning gold parity. An important episode in American history was a monetary switch to bimetallism before the sharp economic downturn in 1893. That crisis (which provoked William Jennings Bryan's famous denunciation in 1896 of the "cross of gold") and the one that followed in 1907 ended the "Gilded Age" of blatant materialism and political corruption first satirized by Mark Twain and Charles Dudley Warner in the 1870s in a novel of the same name. These crises also led to the creation of the Federal Reserve, handing to the public sector the function of lender of last resort previously fulfilled around the turn of the century by Wall Street banks marshaled by J. Pierpont Morgan.

But such local financial volcanoes erupted without threatening the system as a whole. Even repeated crises in Britain itself failed to topple the gold standard, primarily because of the financial support of the Banque de France, the investment of the Indian surplus in London (to the detriment of the Indian economy), and South African gold production. Nonetheless, by the outbreak of the First World War the gold standard was becoming unsustainable as more countries established central banks, complete with gold reserves that were no longer susceptible to the free-flowing influence of London interest rates.

The adjustment mechanisms central to the operation of the gold standard resulted in the *real* interest rate (that is, the nominal rate minus the rate of inflation) being very high. Between 1870 and 1890, average long-term real rates in the major industrial countries were around 4 percent. From 1950 to 1970, the so-called "Golden Age" of rapid economic growth worldwide—and a time when capital markets were highly regulated—real interest rates were about 2 percent. They fell to near zero in the inflationary 1970s. In the period 1981–93, when the international financial market was once again deregulated, the average real rate in major industrial countries was at the historic high of 5.1 percent. Free international capital markets appear to go hand-in-hand with high real interest rates, that is, high returns to rentiers. The reasons are taken up below.

Another question for the new century (especially in light of the Asian, Russian, and Brazilian crises) is whether the local instability/global stability properties of the old gold standard carry over to today. Or whether global stability, imposed a century ago by the hegemonic policies of the Bank of England, is today impossible to sustain in the face of the scale and speed of global financial flows.

Under the gold standard as it functioned between the wars (the gold exchange standard), stability properties were very different. The US had become the biggest international lender, meaning that its national saving (the "source" of funds directed toward financial markets) exceeded its domestic investment (the major domestic "use" of funds after they filter through the financial system). Because the excess of "sources" over "uses" had nowhere else to go, it had to take the form of international lending. Moreover, the US aggregate savings supply rose substantially during a business cycle upswing, so that at the peak both its exports of financial capital and its import demand were high. In contrast to Britain under the high gold standard, capital movements out of and trade flows into the US economy both moved *with* the trade cycle. They thereby tended to stimulate economies elsewhere, with further positive feedback effects on the US—both upswings and downswings were strongly amplified. The US also competed directly in export markets with financial capital importers such as Germany, in contrast to pre-WWI Britain which exported sterling to the countries that produced its imports.

In the interwar years international cooperation was weak, in contrast to the earlier period when the Bank of England could always rely on help from counterpart institutions on the continent. One crucial example was the wave of banking crises that spread across Europe in 1931. Following bank failures in Austria, Germany encountered difficulties in midyear, throwing the Reichsbank into dire need of external credit. France had ample gold reserves (built up through annual trade surpluses that resulted in part because the franc was pegged at a weak level when it re-entered the gold standard). But it attached so many political strings to the credits it offered that the Germans would not accept—money with strings is not liquid. A continent-wide crisis and the spread of the Great Depression worldwide followed.

This collapse was deepened by "currency" or "locational" imbalances in the balance sheets of financial systems in many of the affected countries. In Germany (and elsewhere), a large share of domestic bank deposits was held by foreign investors and banks. At the same time, the German banks' assets were largely domestic. Rising fears of devaluation would lead almost automatically to deposit withdrawals, possibly igniting a bank run and subsequent crisis. Sixty-six years later and half a world away, these same factors exacerbated the Asian crisis of 1997 and spilled over into Russia the following year.

In the United States, the major creditor country, the financial system was fragile for a different reason. Many of its clients had borrowed heavily to undertake financial investments. In the jargon, they were highly "leveraged" or "geared." In principle, such a position cannot be maintained when the value of an investor's collateral assets falls below the level of their debt. In practice, the investor often fails when current income flows (including capital gains) fall short of current interest obligations. After the 1929 Crash, the first condition applied. Through "margin calls" on the loans they had taken out to buy shares when prices were rising, falling share prices turned many previously credit-worthy borrowers into bankrupts. This process of "debt-deflation" (the Yale economist Irving Fisher's term from 1933) was another contributing factor to the Great Depression. A similar process was clearly visible in 1990s Asia.

Finally, the complicated nature of the gold exchange standard worsened its downfall. Each nation could hold its international reserves in either gold or foreign exchange — "gold cover ratios" (of total central bank liabilities) were in the range of 30 to 40 percent in "normal" times. But banking panics reduced the stock of funds banks had available to lend as portfolio owners switched from deposits to currency. At the same time, fears of devaluation led central banks to try to replace their foreign exchange holdings with specie in a "scramble for gold." The worldwide result of these portfolio shifts was an overall contraction in the supply of money and credit that forced prices to fall (exacerbating debt deflation) and output levels to shrink. The monetary authorities' rigid — and, from a modern perspective, irrational — adherence to an outdated system was a final reason for its collapse, as fixed exchange rates under the gold standard transmitted negative demand shocks around the world. Countries that broke from the standard early, such as Britain in 1931, and pursued more expansionary monetary policies fared somewhat better.

One effect of the competitive devaluation and beggar-my-neighbor policies of the 1930s was to encourage wartime economists (led by John Maynard Keynes from the UK and Harry Dexter White from the US) to design a system with fixed exchange rates that did *not* rely on anachronistic national gold hordes. At the famous Bretton Woods, New Hampshire, conference in 1944, they replaced the liberal international financial markets of the gold standard with strict controls on capital movements. These controls were a fundamental characteristic of the new Bretton Woods system. Insofar as its institutional structure reflected Keynesian theoretical concerns of the time, Bretton Woods may be interpreted as a set of rules under which national authorities might, if they wished, pursue full employment policies, free of some of the anxieties that accompany open capital markets. As emphasized in chapter 1, exchange rate stability was central to this system.

The success of the Bretton Woods design is a key factor in evaluating the impact of the subsequent, post-1971, liberalization. Growth and employment rates during the twenty-five years of the system's effective operation from after World War II until about 1970 were at historic highs in most countries, whether developed or developing. Productivity growth was also at an historic high, not only in countries that were "catching-up" but also in the technological leaders. It *was* a Golden Age. How the Bretton Woods system broke down after twenty-five years of extraordinary economic success is a well-known story. For present purposes, the objective is not the resurrection of Bretton Woods — that is economically and politically impossible. Rather, the post-WWII system provides a point of reference from which to study the impact of the reduction in barriers to international capital movements that got underway as it started to fail.

TWENTY-FIVE YEARS OF CAPITAL MARKET LIBERALIZATION

The present wave of capital market liberalization began with the opening of Eurocurrency markets in the 1950s. But the breakdown of Bretton Woods and the consequent privatization of foreign exchange risk truly began the explosion of foreign exchange markets, followed by the creation of global bond markets in the 1980s, and global equity markets in the early 1990s.

The international financial flood of the past twenty-five years rose from a tiny spring — the Eurodollar (later Eurocurrency) markets in the 1950s. A Eurodollar deposit is just a deposit denominated in dollars in a bank outside the political jurisdiction of the United States. British and American authorities winked and nodded at such placements at the outset because they seemed a sensible way for commercial banks to make use of their excess reserves. Many early deposits were made by banks operating for Soviet bloc countries. They moved funds to London because they feared their assets might be expropriated in the US following the failure of the Soviet Union to pay wartime debts. As the name implies, offshore banking operations were originally limited to Europe (with London as the major trading point), but soon they could be carried out worldwide. Net Eurocurrency deposit liabilities amounted to around $10 billion in the mid-1960s and grew to $500 billion by 1980. By the mid-1980s in the industrial countries, bank deposits in currencies other than each nation's own currency amounted to around one-quarter of the total.

A major factor contributing to the growth of Eurocurrency markets was the American "interest equalization tax" of 1964–73, which raised costs for banks to lend offshore from their domestic branches. The resulting higher external rates led dollar depositors such as foreign corporations to switch their funds from onshore US institutions to Eurobanks. A second massive Eurodeposit inflow came in 1973–74 with the onset of "recycling" of Organization of Petroleum Exporting Countries (OPEC) trade surpluses after the first oil shock. The developing country debt boom followed in turn, as rich countries' banks used OPEC's deposits to back massive loans to middle income economies in Latin America and elsewhere. The subsequent crash after the Mexican default of August 1982 led to a "lost decade" of growth in most of the developing world (with Asian economies the major exceptions until 1997, for reasons discussed in chapter 5).

Eurocurrency transactions rapidly taught market players that they could shift their deposits, loans, and investments from one currency to another in response to actual or anticipated changes in interest and exchange rates. These moves were early warnings of a pervasive regulatory problem that dominates the world economy today: *any nation's financial controls appear to be made for the sole purpose of being evaded*. Even the ability of central banks to regulate the supply of money and credit was undermined by commercial banks' borrowing and lending offshore. This process accelerated after the shock of 1973–74. Within ten years, national authorities were forced to scrap long-established interest rate ceilings, lending limits, portfolio restrictions, reserve and liquidity requirements, and other regulatory paraphernalia. These instruments acted on the supply side of financial markets by limiting the ability of private sector players to seek capital gains, hedge risk, or undertake arbitrage. They all could be circumvented by the new freedom to pursue offshore transactions. All finally had to be abandoned.

Dropping their supply-side regulatory tools meant that central banks could now operate only on the demand side of the money market. The only instrument of monetary policy available to them was buying and selling securities to influence short-term interest rates. The result has been higher and more volatile real interest rates. The 1995 Annual Bulletin of the Bank for International Settlements (BIS) commented, ". . . interest rates generally have to become higher and more variable" as they are managed to influence demands for financial assets. The new interest rate regime became the norm in every major economy. The result was a powerful inducement for even greater cross-border surges of portfolio investment. As under the interwar gold standard, central banks in the advanced economies lost much of their power to pursue counter-cyclical monetary policies. And as under the nineteenth century gold standard, high interest rates seemed to settle in for good.

Liberalization and deregulation also changed the way in which commercial banks do business. In the US, the developing country debt crisis was an important cause of the change. So was a 1983 law requiring banks to satisfy capital adequacy requirements on their liabilities according to the "Basel standards" promulgated by the BIS (much more on these below). They moved away from traditional deposit and lending activities toward "off–balance sheet" operations. Although it borders on the arcane, the distinction between off– and on– balance sheet transactions is critical for regulatory purposes. The standard convention is that claims must be included *on* balance sheets if they (or their antecedents) have been acquired with "hard cash." An illustration can be built around the family automobile. As a capital asset it has a proper place on a household's balance. *Off* the sheet are contingent contracts relating to the car — collision insurance is the obvious example. For both the household and the insurance company, the policy sets out specific transactions that must occur if the automobile crashes. They will then show up on income statements and thereby balance sheets in due course. But if there is no crash, the insurance policy remains in an accounting limbo.

The off–balance sheet operations that banks began to undertake were infinitely more complicated than collision insurance, but they ultimately boiled down to contingent contracts. The popular variants included money management and dealing in the over-the-counter (OTC) markets for foreign exchange and for the financial "derivatives" (a portmanteau term for a broad range of contingent contracts, these will be discussed in detail below) that proliferated in response to the interest and exchange rate volatility newly embedded in the system. Off–balance sheet and OTC transactions are opaque and difficult to monitor—let alone regulate. In addition, derivative holdings tend to be very highly geared. Like stock market speculators in the US before the Great Depression, players in derivatives often make relatively small investments in cash and borrow heavily to finance their acquisition of high value assets, with the assets themselves serving as collateral for the loans. The dangers of high gearing on the part of both international and domestic banks and finance houses were clear for all to see in the Asian financial crisis. As the values of their underlying collateral assets collapsed and their guarantors went bankrupt, the liabilities came home to roost. The wind-down of derivative contracts imposed huge losses, amplifying the crisis.

Closer to home, while American (and with a lag, European) banks were changing, so were the portfolio habits of their erstwhile customers. Households transformed themselves from being depositors in banks to investors in pension and mutual funds. According to flow of funds data compiled by the Federal Reserve, over the fifteen years between 1978 and 1993, the share of US financial sector assets held by institutional investors rose from 32 percent to 52 percent; the share of banks fell from 57 percent to 34 percent over the same period. Similar increases in assets managed by institutional investors occurred in Britain, France, and Germany. Pooled money funds moved aggressively toward investments abroad (including emerging markets) and toward much shorter-term placements. In 1993 it was reported that "the typical stock is now held for an average of a little over two years, compared to over four years 10 years ago and seven years in 1960."

THE REGULATION
OF LIBERALIZED MARKETS

The regulatory structure cobbled together in the US after the old supply-side interventions disappeared comprises capital adequacy requirements for banks and privatized monitoring and surveillance at the level of individual financial firms. But important instability problems plague both arms of the new system.

Capital adequacy requirements are pro-cyclical. The credit market will supply capital to the banking system in an upswing and withhold it in a downturn. More importantly, capital adequacy standards would be useless in a liquidity crisis. When there is a loss of confidence, no amount of capital will save a bank or investment firm.

These weaknesses of capital adequacy ratios in volatile financial markets spurred the development of risk management techniques in the hope that they would be a more effective means of reducing both private and systemic risk. The rapid development of markets and financial products together with the competitive pressures of a volatile financial environment pushed the responsibility for risk management to the level of individual firms, subject to regulatory surveillance. In 1996, such privatization of the risk management function was embodied in amendments to the Basel Accord. The idea is that firms should not simply operate on the basis of a mechanical capital adequacy ratio. Instead, they should attempt to estimate their

Value at Risk (VaR) by means of a careful analysis of their assets and liabilities, and estimate the risk to which they are exposed given likely variations in prices. The estimates will be based on the types of financial instruments involved, the characteristics of the counter-parties, and exposure to changes in market conditions including interest rates, exchange rates, and so on. The VaR estimate is then based on a probabilistic measure, itself based on past experience of movements in these variables.

Current procedures reflect the fundamental proposition that financial risk is most effectively managed by those who are exposed to it, and consequently exposed to failure. It is not the task of the financial regulator to coach firms in the management of risk, still less to dictate or even run the firms' risk management function. Instead, the role of the regulator is constantly to examine firms' risk management procedures, to pronounce on their broad adequacy, and encourage development of the best practices within firms.

Putting together an efficient risk management function requires that firms take responsibility for their own failure. The securities regulator is there to provide the ambulance at the bottom of the cliff rather than the fence at the top. Risk management must be supplemented by rules on advance provisions for an orderly wind-down, should the necessity arise. It should also lay down rules for the protection of customers' assets and provide appropriate deposit insurance for individuals and households.

Although significant improvement in risk management techniques and procedures has taken place, this approach still has a tendency to be pro-cyclical. It also suffers from the fact that it is inevitably based on past experience. In a world of rapid financial innovation it is the entirely new event which often poses the greatest risk.

The regulatory structure is under further stress because with market liberalization the distinctions between banks and other financial institutions have become blurred. Money management is now a primary function of *all* financial institutions. Yet regulatory procedures tend to differ between banks, investment houses, insurance companies, savings and loans, and so on. The variety of regulators dealing with these (nominally) different firms creates the possibility of certain activities "falling into the cracks" between particular areas of official responsibility.

Beyond surveillance and regulation of individual firms, regulators must be concerned with risks to the overall financial system. In the US, a case in point in fall 1998 was the intervention of the authorities into the affairs of the Long-Term Capital Management hedge fund[1]. LTCM apparently had debts amounting to hundreds of billions of dollars that were not covered by viable collateral assets. Regulatory surveillance and a timely injection of liquidity meant that the uncovered liabilities did not bring down LTCM's numerous creditors in both the US and Europe (although a few high financial executive heads rolled subsequently). In this case, effective regulation stemmed systemic contagion.

Of course, the failure of particular firms does not inevitably produce systemic risk. Not all players are as proficient at massive borrowing as were the principals of LTCM. The job of the regulator is to introduce safeguards that inhibit the transformation of particular risk into systemic risk. Examples include the legal netting of counter-party exposure and the segregation of client money. More generally, the regulator must take steps to counteract the pro-cyclical stance of firms' internal risk-management procedures. The regulator must be able to take a more balanced medium-term view and must discourage both exaggerated optimism and exaggerated pessimism. He or she must also ensure that appropriate information is available to enable firms to assess risk, and that fair and honest dealing underpins commitments and transactions.

None of the above will, of course, protect a market against overall systemic failure. Effective risk management by firms will diminish systemic risk but it is not enough. A widespread loss of confidence will undermine even the most prudent financial system. The task of responding to such problems takes the regulator beyond the goals of the individual firm and even beyond the scope of regulation, raising general issues for the central bank and government.

Even these high level authorities may today face considerable difficulties in dealing with a loss of confidence. If problems are detected with OTC transactions in derivatives, for example, it may not be easy to find a channel via which the central bank can inject liquidity in a lender of last resort operation. When the Franklin National Bank failed in 1975, the Federal Reserve provided funds to the foreign exchange market by assuming and executing (at a loss) the Bank's foreign exchange book. This form of intervention may well have to be used again. In the LTCM case, the Federal Reserve organized credit injections from the hedge fund's private sector lenders instead of using its own resources, but it could not have done this if it did not have the status of a lender of last resort.

The fundamental riddle posed by systemic risk is that unless they are subject to system-wide interpretation, mere collections of surveillance data say nothing about aggregate dangers. Transparency is not enough. Individual actors can off-load their own risks onto the system. In a common developing country example, banks with external dollar liabilities may well lend in dollar-*denominated* terms to borrowers whose incomes are in local currency (e.g. producers of non-traded goods), thereby "balancing" their own portfolios. In the event of a devaluation, however, the ability of debtors to service their loans would be impaired, in turn imperiling the financial system as a whole. The basic transaction is transparent in this case, and the authorities could take steps (accumulating foreign reserves to back lender of last resort interventions in real dollars and/or encouraging financial institutions to hedge their dollar exposures) to protect the system. With opaque, off-balance sheet transactions the task of the authorities becomes far more difficult.

VOLATILITY AND CONTAGION

Liberalization and the changing regulatory environment have been accompanied by increased volatility of prices and quantities, and its spread (or "contagion") across markets and national borders. In the recent period, increased volatility stands out whether it is measured by short-term movements in exchange rates and interest rates, or by longer swings in market activity. In the major industrial countries short-term volatility, as measured by movement in prices at two-weekly intervals, has tripled in most markets in the past 25 years. And long-term swings have taken the real value of the dollar from an index of 100 in 1980, to 140 in 1985, down to 94 in 1990, and up again to 134 in 1998.

Volatile financial markets generate economic inefficiencies. Volatility creates financial risk, and even if facilities exist for hedging that risk, the cost of capital formation is raised. The impacts show up in developed and developing economies alike. In the face of higher and more volatile real interest rates along with the emergence of "junk bonds" in a deregulated financial system, defaults on US corporate bonds spiked upward after the breakdown of Bretton Woods in 1970, fell back, and then rose steadily through the 1980s. The bond default rate of around 2% per year in the 1990s was exceeded only in the early 1970s (very briefly) and in the Great Depression. Similarly, corporate bankruptcy, at an all time low in the stable years from 1950 to 1970, has now returned to a level characteristic of the deregulated markets of the 1930s.

Volatility fuels contagion. The current regulatory regime does not effectively address this the most dangerous threat of all to the global financial system. In the past, the main strategy against contagion was compartmentalization and segmentation of markets. This was the rationale of the New Deal's Glass-Steagall Act "firewall" between the commercial banking and financial services industries. As late as the October 1987 mini-crash in the US, segmentation among financial markets added to systemic stability. Investors who withdrew funds from equity and derivatives placed them with banks. With encouragement from the Fed, the banks expanded lending to dealers and institutional investors who went back into the stock market, halting asset price declines. With financial firms in the US much more integrated in the late 1990s than in the 1980s, such stabilizing movements of funds would be far more difficult to orchestrate. In continental Europe and Japan, by contrast, universal banking systems in the past were sufficient to stabilize financial systems in which the significance of securities markets was slight.

Following the breakdown of barriers between financial markets—the inevitable outcome of the privatization of foreign exchange risk—and the consequent consolidation of financial conglomerates and the spread of securities markets worldwide, all segments of the system are now tightly interdependent, both nationally and internationally. This new source of huge risks is poorly understood and certainly not fully captured by internal monitoring. Without external checks via clearinghouses or similar institutions, gaps in a firm's own surveillance may go unnoticed. The financial failures in Orange County, Daiwa, and Barings are large but isolated examples. There is a clear potential for system-wide repercussions.

Microeconomic responses can easily escalate into macroeconomic contagion. The stock market crash of 1987 spread rapidly from New York to all financial markets. Recent studies of the 1992 ERM crisis have concluded that systemic contagion makes the link between domestic macroeconomic conditions and the size of currency devaluation, let alone the likelihood of a crisis, tenuous. Indeed, the link may even have the "wrong" sign, with the financially virtuous suffering the greater punishment. The Mexican crisis of 1994 propagated the "tequila effect" throughout Latin America. The Asian financial crisis of 1997 spread throughout emerging markets including Eastern Europe, Latin America, and South Africa.

The prevalence of contagion is a powerful argument against the efficiency of unregulated financial markets, at least in the short run. It might be argued that the damage inflicted upon the real economies of Asia will in turn result in real declines in other economies, and hence falling financial markets are an anticipation of prospects for the real economy. But this simply recognizes the inadequacy of current international institutions in the face of localized financial crises. If a local crisis can precipitate widespread real losses, then it is in the wider interest to ensure that these crises are alleviated. Systemic risk, risk management, and the provision of liquidity via some sort of lender of last resort are problems that must be confronted within the relevant context — the international context.

MORAL HAZARD

The presence of system-wide dangers creates further problems. When regulators try to deal with systemic risk they often have to provide financial guarantees or inject liquidity into threatened institutions. In so doing they inevitably create "moral hazard." The notion of moral hazard comes from the economic theory of insurance. The basic idea is that insurance reduces incentives for prudence — the more fire insurance I hold on my house, the more intriguing the thought of arson becomes. Insurance companies frustrate such temptations by allowing homeowners to insure their properties for no more than 75 percent or so of their market valuations.

Regulatory moves to counter such incentives in financial markets must confront the fact that systemic risk embodies an important element of externality — it is greater than the sum of private risks. In other words, the sum of the risk "managed" by private agents is less than the total risk to the community. And hedged risk is simply spread, not eliminated. The goal of the lender of last resort, deposit insurance, and similar guarantee schemes is to control this "social risk." Moral hazard distorts social risk management by transferring risk from the private agent to the public body. Schemes need to be defined that minimize or otherwise take account of this transfer. Being charged "penal" interest rates for borrowing from the lender of last resort is one such measure. So far as deposit insurance and similar guarantees for various forms of savings instruments are concerned, these protections should be offered to households who should be required to pay for the cover. Institutions should not be similarly guaranteed. In the case of institutions regarded as pivotal to the operation of the economy the government may decide to take over a failing firm and honor its financial obligations, as the Federal Reserve did with Franklin National Bank. As previously noted, such interventions may prove to be particularly important in the case of OTC derivatives markets.

By definition, moral hazard tends to *increase* dangerous risk-taking in the private sector. Yet in a potentially destabilizing positive feedback loop, traditional steps to reduce systemic risk tend to increase moral hazard. In the US, economist Hyman Minsky saw moral hazard in financial decisions rising after the 1930s as a consequence of counter-cyclical policy aimed at moderating real and financial business cycles. At the same time, "automatic stabilizers" such as unemployment insurance were created as part of the welfare state. As is always the case, this economic engineering had unexpected outcomes.

One was a move by corporations toward more financially "fragile" positions, typically based on high leverage.[2] Without fears of price and sales downswings, high risk-high return projects became more attractive. This shift was exemplified by an increased "short-termism" of investment activities, and the push toward merger and acquisition activity in the 1970s and 1980s. Junk bond finance helped these changes take place.

Secondly, the intermediaries financing such initiatives gained more explicit protection from risky actions by their borrowers through lender of last resort interventions by the Federal Reserve. The resulting moral hazard induced both banks and firms to seek more risky placements of resources. Banks, as already discussed, pursued financial innovations. Among them were the creation of money market funds which effectively raised interest rates toward Eurodollar levels in the 1970s, the appearance of investment funds and asset securitization[3] at about the same time, and the later emergence of widespread derivatives markets and hedge funds. One concrete outcome was the savings and loan (S&L) crisis of the 1980s.

Moral hazard is a helpful way to look at history; it can be used to underpin plausible narratives. Extensions out of context begin to stretch verisimilitude. Deposit insurance, for example, certainly played a role in the S&L crisis in the US. In the Garn–St. Germain Act of 1982, depositors were allowed to have any number of fully insured $100,000 accounts with an S&L. With their prudential responsibilities to depositors completely removed by the Act, S&L managers were free to engage in any high risk-high return projects they saw fit—which they immediately proceeded to do, with disastrous consequences.

However, it is quite wrong to extend this observation into the argument that excessive risk-taking is always or necessarily due to the presence of moral hazard. Consider the following examples. Deposit guarantees have frequently been accused of worsening Chile's currency crisis around 1980, but in fact the guarantees had been removed by the authorities explicitly to avoid moral hazard! Similarly, the assertion popular in 1997 that the South Korea government had provided implicit guarantees for banks and industrial corporations does not stand up. Korean conglomerates (or *chaebol*) were supposed to have engaged in reckless investment and be inefficient as proven by their low profitability. But profitability was low only *after* interest payments, not before. Moreover, during the 1980s and 1990s the government did *not* bail out any *chaebol*. In the period 1990–97, three of the thirty biggest went bankrupt. The government did have a history of stepping in to restructure enterprises in trouble, but that left little room for moral hazard— managers knew they would lose control over their companies if they failed to perform.

Despite such shaky empirical antecedents, moral hazard is given a central role in many models of financial crises. East Asian governments are supposed to have self-insured by accumulating international reserves to back up poorly regulated financial markets. National players accordingly felt justified in offering high returns to foreign investors, setting up "spreads" between local asset returns and foreign borrowing rates. Domestic liabilities were acquired by outsiders until such point as the stock of (implicitly) insured claims exceeded the government's reserves. Speculative attacks followed.

The leitmotif of an alert private sector chastising an inept government recurs throughout most economists' discussions of financial crises. In the scenario just presented, the government encourages reckless investment with its implicit insurance schemes. All a sensible private sector can be expected to do is to make money out of such misguided public action! The interesting empirical twist that emerges in the following chapters is that in recent developing country crises, decisions taken by the private sector itself set up incentives that led to destabilizing cross-border financial flows.

THE BENEFITS OF LIBERALIZATION

International liberalization has exacerbated market volatility and greatly increased the dangers of contagion. As argued more fully in chapter 4, results in developed economies have included a shift in the public sector toward less expansionary policies, and in the private sector toward lower investment. Chapter 5 takes up the crises that market liberalization wrought in developing and transition economies.

Nonetheless, liberalization has brought some benefits to some people. The establishment of the currency trading industry and its associated income flows created real purchasing power that did not exist previously. The FIRE (finance, insurance, real estate) sector now contributes more to American GDP than manufacturing, and its foreign exchange operations are an essential component of the sector and hence of the GDP. FIRE incomes largely flow to people at the top ends of national distributions and contribute to increasing inequality. This bias toward inequality could presumably be offset by appropriately progressive tax and expenditure policies, but that has not happened so far. Apart from a wider menu of financial portfolio choices, people in the bottom 90 percent of most nations' income distributions have gained little from the spread of FIRE. A second benefit has been the ability to off-load "risk"—in the sense of price volatility—in foreign exchange markets. Through the use of derivative contracts (forwards, options, and swaps), individual players can hedge against possible future exchange rate disturbances, thereby avoiding unpleasant surprises. Standard calculations estimate the welfare gains from such activities at around one percent of the underlying primary transactions, and a smaller fraction of overall GDP. They do not take into account systemic hazards of the sort discussed above. There is of course an ambiguity to this benefit: hedging is made possible by liberalization, but hedging is necessary because of the consequences of liberalization.

Thirdly, one might expect more widespread financial markets to channel resources where they are "needed," at least in the sense of supporting real investments with high returns. In fact, international capital flows have been "perverse." Throughout the 1980s net flows to developing countries as a whole were near zero, while the US absorbed around $100 billion a year. In the late 1990s the United States still took in two-thirds of the rest of the world's surplus savings, even though its real rates of return were no higher than in other industrialized countries and well below those in the developing world. However, in the late 1980s and early 1990s some tens of billions of dollars of net capital flows did begin to find their way to developing countries. Southeast Asian inflows accelerated after the Plaza Accord exchange rate realignment in 1985, and Latin America received positive transfers after 1990. More foreign resources helped support rapid growth in Asia for a decade before its crisis and permitted exchange rate–based anti-inflation programs in Latin America to succeed.

Finally, market liberalization is generally supposed to enhance microeconomic efficiency, and thereby productivity growth. The benefits are less apparent here. Worldwide growth performance began to deteriorate around 1970, just when liberalization of financial and other markets was getting well underway. Why the post–World War II Golden Age ended is a topic of intense debate. What *is* clear is that deregulation of financial and other markets did not prolong its life.

In sum, forty years of exponential expansion of international capital transactions appear to have created more well-to-do people and perhaps promoted modest market efficiency gains in an environment of generally slow economic expansion. Also, capital flows to "emerging markets" helped inflation and growth performance in some developing economies for a limited period of time.

THE COSTS OF LIBERALIZATION

Were the costs of a similar minor magnitude, the whole enterprise would be of secondary importance. Unfortunately, observed and potential losses are not small. We have already pointed to regulatory problems *within* the financial system. There are also dangerous linkages with the rest of the economy. The East Asian crisis can be tied directly to interactions between liberalized capital markets and macroeconomic instability. This is of global significance. Potential downside risks in more advanced economies are far greater, yet in most discussions have been ignored.

The fundamental issue before us is to attempt to identify the links between liberalization and the deterioration in economic performance that has accompanied the new international financial order. Increased volatility and contagion have undoubtedly made the economies of developed and developing countries less stable. But lack of stability does not necessarily imply worsening economic trends. It simply means that there are larger fluctuations around the trend. However, volatility and contagion may have led to changes in behavior that have in turn resulted in the deterioration in trend performance.

In the developed economies such changes may be observed in both the public and private sectors. In the face of increased risk of financial crises, the public sector has shifted toward a financially conservative stance in which financial stability is an objective superior to the objective of growth and high employment. In the private sector, financial volatility increases risk and discourages long-term investment. Moreover, high and volatile interest rates have a direct impact on corporate cash flow, and hence reduce the supply of funds available for investment.

In developing economies, liberalization has set up incentives for financial systems to behave as they did in Europe and the United States under the gold exchange standard. In some well-known crises, the resulting fragility spawned disaster. In important examples such as Brazil, both the trend growth rate and the income distribution have deteriorated. As noted above, the economy went through a "lost decade" after the debt crisis of 1982 and may well suffer another after the currency crisis of 1999. Elsewhere in the world, with sub–Saharan Africa as the main example, governments in advanced economies have cut back foreign aid programs as a consequence of their new fiscal rectitude. Their private sectors have not seen fit to replace such public capital outflows and the recipient countries have suffered.

These proposed relationships linking liberalization to the deterioration in trend performance are, of course, just hypotheses. Whether they can be substantiated is investigated further in the chapters that follow.

NOTES

1. Although they emerged a decade earlier, hedge funds appeared on the general public's radar screen with the ERM crisis in 1992, when they made massive profits on the pound sterling's fall. Despite their benign name, hedge funds thrive on speculation. They are basically closed-end mutual funds which sell their shares to wealthy investors who are willing to bear high risks in exchange for (possibly) very high returns. Prior to the LTCM event, they had been very lightly regulated.

2. An extreme example is a position in which expected income flows fall short of expected interest obligations in at least some future time periods. Minsky calls this "Ponzi finance." See chapter 5 for developing country examples. The eponymous

Carlo Ponzi operated in Boston in 1920. His own scheme involved continual new borrowing to pay his prior investors high returns based on purported arbitrage among arbitrary valuations that had been given to international postage stamps. When federal authorities raided his premises he had less than $100 worth of stamps on hand.

3. Securitization is the bundling of financial sector assets such as consumer credits into a package for resale to third parties. Diversification across a large number of bundled credits presumably reduces the package's aggregate risk. However, this clearly did not happen with the developing country loans that had been securitized prior to the wave of crises in the 1990s.

3—Exchange Rates and Capital Controls

The prime mover behind the behavior of the international financial system is the exchange rate regime.

The privatization of risk implicit in floating exchange rates demands a liberalized capital market. This combination transforms the exchange rate into both an object of enormous potential profit (an incentive to speculation) and an object of fear (a risk that must be hedged).

The mirror image of this phenomenon is the requirement that fixed rates be protected by capital controls. In a liberal financial environment, misalignment of a fixed rate can provoke overwhelming destabilizing capital movements and precipitate a crisis. Small wonder that when financial eruptions spread beyond national borders they almost always involve major shifts in exchange rates, with consequent revaluations of assets and liabilities, and significant financial disruption.

The answers to two questions are fundamental to an understanding of the international financial system: how are exchange rates determined, and what do they do?

Despite the pivotal role that both the levels of exchange rates and their changes play in the international economy, satisfactory explanations of how they are determined are notable by their absence. The initial part of this chapter first explores why exchange rates between different countries' currencies are at the levels they are, and second, how and why the levels are changing. The arguments are somewhat analytical but worth mastering, given the global significance of exchange rate movements in an era of unregulated international financial flows.

With respect to today's liberalized capital markets, three central conclusions emerge:

> *First*, exchange rates are *not* determined by so-called market "fundamentals," but rather by investors' expectations

and conventions as they interact in cross-border "forward" markets for foreign exchange and other assets.

Second, as key components in a financial beauty contest, conventions can change (sometimes very rapidly) in response to shifts in fundamentals, but such changes are historically contingent and impossible to foretell in detail by the vast majority of market players. Indeed, the distinction between conventions and fundamentals is blurred because they play off against each other in the beauty contest.

Third, when conventions do shift, they can feed back on market performance and the fundamentals themselves in highly destabilizing fashion.

Part of this *in*determinacy of an exchange rate between two currencies resides in the degree of "openness" of the economies concerned. Depending on time and place, both the current and capital accounts of an economy's balance of payments can lie along a spectrum ranging from essentially unregulated or "open" to highly restricted or "closed." As emphasized in chapter 2, controls on cross-border financial movements are key factors in determining openness. Changes in control regimes have been responsible for destabilizing financial markets in developed and developing economies, as will be described in chapters 4 and 5.

How capital controls operate and how they can break down are topics covered later in this chapter, beginning with their post–World War II history in the United States (now mostly forgotten) and then going on to experiences in representative developing countries. The discussion concludes with an examination of proposals for a "Tobin tax"—a levy aimed at restraining capital market transactions by making them more costly—and other means for regulating cross-border capital movements in the industrialized world.

THE DETERMINATION
OF EXCHANGE RATES

One standard line of argument about the determination of exchange rates is based on arbitrage in financial and commodity markets. A second approach focuses on stock and flow balances involving asset portfolios, or the "home" country's accounts with the rest of the world.

Arbitrage involves a (nearly) simultaneous purchase and sale in separate markets in order to profit from a price differential between them. A foreign exchange dealer may, for example, buy sterling with dollars, use the sterling to buy euros, and then spend the euros to buy dollars, making a profit from misalignments in the triangular transaction.

Much current analysis of financial markets—including the famous Black-Scholes formula for pricing derivatives—is couched in terms of a highly mathematical theory built up since the 1960s. *The* basic assumption it makes is that all arbitrage opportunities are seized by market players. There are no misalignments in multilateral markets. Markets are "efficient" in that sense. Even small misalignments are ruled out.

This "complete arbitrage" hypothesis was applied to currency markets in the 1920s by Keynes. It gives a rule known as "uncovered interest-rate parity" by which the exchange rate can be calculated as an asset price from expected changes in its value over time. At about the same time the Swedish economist Gustav Cassell advocated another exchange rate rule known as "purchasing power parity" based upon arbitrage in commodity markets. Exchange rates should be such that tradable commodities command the same prices in any country. Neither parity condition is observed in practice, rendering their underlying assumptions somewhat dubious. But both are commonly used as exchange rate fundamentals, i.e. from time to time one or another parity is *believed* to be true by market players. If one of the hypotheses is badly violated, the market may conclude that the current exchange rate is at an inappropriate level.

Other theories about how the exchange rate is determined concentrate on its relationship to macro-level market aggregates such as the trade balance, the composition of asset portfolios, or the overall balance of payments. If the rate is allowed to "float" or change freely, it is *supposed* to arrive at a level that "clears" these macro balances. If the rate is fixed, the macro balances may fail to achieve equilibrium in well-determined ways. It will be shown below that these are not satisfactory approaches to exchange rate determination. In fact it turns out that in today's markets the exchange rate is *extrinsic* to all three balances. They arrive at their observed positions through variation of other macro variables such as interest rates or the general level of economic activity. A floating exchange rate is not a "price" that adjusts to equilibrate markets. Apart, that is, from the markets in which its own future values are set.

However, the exchange rate is influenced by observed macro performance via the impact of the conventional "fundamentals." And these fundamentals may in turn be influenced by the exchange rate. For example a large current account deficit (or its mirror image, a capital account surplus) is often seen as an adverse fundamental. Similarly, as will be shown in chapters 4 and 5, certain portfolio positions can be interpreted as fundamental as well. These fundamentals feed into the beauty contest determining the dynamics of the financial markets. Shifts in conventional views about how current fundamentals influence expected forward values of the exchange rate can be highly destabilizing both to the exchange rate and to the economy as a whole.

Two other analyses of the behavior of exchange rates are worth mentioning. *First*, "twin deficit" models assume that the balance on external accounts is determined by the fiscal balance, which immediately emerges as another fundamental. In particular a deterioration in the external position is attributed to growing fiscal deficit. *Second*, the so-called "trilemma" suggests that three component policies — liberal capital markets, a fixed exchange rate, and an independent monetary (or indeed, fiscal) policy—may be mutually incompatible. Any two out of the three are possible at the same time, but not the third. Again, the state of expectations in the market is the ultimate arbiter.

THE BALANCE OF PAYMENTS

A seldom-acknowledged fact of economics is that one of the best ways to solve a problem is to get your accounting right. This is nowhere more true than in analyses of international trade and finance.

A country's balance of the payments with the rest of the world (ROW) comprises three main accounts—for trade in goods and services, for "factor payments" such as interest, wage remittances, and dividends, and for movements of capital. The sum of the first two accounts, the "current account," is equal to a flow of payments into and out of the country. To the extent that national spending exceeds income, the gap must be covered by borrowing on capital account. To the extent that national income exceeds spending, then the surplus must flow into lending to the ROW. The capital account is made up of a wide variety of portfolio flows, but the overall balance must, as an accounting identity, be equal and opposite to the current account, once changes in foreign exchange reserves are taken into account, too.

Table 3.1 shows how these flows fit together for the home country and ROW, on the simplifying assumption that the only financial claims between the two are interest-paying bonds issued by their respective governments. Factor payments apart from interest are thereby ignored. It is useful to think about the balance of payments in terms of inflows (or "sources") and outflows (or "uses") of funds. The main sources of funds are exports, interest (plus remittances, dividends, etc.) paid by the ROW to the home country on its holdings of assets abroad, plus the home country's borrowing, i.e. increases in its debt (liabilities) to the rest of the world (including claims owed to the

Table 3.1

Components of the Balance of Payments (in $, or "home currency")

Inflows (Sources)	Outflows (Uses)
Trade Account	
Exports ($)	e[Imports (¥)]
Factor Payments	
e[Interest to home non-financial sector (¥)]	Interest to ROW non-financial sector ($)
e[Interest on home reserves (¥)]	Interest on ROW reserves ($)
Capital Account	
Increase in home debt to ROW non-financial sector ($)	e[Increase in ROW debt to home non-financial sector (¥)]
Increase in ROW reserves ($)	e[Increase in home reserves (¥)]

ROW non-financial sector and the foreign reserves[1] of the ROW). The main uses of funds are for imports, interest payments on the home country's debt, and lending, i.e. increases in the home country's claims on the ROW (including home's international reserves).

The accounting convention is that the totals of sources and uses must be equal. Sometimes this rule leads to unusual combinations of flows. For example, the home country might be running a current account deficit (outflows exceed inflows on the combined trade and factor payments accounts) along with a *larger* capital account surplus (the increase in home debt to ROW exceeds the reverse flow). If ROW's reserves stay constant, then home's reserves must be rising. Such configurations are rarely permanent but bring a pleasant sense of (false) security while they last. As will be seen in chapter 5, they were essential features in the early stages of several developing country crisis scenarios.

A final, crucial bit of accounting is that some flows are denominated in terms of the home currency ($) while others are in ROW terms (¥), as indicated by the parentheses at the end of each entry. The ROW flows in yen are converted to dollars via multiplication by the spot dollar/yen exchange rate, e, as a scaling factor between two sets of prices. Home and ROW have their own pricing systems, and the number e translates from one to the other. By way of illustration, the dollar/yen rate early in 1999 was about 0.009 — one yen would buy 90 percent of a US penny. In standard (and confusing) usage, a *weaker* dollar corresponds to a *higher* exchange rate. If the rate were to rise above 0.009, the yen would buy a bigger fraction of the penny, the yen would be stronger and the dollar weaker.

There is no compelling reason why each yen entry in the balance of payments should be converted to dollars by the *same* factor. A country's trade and banking authorities could in principle dictate different conversion factors for different sorts of payments (different categories of goods and services, different forms of factor payments, different financial flows, etc.). Such "multiple rate" systems have been used in many times and places. They are always subject to evasion because they set up arbitrage opportunities between different transactions across the same borders — cheap loans might be taken out to finance dear imports or vice versa. In a relatively closed economy such maneuvers are difficult to arrange. In the current international environment with its open economies, multiple rate systems are extremely vulnerable to arbitrage. But they existed worldwide in the not-so-distant past, and if for some reason national economies are re-closed to external transactions in the future, they could appear again.

EXCHANGE RATE REGIMES

Present-day exchange regimes come in two fundamental varieties — fixed and floating.

A "fixed" exchange rate sets a value for the local currency in terms of the currency of some other country (or a weighted average of other countries, if a "basket peg" is adopted). As a variation on the fixed theme, the rate may be allowed to fluctuate within a band or be revised from time to time to guide its real value in a certain direction. One such scheme is a "crawling peg" in which small, frequent exchange rate changes are used to offset a differential between inflation rates in the home country and the rest of the world.

Since the market in which currencies are bought and sold never closes, a fixed value of the exchange rate must be maintained by interventions in the market, typically undertaken by the home country central bank. Examples include sales or purchases of reserves, or interest rate adjustments, which attempt to balance the supply of the currency with the demand for it at the prevailing fixed exchange rate. Market players may support or attack a fixed rate by buying or selling assets denominated in the home currency, but that does not mean that the rate will change (once it hits a boundary of its band, at least). Rather, the country concerned will accumulate or lose reserves. This will have further implications down the line. For reasons discussed later, many developing countries pursue fixed rate schemes of one form or another. The sustainability of the rate today or tomorrow depends, as we shall see, on players' *perceptions* of the economy's fundamentals.

Since the early 1970s the developed countries have floated their exchange rates, managed with greater or lesser concern by the authorities. In early 1999 the major floating currencies were the dollar, the yen, the euro, and the pound sterling. Since the mid-1970s the United States has not been greatly concerned with the real value of its exchange rate (recall the numbers illustrating the dollar's volatility in chapter 2). So the US comes closest to having a "pure" floating regime, but other rich countries including "Euroland," (the eleven nations which initially adhered to the euro), are not far behind.

In the wake of massive reserve losses in their recent crises,

Mexico, some East Asian countries, Russia, and Brazil have also adopted floating rates. How closely they will be managed or removed from immediate market pressure by capital controls remains to be seen.

ASSET PRICES, EXPECTATIONS, AND EXCHANGE RATES

As emphasized in the introduction to this chapter, despite the enormous importance of exchange rates to the international financial system, experts have a hard time explaining their behavior. A floating rate however clearly behaves as an "asset price" in the sense that its present level depends on expected future returns to holding assets valued in home or foreign money. These returns are quoted in forward or futures markets (the distinction between the two being that futures markets have more formalized trading rules). Indeed, a floating rate regime cannot function in the long run without forward transactions. As we will see in subsequent sections of this chapter, fundamentals cannot directly determine the exchange rate. This means that there is *nothing* an exchange rate can plausibly float against except its own expected future values.

How asset markets behave is a subject of continuing controversy. Analysis of the exchange rate as an asset price can be neatly encapsulated between two books by Keynes—his *Tract on Monetary Reform* (1923) and *The General Theory of Employment, Interest, and Money* (1936). The former concentrates on how rational investors will pursue arbitrage strategies to determine exchange rates. Via the beauty contest, the latter shows how investors are not so rational after all.

To grasp the concept of an asset price, consider how to determine the market value of a rental apartment building in New York City. A real estate investor who is considering buying the building would have to take into account the costs of borrowing or returns from alternative placements (say an interest rate i of 5 percent) together with an additional carrying cost reflecting risk and the aggravation of dealing with tenants, the mayor and his employees, and other distractions (say the cost rate is $c = 5$ percent). Suppose the yearly rent roll and maintenance costs are R and M respectively. Then the value V of the building should be given by the discounted sum of its net returns $(R - M)$ over time. The relevant discount rate is the sum of interest and carrying costs, $i + c$. For a long-lived asset like a building, its value V will be given by the (approximate) formula $V = (R - M)/(i + c)$, i.e. the value is the net return flow "capitalized" by the discount rate. With the numbers just quoted, the building's value would be its net income stream multiplied by a factor of $1/(0.1) = 10$.

A slightly more general formulation sets an asset price V equal to an expected net return flow R^{exp} capitalized by interest and carrying costs, $V = R^{exp}/(i + c)$. The expectations may be more or less definite — rent rolls in New York City are fairly well determined, potential capital gains on Bangkok real estate in the mid-1990s obviously were not. For given expectations, the formula also shows that an asset price such as V can be expected to vary inversely with its discount rate such as $i + c$. This fundamental relationship underlies a number of conclusions to be presented below.

Keynes presented an alternative formulation of the same calculation in *The General Theory*. What he called the "own-rate of return" on an asset is $i = (R^{exp}/V) - c$, that is, the net income per unit value minus the carrying cost. Keynes's point was that asset prices like V "should" adjust to bring revenue streams net of carrying costs into broad alignment with one another and with "the" interest rate as well. The quotation marks around the "should" are meant to call attention to the fact that arbitrage very often fails (in part for reasons he advanced in his beauty contest). Fully arbitraged asset prices represent a "central tendency" or "center of gravitation" in the market that is often honored in the breach.

The exchange rate becomes an asset price when it responds to potential capital gains or losses in forward markets. Consider a Japanese investor who wants dollars in one month's time. He or she has two basic options. The first is to buy dollars now at the spot exchange rate e and hold them at the American (monthly) interest rate i. The total dollars available at the end of the month will be $e(1 + i)$. The alternative is to hold resources in yen at an interest rate i^* and then buy dollars at the *expected* forward rate $f = e + \triangle e^{\mathrm{exp}}$ where $\triangle e^{\mathrm{exp}}$ is the expected change in the dollar/yen exchange rate (the symbol "$\triangle$" preceding a variable is standard notation for its change over a period of time). The total at hand after a month would be $f(1 + i^*)$.

Complete arbitrage over time in forward markets should insure that returns to both these two strategies are equalized, or $e(1 + i) = f(1 + i^*)$. Under normal conditions both the expected exchange rate change and the monthly interest rate will be around a percentage point or less. The product i^* ($\triangle e^{\mathrm{exp}}$) of these two valuation changes per month will be "small" (well less than 0.01 percent) and can be ignored. If this is true, then a bit of algebra applied to the arbitrage condition above shows that $e = \triangle e^{\mathrm{exp}}/(i - i^*)$. The current exchange rate should be equal to its expected change, capitalized by the difference between the two interest rates.

There are two interpretations of the $\triangle e^{\mathrm{exp}}$ term. The first one applies to exchange markets among industrialized countries. They are usually "thick" in the sense of having a large volume of daily transactions and a wide spectrum of forward contracts. There is free capital mobility and an absence of political or country risk (of the imposition of capital controls, for example). A corollary is that future values of the exchange rate can be readily "hedged" by setting up forward contracts.

In a simple example of hedging, suppose that a Japanese company agrees to pay an American software house ¥10,000,000 in twelve months to use its products for one year. The current dollar/yen rate is 0.009, making the contract worth $90,000. To protect its position, the American company may want to enter into a contract with a counter-party (perhaps the Japanese company itself) to exchange future yen for future dollars at the current spot rate. *If this contract were costless*, a year from now the counter-party would pay to (or receive from) the American company an amount of cash equal to ¥10,000,000 times the difference between the current rate and the spot rate at that time. If the dollar strengthened so that the rate a year hence were 0.008, then the US company would make only $80,000 from its ¥10,000,000. But as a result of the hedging contract, the counter-party would be obligated to pay 10,000,000 x (000.9 - 000.8) = $10,000, offsetting the exchange loss the American firm would otherwise have suffered.

Of course, in the real world contracts that do not involve "transactions costs" do not exist. However, the volume of trading in currency markets among Europe, the US, and Japan (at least) is so great that hedging contracts can be set up with costs on the order of 0.1 percent or less of the amounts being hedged. When forward values of the exchange rate can be "covered" in this sense, we have a case of *covered* interest-rate parity. In effect, pairs of contracts exist which differ *only* with respect to currencies of denomination and interest rates — say dollar and yen deposits at the same branch of the same bank. The members of the pair are subject to identical credit risks, capital controls, and explicit taxes. The Japanese investor or the American software firm can choose either one (or both) as a place to park funds.

But the exchange risk remains. It has simply been shifted onto the counter-party who is exposed to the *uncovered* interest rate parity or UIP case. The expected change in the exchange rate Δe^{exp} unavoidably depends on the outcome of all investors' expectations about the future (the sum of average opinion). In own-rate form $i = i^* + (\Delta e^{\text{exp}}/e)$, Keynes's relationship says that the home interest rate will exceed the ROW rate whenever the home currency is generally *expected* to depreciate or weaken, i.e. Δe^{exp} is expected to be positive. A Japanese investor who goes into dollars subjectively anticipates a capital loss and has to be compensated by an American rate i that exceeds i^*. The "spread" between interest rates will become greater as $\Delta e^{\text{exp}}/e$, the expected relative or percentage change in the exchange rate, rises. If arbitrage is complete, one implication is that e will "jump" in response to a change in expectations if interest rates remain unchanged.

"Testing" the validity of interest rate parity models has been a playground for econometricians over the past few decades. They have enormous fun trying to formulate and quantify expectations. They have shown that covered parity in "thick" markets for the currencies of developed economies does indeed appear to be widely observed. At least, this is true when markets are behaving in tranquil fashion. Then covered interest rate differentials have become negligible in countries with unrestricted capital flows. On the other hand, the evidence indicates that UIP does not hold—expected exchange rate changes (however measured) do not reliably correlate with interest rate differentials.

The fact that UIP is not generally valid, and hence that interest rate spreads are not always closely tied to expected exchange rate changes (and vice versa), has profound implications for the global political economy. As will be seen in chapter 5, the presence of large return spreads between domestic assets and foreign borrowing costs is an *excellent* predictor of financial crises in "emerging market" economies. But what the spreads reflect is not arbitrage but the presence of extremely high return differentials that cannot possibly persist. Substantial violation of UIP signals potential exchange rate problems, but it is no reliable guide as to when and how dramatically they will occur. When a crisis strikes and depreciation is unavoidable, then Δe^{exp} suddenly shoots upward. The own-rate formula indicates that a spike in the home interest rate i or the spot rate e cannot be far behind. To begin to reestablish "normal" arbitrage, the home country is pushed by the market toward tightening credit, devaluing the currency, or both. Only an economically powerful country or one that imposes capital controls can avoid such pressures.

COMMODITY ARBITRAGE
AND PURCHASING POWER PARITY

Arbitrage in commodity as opposed to asset markets underlies a long-run theory of exchange rate determination that may be traced back to the sixteenth century and was popularized in the twentieth century by Gustav Cassell. The basic idea is that the dollar should buy as much of a traded good in a foreign country as at home. If P and P^* are the home and foreign price indexes respectively, then the spot exchange rate e should satisfy the relationship $e = P/P^*$. This is "purchaser power parity" (PPP). If P exceeds eP^*, then the home country should be inundated with goods from its foreign providers until P is forced down or e up to restore market balance. If the latter adjustment occurs in an inflationary context, the exchange rate should rise along with the domestic price level (perhaps with fluctuations around the trend or "overshooting" when e jumps to satisfy UIP in response to shifts in the expected rate of inflation). Purchasing power parity is a "fundamental" that is conventionally supposed generally to hold. In the "overvalued" $P > eP^*$ case, violation of PPP should be associated with a widening trade deficit, so that two well-known fundamental indicators reinforce one another.

However, despite its long pedigree and the fact that it is widely believed to hold, PPP does not apply in practice. Two examples:

> The introduction of the euro prompted a flurry of international price comparisons. They showed that prices for the "same" consumer good across the eleven countries that joined together to form the single currency zone of Euroland spanned a range of 50 percent up or down from the middle. The range for producers' goods was almost as wide.

> In a longer run, the association of PPP "overvaluation" with a wide trade deficit does not always hold. By most price comparisons the US is "undervalued." In one frequently

quoted example, price quotations in the local currency for many consumer goods in the UK and US are just about the same numbers, although in exchange markets it costs about $1.60 to buy one pound. At the same time the chronic US trade deficit signals that the dollar is too strong.

A plethora of similar observations may be found throughout the literature. The market's enforcement of the "law of one price" across borders or even within one country is notably lax. Even so, a persistently higher rate of inflation at home than abroad is usually interpreted as an unfavorable "fundamental," and accordingly the market requires that the exchange rate adjust. Many developing countries have countered such a tendency with crawling peg regimes in which the exchange rate is adjusted frequently to keep P approximately equal to eP^* and maintain purchasing power parity.

COMMODITY MARKETS

Outside of forward currency markets, is the exchange rate "just" a scaling factor or is it a price? If so, then the price of what? Which market(s) does it clear? These questions set the stage for a number of arguments asserting that the spot rate clears markets less ethereal than those for its own expected forward values. To describe them, we have to consider how commodity markets operate in the first place. In keeping with the economists' predilection for bucolic examples, consider Unhygienix, the fishmonger in the famous French village of Asterix the Gaul (in the English language version, alas). Three points about the village's economic operations bear note:

The first is that price changes are supposed to help clear markets. If Unhygienix stocks too many fish, he won't be able to sell them at the going price. Standard theory says that he should cut his markup to allow the price to fall and the villagers' demand for fish to go up until the excess supply is eliminated. If the stock of fish is initially too low, then Unhygienix and his wife Bacteria can charge more, and possibly also get more turbot from their wholesalers.

Secondly, the fish market cannot fail to clear just by itself. The basic reason is that one person's sales in one market provide the income that he or she can use to make purchases in other markets. Those who spend on fish may make their money selling wild boars. Those who spend on wild boars may make their money selling fish. The total amount available to spend on fish is equal to the total value of wild boar sales. And the total amount available to spend on wild boar is equal to the total value of fish sales. So if the total demand for fish is equal to the total supply, then at the same time the total demand for wild boar is equal to the total supply of boar, too. But if summing across these transactions shows that the villagers as a totality want to spend *more* on fish than Unhygienix has on hand at his current prices, then they must also want to spend *less* than the value of available supply of wild boar at the ruling price. An excess demand for fish is accompanied by an excess supply of wild boar. Put more abstractly, the same point is that if in $N - 1$ of the village's N micro markets demand equals supply (that is, the markets clear at current prices), then so must the N-th because there is no way that it can be out of balance if demand equals supply in all the others. In keeping with the Gallic theme, this truism is known as Walras's Law after the nineteenth-century French economic theorist, Léon Walras.

Finally, while changes in prices often play a role in market adjustment, this is not always so. Suppose that Unhygienix sets a customary price for his fish, as does the strongman Obelix for his wild boar. If there is an excess demand for fish, Unhygienix may be able to bring in more; an excess supply can be made into fertilizer. Obelix is strong enough to catch boars on demand; any excess supply can go into inventory. The fish/boar relative price does not have to move to encourage these supply and demand responses to happen. In a village context, at least, word-of-mouth communication among customers and tradesmen could be sufficient reason. In a modern industrialized economy, business enterprises usually do not raise prices when inventories of the goods they produce start to fall in response to higher demand. Rather, they run extra shifts and hire more workers to step up production to meet demand pressures. When inventories rise, production is cut back.

THE TRADE ACCOUNT

These observations shed light on the trade account, a macro-economic relationship involving markets for thousands of imported and exported commodities. A change in the exchange rate will affect domestic prices of all these traded goods—in that sense the exchange rate is a *macro* price. But movements in the exchange rate shift the prices of all traded goods relative to prices of what? In its modern form, the answer was provided by Australian economists W. E. G. Salter and Trevor Swan in the 1950s. It is that the exchange rate has to fluctuate relative to the prices of non-traded goods—domestically marketed commodities and services such as (usually) haircuts and unskilled labor. By Walras's Law extended to the macro level it is generally assumed that if markets for non-traded goods clear, then so will markets for traded goods. Devaluing the local currency makes traded goods more expensive for consumers and their local production relatively more profitable; it also reduces the real wage (because some goods have gone up in price relative to the wage) and hence purchasing power. All these changes are supposed to cut imports, stimulate import-competing and export industries, and reduce the trade deficit.

Salter and Swan's line of reasoning suggests that a floating exchange rate could adjust "in the market" to clear the trade account. A large deficit presumably sets up forces that push the spot rate e upward (the currency weakens), switching the resource allocation from non-traded toward traded goods and causing the deficit to fall. This story sounds plausible, but the fundamental problem is that it became irrelevant to developed economies after capital markets were decontrolled.

As was described in chapter 2, the volume of annual currency trading around 1970 was less than double the yearly value of foreign trade and long-term investment. Now it is eighty times as large. For industrialized countries at least, the trade account makes up such a tiny fraction of total external transactions that it cannot possibly play a central role in determining the exchange rate. Either the exchange rate is fixed by the authorities, or it is determined in asset markets. With the rate determined one way or the other, domestic prices and outputs adjust so that markets for non-traded goods clear. As will be shown below, the current account of the balance of payments comes out as a consequence.

However, for many developing economies the story is the other way around. Their trade often dominates their external transactions. Forward markets based on currencies even as important as the baht or rupee are "thin," and subject to large, destabilizing fluctuations. So the commodity markets play a significant role in exchange rate determination. Rather than suffer the instabilities of a floating rate, the better part of valor in countries like Thailand or India may be a fixed rate with crawling peg adjustments or a "dirty" (closely managed) float. In line with the fish vs. wild boar story above, pegging the exchange rate throws the bulk of market adjustment onto output as opposed to price changes. In a fixed rate system, devaluation may well improve the trade balance by driving down local real wages, cutting effective demand, and reducing imports by throwing people out of work.

With a fixed rate, the ratio of a non-traded goods price index to its traded goods counterpart (say the ratio between the consumer and wholesale price indexes) becomes a "fundamental."

If the ratio is judged to be "too high," depreciation is a policy option. However, it is commonly rejected by local authorities who may fear the inflationary impact of a weaker exchange rate pushing up import prices. Yet depreciation may be enthusiastically recommended by representatives of the International Monetary Fund because they often see attacking trade deficits as their main task.

In practice in both rich and poor economies, neither a big trade deficit nor high prices of non-traded relative to traded goods necessarily lead to exchange rate adjustment. With an income level in the middle, Argentina for years had a large deficit and skewed traded/non-traded prices after it pegged its peso rigidly to the dollar in 1991 as part of an anti-inflation package. Thanks in part to generous capital inflows and high unemployment, it had enough foreign exchange on hand at (almost) all times to cover its external obligations through 1998. The future will tell whether the January 1999 devaluation by Brazil — Argentina's biggest trading partner — will force this situation to change.

PORTFOLIO BALANCE

Another of Keynes's contributions in *The General Theory* was to emphasize that prices and rates of return on assets (which, as we have seen, are generally related inversely) are determined in markets for stocks and not flows. The interest rate on Treasury bills is set by transactions involving the whole stock of bills, *not* the flows or changes in the stock auctioned or retired by the Treasury this week. Transactions in a new financial security would just add one more market to the total number of markets in the economy for goods, services, *and securities*. Walras's Law applies, so that only N - 1 of N markets have to clear via adjustment mechanisms such as changing interest rates and prices. For securities considered in isolation (as in the discussion immediately following), the law basically states that each actor's net worth is the difference between the values of his or her assets and liabilities, and that all securities must be held in asset portfolios. There are no financial "black holes."

Consider the special but illuminating case of a closed economy in which there are just two markets for financial claims, say the markets for interest-free money (admittedly an anachronism in the late twentieth century) and bonds. A higher level of economic activity usually leads to an increase in money demand to permit a greater volume of transactions involving goods and services. Asset-holders will try to switch their portfolios from bonds. Because the entire stock of bonds has to be held, their price will fall or, looking at the same thing the other way around, the interest rate will rise. An increase in the money supply engineered by Federal Reserve open market bond purchases will similarly cause the bond price to rise and the interest rate to fall in the standard recipe for expansionary monetary policy. The adjustment can be viewed as happening in either the bond or money market, with the other tagging along.

Now consider asset market interactions between the home and ROW economies. There are four assets—moneys and bonds in the two countries. It is simplest to assume (harmlessly for the analysis but incorrectly, as we have seen in chapter 2) that money supplies are only held domestically while asset-holders in both countries have both sorts of bonds in their portfolios. Demand for the home bond can be assumed to rise with its interest rate i and the spot exchange rate e and to decline with the ROW rate i^* and expected home depreciation Δe^{exp}. That is, asset-holders will shift their portfolios toward the home bond when its return goes up. They will shift away when the foreign return rises *or* when they fear a capital loss on the home bond due to an expected devaluation. The proportional impact of the expected capital loss will be lessened by a higher value of e, so an increase in e, i.e. a devaluation of the spot rate, could be expected to increase the demand for home bonds. Although the discussion to follow highlights these "substitution" effects, devaluation also has "income" and "wealth" effects that are crucial to its political economy. A weaker home currency tends to reduce real income flows and the real wealth of households and business. These changes go together with devaluation's substitution effect to put downward pressure on home interest rates. Its adverse income and wealth effects also explain why the decision to devalue a pegged exchange rate is politically fraught.

Interpreted superficially, this two-country accounting framework suggests that the level of the exchange rate is set by clearing of *current* asset markets as opposed to forward markets as in UIP. That is, a straightforward application of Walras's Law seems to imply that there should be three independent asset markets, say for home's money and bonds and for ROW's bonds. Given the expected change in the exchange rate, clearing of these three demand-supply balances should determine the two interest rates and the spot rate.

As it turns out however, such an application of Walras's Law is incorrect. Taking portfolio allocations and balance sheets fully into consideration, it is straightforward to show that the model can really only determine the two interest rates. As we have seen, in a closed economy Walras's Law says that if the market for money clears, then so does the market for bonds. Just adding a second economy scaled to the first by the exchange rate does not alter this basic situation.

To trace through the details with a *given* spot rate, suppose that the central bank creates money (deposits it in bondholders' accounts) to buy home bonds in an open market operation. As discussed above, the bond price will rise and the home interest rate will fall. Home portfolios will shift toward home money and ROW bonds until the home money market clears. Foreign portfolios will also shift toward ROW bonds. The combined new demands from home and the ROW will drive up the latter's bond price or reduce its interest rate until the foreign bond market clears. But by Walras's Law applied to the foreign economy, then its money market has to clear as well. All four financial markets rebalance *without* any need for the exchange rate to change—it is irrelevant to the adjustment process.

Nor does the exchange rate play any role in equilibrating the balance of payments over time. In one standard scenario, suppose that the home country runs a current account deficit. Its foreign reserves will fall, leading to monetary contraction and a higher interest rate i. If the UIP formula applies, the expected change in the exchange rate Δe^{exp} will become positive, presumably causing the spot rate to depreciate over time. A weaker rate should lead to better trade performance, reserve inflows, and a long-run position in which the current account is balanced and the exchange and interest rates are stable. This scenario suggests that stock-flow adjustments in the presence of capital mobility will generally move the exchange rate in the "right" direction to eliminate a current account deficit in the long run.

This story is comforting, but wrong. The United States, for example, has run substantial trade deficits since the 1970s with two depreciation-then-appreciation cycles with periods exceeding ten years. Medium-term volatility characterizes dollar exchange rate dynamics, not unidirectional adjustment leading the external balance to improve. In one more example of this chapter's basic theme, portfolio adjustments do *not* provide a way for a "fundamental" external deficit to generate an exchange rate adjustment that will make the deficit disappear.

OVERALL BALANCE

The best-known approach to open economy macroeconomics was proposed independently by J. Marcus Fleming and Robert Mundell in the 1960s. They too were attempting to build a theory to explain the determination and role of the exchange rate. In the absence of "perfect" capital mobility (which would set $i = i^*$ and $\Delta e^{\text{exp}} = 0$ automatically) they claimed to show that the spot rate would adjust to bring the capital and current accounts of the balance of payments into equilibrium.

They were wrong, essentially because (by Walras's Law applied to financial and commodity flows) when all other macro balances in the economy are satisfied, then the balance of payments has to be satisfied as well. Shifts in the exchange rate are not needed to make "the foreign exchanges" clear. The key to understanding why is to consider how the economy's whole set of macro relationships fit together, how outcomes are dependent on one another. The relevant relationships may be marshaled under four headings: (1) determination of the level of economic activity from macroeconomic equilibrium in markets for goods; (2) linkages of changes in stocks of assets and liabilities with savings flows from the price/quantity side of the system; (3) clearing of financial markets in terms of flows; and (4) how all these relationships feed into one another.

Macroeconomic Equilibrium

Fleming and Mundell saw the world in Keynesian terms: the level of economic activity is determined by effective demand. Demand is driven by relatively stable "injections" such as investment (gross fixed capital formation plus inventory accumulation), government spending, and exports. For these demands to be met some share of national output must *not* be consumed, that is, it must be saved or transferred to the government via taxes, or demands must be met from the rest of the world via imports. If saving, tax, and import "leakages" increase with output, then output adjustment becomes a mechanism—*the* mechanism according to Keynes—to equate total injections with total leakages.

Price changes may or may not ease this process, in line with the fish/wild boar discussion above. Suppose for example that prices are determined by the interaction of effective demand with the impact of money wages on the levels of real incomes. In one highly relevant scenario, devaluation cuts the real wage by driving up prices of traded goods. If labor reacts by pressing for money wage increases and producers pass such cost increases along into prices, then the stage is set for a wage-price spiral having little to do with equilibrium in labor and commodity markets. The changes in income distribution induced by inflation may in turn influence the level of effective demand via the levels of injections and leakages, and affect distribution once again.

Macroeconomic equilibrium is defined by the equality of the value of total savings in the economy to the value of total investment. Four saving flows are often identified, for households and unincorporated business, incorporated business, government, and the rest of the world. They are defined as follows:

Household: S_{hh} = wages + dividends + rents + unincorporated business income + net interest + transfers - consumption - taxes

Business: S_{bus} = gross profits (of nonfinancial and financial corporations) + net interest - dividends - rents - taxes

Government: S_{gov} = taxes + central bank and other public sector profits + net interest - current spending - transfers

Rest of world: S_{row} = imports + interest paid to ROW - exports - interest received from ROW

The definition of S_{row} maintains the assumption of Table 3.1 that bonds are the only claims held across borders, with interest payments as the corresponding income flows. It is easy to verify that "foreign saving" S_{row} equals the current account deficit as defined above. If the home country spends more income abroad than it receives then it is dis-saving internationally. Saving from the ROW has to make up the gap.

The macro equilibrium condition mentioned above states that investment injections are just met by saving leakages,

$$PI - S_{hh} - S_{bus} - S_{gov} - S_{row} = 0 \qquad (1)$$

where I stands for real investment and P is a price index. If P is determined via money wages as discussed above and I responds to firms' expectations and (in Keynes's phrase) "animal spirits," then savings levels adjust via changes in output to bring about the equality in formula (1).

Flows of Funds

The next step is to recognize that savings flows must be used to build up assets or retire liabilities. Each sector has a "flow of funds" relationship of the form

Saving + $\triangle$ Liabilities = $\triangle$ Assets

where the "$\triangle$" term signals changes in stocks of liabilities and assets over a period of time (typically a quarter or a year in the reported data). Cumulated over the period, the flow of saving plus increases in liabilities (or gross borrowing) serve as sources of funds for acquisition of new assets (lending), the uses of funds. As usual, the sources = uses equality emerges as part of the economy's overall macro balance.

Among the asset changes for business will be capital accumulation, or the value of investment PI. There is also a flow of funds equation for a fifth, or financial, sector subject to a standard accounting convention that its saving is zero. This convention is assured by crediting the profits of private financial firms and the central bank to business and government saving flows respectively, as in the definitions above. The financial sector's flow of funds basically states that any new loans or credits that it offers have to be backed by new liabilities or deposits.

Finally, it makes sense to look in detail at the flows of funds balance for the rest of the world. Rearranging the entries in Table 3.1 (omitting the exchange rate multiplications for simplicity) shows that

$$S_{row} + \text{Change in ROW debt to home} + \text{Change}$$
$$\text{in home reserves} = \text{Change in home debt}$$
$$\text{to ROW} + \text{Change in ROW reserves} \qquad (2)$$

To the left of the equals sign, home's current account deficit and its acquisition of new liabilities issued by ROW (that is, borrowing by ROW from home) are sources of funds for the ROW. It can use this money to build up assets in the home economy. The entries on the right-hand side of the equality show how the ROW allocates these resources across its new claims on home. Equation (2) is home's balance of payments, restated from Table 3.1. But it is also just ROW's flow of funds account with the home economy, no different in principle from those of home's household, business, government, and financial sectors.

This observation suggests that the balance of payments must be satisfied when home's financial and commodity markets clear. Summing changes in sources and uses across the five groups of financial actors, it must be true that △Assets = △Liabilities overall since one group's new claims are the others' new obligations. In light of equation (1) for commodity market balance therefore, if four of the flows of funds are satisfied then so will be the fifth in another variation on Walras's Law.

Clearing of Asset Markets in Terms of Flows

Now we can bring in markets for assets. From the discussion above of the portfolio balance model, we know that if (say) the home country's money market clears in terms of stocks, then so will the market for bonds. For present purposes, an essential extension of this statement is that if demand-supply balances for stocks clear steadily over time, then so will balances for changes in stocks, or flows. For example, the money created by a Federal Reserve open market operation of the sort discussed above will be absorbed into private sector money holdings without significant delay. Moreover, when flow balances for financial claims clear steadily, they feed automatically into the flows of funds equations. In any financial system, flow asset market balances and changes in portfolio composition weave together in a seamless web.

The Balance of Payments

So how exactly does the balance of payments figure in this tapestry? The details boil down to an extensive application of Walras's Law. Suppose that equality does not hold in equation (2). That means that changes in the claims included in the accounting—debt and reserves—do not offset home's current account deficit or S_{row}. Therefore some other transaction must be occurring. On the current account side of the ledger it could be smuggling. The officially recorded value of S_{row} is not correct because illicit commodity transactions are taking place. But it is far more likely with liberalized financial markets that the discrepancy will show up in the capital account.[2] To make the argument concrete, let us suppose that the home country is running up external arrears by not meeting its contracted payment obligations on outstanding debt. There are two possible forms of repercussion on home's flow asset market balances and flows of funds. One is that some other flow of funds relationship will fail to balance. The other is that if home's domestic flows of funds equalities hold, then some flow market balance for a financial asset must fail to clear.

Consider the second case. The obvious counterpart to a non-clearing balance of payments is the domestic bond market. The run-up in external arrears would be reflected into a flow excess supply of home bonds—foreigners are not picking up enough domestic securities to provide home the wherewithal to meet its external obligations. Under such circumstances (as discussed above), a spot devaluation could be expected to make home bonds appear cheaper for foreigners, thereby increasing their bond demand and removing the disequilibrium. As a consequence, the balance of payments would clear.

The rub is that if home's other financial markets are clearing, this sort of adjustment *cannot* happen—we know from the analysis of the portfolio balance model that if the home money market clears then so will the market for bonds. And with both money and bond markets in balance, there is simply no room in the accounting for a balance of payments disequilibrium.

The other possibility is that the non-clearing balance of payments is reflected into another flow of funds relationship subject to the overall macroeconomic equilibrium condition (1). For example, one can imagine and even observe (as in the developing country experiences recounted in chapter 5) situations in which the home country runs up external arrears at the same time as the domestic business sector borrows in anticipation of investment projects that aren't working out. An exchange rate realignment might even reverse such simultaneous buildups of external and internal bad debt. But at the macroeconomic level such situations are unusual—the banking sector at home is *not* usually in the business of providing nonperforming loans to corporations. In harmonious times the balance of payments emerges automatically from output and asset market equilibria. There is *no* need for the exchange rate (or any other variable) to adjust to ensure that external balance is satisfied.

THE TWIN DEFICITS

To summarize, the exchange rate is not determined in asset or commodity markets apart from transactions involving its own forward values. On the other hand, market relationships do suggest the existence of "fundamentals" that may well influence how a floating rate is determined via forward contracts. The price-based fundamentals mentioned so far include PPP, UIP, and the ratio of non-traded to traded goods price indexes. On the quantity side, we have the current account deficit. In present-day discussion, the fiscal deficit is often treated as another fundamental factor influencing expectations about the exchange rate.

A couple of channels are usually mentioned. One presupposes that the government mainly borrows from the banking system to finance a revenue shortfall. The resulting expansion in bank loans or assets has to be accompanied by greater liabilities, usually money. If "printing money" drives up the domestic price level (which may or may not happen) and the nominal exchange rate does not increase at the same rate, then PPP violation, an increasing ratio of non-traded to traded goods prices, and a widening trade deficit are supposed to loom.

The other view is based upon the investment-saving balance (1). Suppose that the value of investment PI is stable. Then a reduction in S_{gov} due to a bigger fiscal deficit must be met by higher saving from other sources. Greater economic activity spurred by the fiscal stimulus might be expected to raise saving from households, business, and the rest of the world all together. In Reagan-era discussion however the focus was on foreign saving—a lower level of S_{gov} was supposed to be matched by a "twin" increase in S_{row}. In practice, a close linkage was not observed, but that did not prevent twinned deficits from becoming part of the conventional wisdom.

THE TRILEMMA

Closely related to the twin deficits is a macro policy "trilemma" among (1) full capital mobility, (2) a fixed exchange rate, and (3) an independent monetary and fiscal policy. Supposedly only two of these policy lines can be consistently maintained. If the authorities try to pursue all three, they will sooner or later be punished by destabilizing capital flows, as in the run-up to the Great Depression around 1930 and Britain and Italy's difficulties during the ERM crisis more than sixty years later.

A trilemma exists in the eye of a beholder. Capital mobility and a fixed exchange rate are objective factors, but what is an "independent" monetary and fiscal policy? Typically the argument is that monetary and fiscal policy must agree with what the market "believes" to be reasonable and consistent objectives. In particular, monetary and fiscal policy must not be "excessively expansionary." Monetary stimulus would be associated with low home interest rates, which could lead to problems with UIP. Fiscal expansion might lead to problems with the trade deficit and/or PPP. These developments begin to threaten macro stability when players with significant market power begin to sense that at the fixed rate, the home country's current account deficit (or, perhaps, the fiscal deficit) cannot be financed by plausible levels of new foreign borrowing. They begin to divest assets denominated in the home currency in anticipation of the capital losses they would suffer if and when there is a devaluation. A crisis hits when reserve losses accelerate, the market raises its estimate of Δe^{exp} in the UIP calculus, and more players start stripping assets. The authorities are forced to devalue, interest rates soar, and the successful attackers sit back to count their profits.

How does the market decide when a trilemma is ripe to be pricked? The fact that no single form of transaction or arbitrage operation determines the exchange rate means that governments have some leeway in setting both the scaling factor between their country's price system and the rest of the world's and the rules by which it changes. However, their sailing room is not unlimited. A fixed rate is always in danger of violating what average market opinion regards as a fundamental. In a variation on the trilemma theme, even a floating rate amply supported by forward markets can be an invitation to extreme volatility. Volatility can lead to disaster if asset preferences shift markedly away from the home country's liabilities in response to shifting fundamentals or adverse "news." Unregulated international capital markets are the root of the trilemma.

THE BEAUTY CONTEST

Market players may well be "rational" in the sense that they tend to follow arbitrage rules like those underlying UIP, but rationality is not a sufficient description of the outcomes of their collective behavior. Even when the market behaves smoothly, interest rates and expected exchange rate changes ultimately depend on decisions of players regarding compositions and quantities of the bundles of domestic and foreign assets they hold. Convention plays the major role in such choices. The pricing of financial assets is a beauty contest.

Markets driven by average opinion about what average opinion will be demonstrate two special behavioral patterns. In "abnormal" times they can be volatile and prone to severe loss of liquidity when all opinion shifts the same way. The liquidity squeeze can drive up the cost of capital, reduce investment, and slow growth in the medium run. East Asian economies were hit by precisely such a loss of liquidity in 1997.

In "normal" times, the self-fulfilling prophecies of the market can sustain reasonable stability: "We should not conclude from this that everything depends on waves of irrational psychology. On the contrary, the state of long term expectations is often steady . . ." argued Keynes. Because it is shared by "a large number of ignorant individuals" (be they highly paid Wall Street professionals or otherwise), market opinion crystallizes around "convention" as expressed in simple slogans or views of the fundamentals. "Safe haven" assets in Switzerland or the US are safe so long as most players believe them to be so.

The fact that conventions can change unexpectedly and rapidly is the key to the trilemma. Most international crises in recent years have occurred in countries with open capital markets and more or less fixed exchange rates. The real question has to do with the *perceived* policy stance of the governments concerned—why did the "Asian miracle" turn virtually overnight into "crony capitalism"? As will be seen in chapter 5, underlying trends in the region were not fully favorable during the 1990s, but they did not affect the "miracle" of conventional wisdom until mid-1997. "[T]he mass psychology of a large number of ignorant individuals" was difficult to budge, until, that is, it reversed itself completely.

THE TECHNOLOGY FACTOR

Keynes was writing sixty-five years ago. Even if his description of market psychology is correct, it could be that institutional or technological changes have made it irrelevant to financial markets (especially currency markets) today. But he was not wrong. Evolution along both lines has made the system more subject to systemic risk than it was in the speculative heyday of the 1920s.

The beauty contest magnifies local prejudices. A person responding to the contest who knew nothing about English tastes in women's faces could do no better than pick the most beautiful photo according to his or her own preferences. To get past Keynes's first degree you have to know something about what everyone else is thinking. Modern communications technology has made transmission of the current play of preferences much more rapid and widespread than in the past, adding to the contest's instability. The currency devaluations in Asia after the 1997 crisis were far greater than warranted by all calculations of fundamentals — substantial "overshooting" was built into the reversal of conventions.

A second form of innovation has taken place within the financial industry itself. Recall the simple problem confronting the Japanese investor discussed above in connection with UIP. The proliferation of derivative contracts coupled with computer technology to solve high-dimensional optimization problems have amplified the arbitrage maneuvers that such a player can consider across enormous ranges of space, time, and contingent events. Does this mean that financial markets, at least, work any better?

The answer in fact may be no. One use of derivatives has been to create "towers of leverage" far taller than those that helped bring down the American financial system in the 1920s. The episode of the Long Term Capital Management hedge fund in the fall of 1998 (discussed fully in chapter 4) is only the most striking example. As regulatory compartmentalization has been broken down, the irony is that the greatest systemic damage has been done by instruments ostensibly invented to *spread* risk over risk-averse individual investors. As will be seen in chapter 5, the *inability* of derivative contracts to allow important players to hedge worsened the Asian crisis.

Keynes's basic insights remain valid and have not been abrogated by the latest technological tricks. Today's financial crises thrive on technology but don't deviate from the familiar pattern. From the Silver Train (*Silberzug*) steaming from Vienna to

Hamburg in December 1857 in a lender of last resort operation, through desperate telegrams to New York from Flem Snopes in Yoknapatawpha County, Mississippi, to cover margin calls in 1929, to frantic Mexican nationals electronically switching from pesos into dollars in anticipation of the December 1994 devaluation, the last gasp is the same. New technology facilitated each event and made it far more stressful when it happened.

CAPITAL CONTROLS

Given the power of changes in convention to magnify market crises, an immediate question might be: Why do intelligent and well-informed national policymakers expose their countries to the perils of the trilemma by adopting liberal capital markets and/or fixed exchange rates? A full consideration of these issues, particularly with respect to the exchange rate regime, must await further discussion in the following chapters. But given the role which financial market liberalization plays in the overall argument of this chapter, this is an appropriate point to consider the pros and cons of capital controls.

First, by way of review, several techniques can be used to close an economy. On trade account, quotas or more generally quantitative restrictions (QRs) are aimed at holding down imports and exports definitively. They may impinge on the capital account if they are tied to trade finance. Very high import tariffs or export tax rates are used at times to the same ends.

Capital controls as such put limitations on quantity, conditions, and destinations of capital flows. Recent literature distinguishes between market-based and non-market based (or QR type) controls. A tax on some form of financial flow (for example short-term borrowing by national firms from foreign banks) is said to be market-based because it operates by altering the cost of foreign funds. An absolute prohibition of such transactions is deemed to be a "non-market" intervention.

So-called exchange controls are an extreme form of capital

controls. They require that some or all foreign currency inflows be surrendered to the central bank or a government agency which will determine their use. The absence of exchange controls means that a currency can be exchanged freely for a variety of uses, or that it is "convertible."

THE UNITED STATES
AND CAPITAL CONTROLS

Countries pass through stages in their use of capital controls. As it struggled to deal with a long-term deterioration in its balance of payments after World War II, the United States provides an interesting history. Prior to the late 1950s, its strong surplus on trade account partially offset other outflows, notably government spending abroad including Marshall Plan aid in the late 1940s and external military and foreign assistance thereafter.

The US external position began to deteriorate simultaneously with the movement of European currencies toward trade account convertibility which was completed in late 1958 (capital controls, as noted in chapter 2, persisted a decade or so longer). Europeans were no longer so eager as before to accumulate dollar liabilities exported by the US and began seeking alternatives. Given folklore about the glories of the gold standard and the quirks of the Bretton Woods system via which the dollar was pegged to gold and all other currencies were pegged to the dollar, foreign central banks began to use their dollar balances to buy gold. The US gold stock fell by $2.3 billion in 1958—the first year of the run—and losses for the next fifteen years were on the order of a billion dollars annually.

The US responded to this problem in several ways. Internationally it pushed for the creation of a global financial safety net. Much of this effort took place during the Kennedy administration, with C. Douglas Dillon and Robert Roosa at Treasury as the leading actors. Swap arrangements, or standby credit lines, were negotiated among central banks for possible use to counter gold and/or currency runs. These were complemented by General Arrangements to Borrow (GAB) set up among the Group of Ten rich countries in 1961. This amounted to a credit line to the IMF to be used against payments crises, backed by the G-10 members. After being dormant for decades, the GAB was used to raise funds for the unsuccessful effort to stop the Russian crisis in the summer of 1998.

Another policy line advocated by some members of the Kennedy-Johnson administrations was to create an international reserve asset or even a global central bank with liquidity-creating powers, as suggested by Keynes prior to the Bretton Woods discussions and by Yale economist Robert Triffin in the 1950s. Increasingly impatient with the US deficit, some European nations began to advance similar ideas by the middle of the decade. In 1967, after a maze of negotiations complicated by Charles de Gaulle's obsession with putting the world back on a strict gold standard, the US finally agreed to the issuance of Special Drawing Rights (SDRs) in modest quantities by the IMF. (The odd name was a linguistic ploy to mollify the French for losing the argument over gold.) An SDR is basically a credit to a deficit country created by the Fund which can be transferred to some strong currency country to raise resources to be used to finance the deficit. Since their invention SDRs have withered on the vine, but presumably the mechanism to create them could be revived if the international system ever feels a need to create a reserve asset.

In sum, American concerns in the early 1960s about possible dollar instability led to the construction of much of the anti-crisis apparatus deployed—without much success—against the Asian, Russian, and Brazilian crises in the late 1990s. Other moves by the US helped bring about the end of the Bretton Woods system. A "gold pool" was created in 1961 via which other countries agreed to contribute to the defense of the $35-per-ounce gold price. In 1968 the US renounced its obligation to sell gold to private purchasers, and, as noted above, in 1971 it closed the gold window to official purchasers as well. That year marked the imposition by President Nixon of a 10 percent import surcharge, in violation of all established rules for international trade.

The gradual delinking of the dollar from gold ran parallel to a decade-long national effort to hold down the external deficit, mainly by using capital controls. In 1963, President Kennedy proposed an interest equalization tax aimed at discouraging foreign bond offerings in the US. After its enactment in 1964 the tax was instrumental in spurring the growth of Eurocurrency markets in London as outlined in chapter 2. Voluntary restraints on banking and corporate funds transfers abroad followed in early 1965. After successive rounds of tightening, the "voluntary" program became fully mandatory in 1968. Other moves included restrictions on duty-free imports by American tourists and various bilateral deals to induce countries not to trade in dollars for gold.

These maneuvers did not succeed in reversing the deficit. The trade balance turned negative in the late 1960s, and the government account continued to be strongly negative, especially during the period of the Vietnam War when capital controls were strengthened. But then, beginning in the late 1960s, the whole policy line reversed. The intellectual origins came from a suggestion by MIT economist Charles Kindleberger and others that as the key currency the dollar fulfilled a need for international liquidity. There was no need for the dollar to be tied to gold. With the dollar's artificial link with gold severed, the US would be free to pursue a "passive" payments strategy. Abolition of capital controls in 1974 firmly established the new policy regime.

Through the rest of the 1970s the new American unconcern with the balance of payments was associated with a weakening dollar and a gradual improvement in the trade balance. The floating exchange rate system seemed to be "working" as the rest of world was willing to hold increasing stocks of dollar liabilities in line with Kindleberger's prediction. However, fears of a run against the dollar remained. They were finally eliminated by Federal Reserve Chairman Paul Volcker's interest rate shock of 1979. Short-term rates of over 20 percent pulled capital toward the US and provoked a deep recession. Consistent with UIP, the exchange rate appreciated. Together with the highly expansionary fiscal policy put into place soon after by President Reagan, the strong dollar led to massive foreign borrowing by the US throughout the 1980s. The passive policy triumphed, but as we will see in chapter 4 the buildup of foreign debt it set off may soon threaten the hegemony of the dollar. The US—and the rest of the industrialized world—may not have seen the last of capital controls.

CAPITAL CONTROLS AROUND THE WORLD

Meanwhile developing countries have only recently abandoned, or still maintain, a variety of control regimes. Latin American countries have traditionally utilized market-based controls, putting taxes and surcharges on selected capital movements or tying them up in escrow accounts. Non-market based restrictions were more common in Asia. As recounted in chapter 5, their abrupt abolition in the early 1990s in most of East Asia fed directly into the crisis of 1997 there. Elsewhere, China and India retained controls and escaped relatively unscathed. Time will tell whether Malaysia's reinstatement of controls after the crisis was an effective move.

To give some feel for the types of controls currently in play, sketches of Malaysia's and Chile's systems follow, in part because they have figured widely in public discussion. Consideration is then given to Yale economist James Tobin's proposal for a tax on capital movements across borders in industrialized economies, and to suggestions for limiting destabilizing capital outflows from advanced to emerging markets.

Malaysia

Prior to the Asian crisis, Malaysia had not gone as far as its neighbors in liberalizing capital movements. It retained restrictions on external borrowing by national firms unless they could demonstrate the capacity to earn enough foreign exchange to service their debts. The economy thereby was not as badly exposed in the short term as those in Thailand and Korea.

After the crisis hit, Malaysian authorities imposed exchange controls, in effect making ringgit held outside the country inconvertible into foreign exchange. After the ringgit devalued, exporters were required to surrender foreign currency earnings to the central bank in exchange for local currency at the new pegged rate. The government also restricted the amount of cash nationals could take abroad and imposed prohibitions on repatriation of earnings on foreign investments held within the country for less than a year. However, no limitations were placed on inflows and outflows of capital for commodity trade and long-term investment.

For those with enough financial ingenuity, opportunities for arbitrage implicit in such restrictions can "always" be exploited. However, in the Malaysian case they apparently were not. The authorities were able to stabilize the currency and reduce interest rates, leading to a degree of domestic recovery. The contrast with Chile's more market-based approach to limiting capital inflows is illuminating.

Chile

As discussed more fully in chapter 5, many Latin American economies started to receive large capital inflows in the early 1990s after a decade of financial drought. Fearing an uncontrollable flood of foreign exchange, Chile attempted to limit such inflows beginning in 1991. The basic tool it utilized was an unremunerated reserve requirement on external capital held in the country for less than a year.[3]

One positive outcome of this policy was a relatively high ratio of direct to portfolio investment throughout the 1990s. Despite attempts to stimulate foreign investment by Chilean nationals however, much of the inflow had to be absorbed in the form of reserve increases at the central bank. Higher reserves fed directly into a bigger money supply, leading the monetary authorities to fear rising prices. True to the inflation obsession of their tribe, the governors of Chile's "independent" central bank began to "sterilize" the inflows by limiting money creation. They sold government bonds from their portfolio. As could be expected, bond prices fell and interest rates shot up, especially in 1995–96 when (despite the reserve requirement) short-term inflows soared. This situation reversed in 1997 due to contagion from the Asian crisis. A subsequent sharp drop in the price of copper (Chile's main export) led to scrapping of the control regime in 1998. A resumption of inflows in the first part of 1999 was leading to discussion of its reinstatement.

Chile's experience with market-based controls suggests that they can help hold down volatility and push foreign investors in the direction of taking a longer-term perspective. But by themselves, Chilean-style inflow restrictions did not assure policy autonomy, as demonstrated by the monetary authorities' felt need to sterilize reserve increases. At least while the capital market boom was peaking in the mid-1990s, tougher restrictions on incoming flows may have been in order.

Tobin Taxes

A "Tobin tax" is a small (say 0.1 percent to 0.5 percent) levy on *all* foreign exchange transactions undertaken by national financial actors. If successfully applied to offshore transactions it could be a component of an internationally effective regime for financial regulation. The goal of the tax is to cut profit margins on short-term trading (which often takes the form of "round-tripping" among different currencies) without reducing returns on long-term investments. According to most estimates the worldwide revenues could be substantial, on the order of $100 to $200 billion per year.

Especially if international arrangements could be negotiated to put the tax revenue stream to good use, Tobin's proposal cannot be dismissed as a bad idea. It resembles Chile's scheme for controlling capital inflows in this regard. The real question is whether it is an overwhelmingly *good* proposal. Three observations are worth considering:

> Concentrating on a tax diverts attention from the really serious international financial question, which is how to establish an effective offshore regulatory system. It may be that a levy on transactions is not the best policy toward this end. Like most fiscal instruments, it is not easily modified once put into place and cannot be adjusted to deal with problems in specific financial markets and/or firms.
>
> Broad taxes can have unanticipated spillovers. Recall how President Kennedy's interest equalization tax (with a design bearing a family resemblance to Tobin-style proposals) stimulated the growth of Eurocurrency markets with enormous systemic repercussions.
>
> A modest transactions tax cannot stop speculators from betting on large exchange rate changes. If massive speculation is to be aborted, "boulders" as opposed to "sand" in the wheels of international finance would be needed.

The bottom line perhaps is that a Tobin tax cannot be the centerpiece of a new financial order, but as a disincentive to destabilizing capital movements it could play a supporting role.

Restrictions on Outflows from Industrialized Economies

More relevant to global financial stability are schemes aimed at restraining speculative capital movements from rich to poor countries. For example, in a variation on the Chilean theme, institutional investors taking positions abroad might be required to hold deposits in commercial banks at home in proportion to the riskiness of their positions as assessed by their national regulatory authorities. The deposits could earn interest, but at a rate below the average on the investors' other assets. Such a mechanism would reduce incentives for all financial institutions to take overly risky or excessively geared positions in foreign financial markets.

Another approach is to limit the use of "put" options in borrowing countries' sovereign debt instruments.[4] Creditors would not be allowed to get their money back early in specified circumstances, for example if the borrowing country's "fundamentals" deteriorate. "Call" options which would give borrowers a contractual right to delay payments under adverse conditions are another possibility under discussion.

Unsurprisingly, financial institutions in developed economies resist such restrictions on their freedom to maneuver, but the consequences of their actions in the recent crises in developing and post-socialist economies suggest that such interventions could enhance the social good.

SUMMARY

The arguments in this chapter have been lengthy and complex. For future reference, here in brief are the essential points:

Floating exchange rates are *not* determined by market balances directly influenced by the fundamental characteristics of the economy concerned. Instead, they emerge from forward asset markets in a complex interplay with their own future values and levels of other asset prices as "expected" by players in those markets.

Policymakers can try to determine exchange rates in a fixed rate system, but can only succeed in the medium to long term if capital movements are subject to controls. And controls can at times be overwhelmed by market forces.

In the absence of controls, on- and offshore regulation can help deter destabilizing capital surges, or at least those that result from "normal" financial storms. As pointed out in chapter 2, in abnormal storms all regulatory attempts can easily fail.

In another memorable passage from *The General Theory*, Keynes wrote, "Speculators may do no harm as bubbles on a steady stream of enterprise. But the position is serious when enterprise becomes the bubble on a whirlpool of speculation. When the capital development of a country becomes a byproduct of the activities of a casino, the job is likely to be ill-done." Liberalization of international capital markets and speculation in exchange rates have extended the reach of the casino from mere countries to the entire world. The task for the future is to keep the resulting tendencies toward destabilization and the hindrance of "capital development" under control.

NOTES

1. Foreign reserves are like uncashed checks. When the ROW holds dollars in reserve, it may, for example, have supplied goods or services that US citizens have bought with dollars, but is not using those dollars to buy US goods. These uncashed checks are the equivalent of a loan to the US.
2. Or, in practice, in the ubiquitous "errors and omissions" entries that proliferate in all accounting schemes when they try to cope with available data.
3. As noted above, restrictions of this type have a long history in Latin America. Brazil and Colombia adopted policies similar to Chile's at about the same time, but they have been much less widely noted internationally.
4. In financial jargon, a "put" is an option to sell the security in question under contracted circumstances, and a "call" is an option to buy.

4—Developed Countries and the New Financial Order

The new financial order has changed the ways in which modern economies work, and accordingly it has had a major impact on their performance. Financial innovation has not only created entirely new financial services industries, it has changed the manner in which industrial and commercial activities are financed and the way households conduct the financial aspects of their lives. In many areas, financial innovation has boosted economic opportunity. It has also changed the parameters within which governments operate. Most notably there is now no such thing as domestic monetary policy divorced in form and content from monetary events outside national borders. International capital markets reach into the financial heart of Middle America.

Those markets are more volatile, their crises more frequent, and their consequences more severe than ever before. Crises, whether associated with major swings in macro variables such as exchange rates or stemming from the failures of individual firms, are the most visible consequence of capital market liberalization. But they are probably not the most important. If greater volatility and occasional sharp crises are simply new, dramatic fluctuations around a growth trend that is unaltered, or even enhanced—then volatility is simply the price being paid for superior long-term performance. But that is not the case. National and international market liberalization has been accompanied by a widespread slowdown in investment and growth. The factors linking liberalization to slow growth are complex and controversial, and laying all the blame at the door of a single change in economic organization (albeit a hugely important change) would put more weight on a single argument than it can reasonably bear. Nonetheless, clear connections are evident between the new international financial order and the slowdown in growth and increase in unemployment that the majority of major industrial economies have suffered over the past twenty-five years.

CRISES

The first banking crises of the new era occurred in the US and in Germany in June 1974. In the US the failure of a relatively small bank, Franklin National, threatened not only the future of similar US banks but also the entire Eurodollar market. In Germany the closure of the Herstatt Bank almost resulted in the collapse of the *American* bank-clearing system.

In both instances the fundamental point at issue was the same: would the relevant central banks, the Federal Reserve and Bundesbank, act as lenders of last resort not only for the domestic liabilities of their respective national entities but also for the foreign liabilities? It was hesitation on the part of the Bundesbank that did so much damage in the United States.

Central bankers around the world could see that the era of *national* monetary policy had ended and with it had gone the purely national role of the lender of last resort. In managing the collapse of Franklin National the Fed acted as an *international* lender of last resort. This was necessary to maintain confidence in the dollar, the New York money markets, and the US banking system as a whole. Moreover, the Fed was made painfully aware that it could not fulfill its new role alone. The successful windup of Franklin National's affairs required cooperation from the Bank of England and the concerted support of all the other major central banks. A new forum was required so the newly needed cooperative rules of the game could be worked out. In early 1975 the Committee on Banking Regulations and Supervisory Practices was established at the Bank for International Settlements in Basel. It would be both a forum for the development of collective action among lenders of last resort and the vehicle for the regulatory cooperation that is the other side of the lending coin.

Further crises were to follow. The international debt shock of 1982 introduced a new dimension—the financial systems of the developed economies were not only vulnerable to shocks within their collective borders, they could also be brought down by events in developing countries. The possibility of a Mexican default in autumn 1982 threatened not only the future of US banking but of banks throughout the world. Again, concerted action led by the Federal Reserve, the Bank of England, and the Bank for International Settlements averted a crisis— just. The Fed and the Bank of England argued for the enforcement of new capital adequacy standards for banks. Unable to convince others, in 1987 they signed a bilateral agreement fixing the 8 percent ratio of bank capital to assets, as adjusted for risk, that is still the norm today. Once the standard had been set, other countries were eager to sign up to secure the "respectability" that went with acceptance of the new norm.

The next crisis was the stock market crash of 1987. This event taught the world about contagion. The collapse began over fears about the dollar exchange rate. Fearing foreign exchange losses, investors sold US securities. The stock market crashed in mid-October, with repercussions that spread rapidly to markets around the world even though they did not suffer from the foreign exchange uncertainties that destabilized Wall Street. Asset prices were marked down everywhere with no reference to the "fundamentals" in any particular country. It was a classic example of contagion, of a beauty contest in which markets were reacting to the news of markets. The news spread rapidly. The correlation between *hourly* changes in London and New York became much closer after the crash, and the greater the volatility, the closer the relationship became.

Further crises would illustrate the reality of the new financial order. The ERM crisis of 1992 saw Italy and the UK ignominiously ejected from the exchange rate mechanism of the European monetary system. The British government's attempt to maintain a monetary policy stance that was internally contradictory was brutally exposed by the foreign exchange markets in a classic example of the policy trilemma discussed in chapter 3. At one and the same time the UK government had attempted first to use monetary policy to maintain a fixed parity between the pound and the deutsche mark, and second to weather a severe domestic recession characterized by rising unemployment and falling asset values (particularly housing prices). The level of interest rates required to maintain the external parity exacerbated domestic economic problems. With growing nervousness in the currency markets during the summer of 1992, the policy stance became literally incredible. No one could possibly believe that the government was prepared to raise interest rates to protect the exchange rate while further depressing domestic asset prices and so deepening the recession. It was this contradiction that was exploited by financial markets in a speculative run that forced the pound out of the exchange rate mechanism (ERM) and precipitated a 20 percent devaluation against the Deutschemark. George Soros is said to have made $1 billion betting against the pound.

But the key point is that the ERM crisis was not a purely "national" event. It represented the failure in the new financial order of international cooperation (the European Monetary System) to maintain a structure of fixed but changeable parities in the face of speculative attack. In the European Union it strengthened the resolve of those who looked to a single currency, the euro, as a means of (partially) insulating domestic financial systems from currency speculation.

The new financial order also produced an entirely new form of crisis in developed economies, originating in highly leveraged derivatives markets.

DERIVATIVES

A derivative is an asset with a value that depends on the value(s) of one or more *other* variables. These other variables are the "bases" of a contract between two or more players. Each party to the contract receives payments or incurs costs over time depending on the values that the basis variables assume.

"Now what news on the Rialto?" asks Solanio in Shakespeare's *Merchant of Venice*. The state of play in contingent contracts of the sort today called derivatives surely figured in Solanio's question—after all, his friend Antonio's shipping interests had a highly uncertain future which he could have hedged or insured.[1] In sophisticated financial centers, derivative instruments have been around for a long time. Post-Venice, fully established markets in derivatives appeared in Chicago in the mid-nineteenth century. Trading in grain and livestock futures soon came to be dominated by financial players, but such contracts were originally developed as a way for farmers to hedge risk. A farmer could sell his corn forward at a specific date for a given price, thus insulating the farm against price fluctuations. Those who agreed to buy the grain at the fixed price were in effect taking on the farmer's risk. If, when the harvest was in, the actual price was lower than that agreed, they would still be forced to buy the corn at the previously contracted high price. Of course if the actual price on the day the contract closed was higher, they would make a profit. The risk did not disappear, it was assumed by those willing to shoulder risk, for a fee, and they would offset their exposure to risk by spreading it through another range of transactions.

The development of futures markets was of social benefit. It was important to society that every year farmers had sufficient capital to plant the seed for the autumn harvest. If farmers bore all the risk and then were bankrupted by a particularly low price, seed would not be planted and the whole community would suffer. By spreading the risk, farmers are protected against price fluctuations (though not harvest failure) and the likelihood of bankruptcy is reduced.

Such futures contracts are akin to the classic model of insurance, where risk is diversified and the impact of loss (of money, or health, or even life) is shared by a broad section of society.

Like other derivatives, futures contracts can be highly leveraged. The risk involved is the likely movement of the price one way or another. In normal times the price might move by say 10 percent. Hence the potential gain or loss is the 10 percent margin between the price fixed in the futures contract and the actual price which rules on the day it expires. So a speculator whose capital is just $100 might promise to buy $1000 worth of future corn with an eye to immediate resale. If the price rises by just 1 percent to $1010, a 10 percent profit is made on the $100 investment. If the price rises by 10 percent the speculator makes a 100 percent profit. If the price falls by 10 percent the speculator loses all the capital used to back the transaction. If the price falls by 20 percent, then losses will spread from this transaction to other business the speculator may be involved in. If the price falls to zero, then $1000 of losses must be covered somehow. The stakes are high.

Derivative contracts can be written on any bases — on movements in interest rates or currency exchange rates or on the level of a stock exchange index, or, in one interesting example, a Salt Lake City bank issued a certificate of deposit with its interest rate linked to the number of victories by the Utah Jazz basketball team. On the one hand derivatives provide the opportunity of hedging risk, on the other they are vehicles for assuming risk in the hope of profit, i.e. for speculation. Less than 30 percent of contracts, such as futures contracts in commodities or foreign exchange, are highly standardized and traded on futures markets. The rest are specific contracts between buyer and seller designed to meet the particular risk profile which one side wishes to hedge and the other is willing to carry. These specific contracts are known as over-the-counter, or OTC contracts. OTC contracts pose regulatory problems since their value is not continuously assessable in an open marketplace.

Privatization of foreign exchange risk in the wake of capital market liberalization has caused an enormous expansion in the scale and variety of derivative instruments. The notional principal outstanding in financial derivatives (equivalent to the $1000 in the example above) has risen from just over $1,000 billion in 1986 to more than $100,000 billion (three times the world's GDP) in 1998. This colossal expansion is a direct result of the greater foreign exchange risk the private sector now has to bear and the volatility now typical of virtually all financial markets.

As noted in previous chapters, the new financial order has been characterized by significantly larger fluctuations in exchange rates and greater variability in interest rates. Around 85 percent of America's *Fortune 500* companies make some use of derivatives to insulate themselves from swings in interest rates and currencies. The growth of derivatives markets is part of the process of liberalization. In a world of fixed rates and capital controls, derivatives had a far smaller role than they do today. It is clearly true that liberalization of capital markets has created the *possibility* of many derivatives. It is equally true that fluctuating rates and liberalization have created the *demand* for derivatives.

An important issue is whether derivatives markets have, in their own operations, created new risks, especially systemic risks. This concern is well-founded. While the underlying risk associated with any given asset may not have changed, the sheer complexity of the structure of derivative positions limits the ability of firms to monitor and manage risk effectively. The well-publicized abuses of derivatives markets in the cases of Orange County and Barings Bank indicate the difficulties that senior executives may have in understanding what is being done in their names. Regulators face similar difficulties.

The collapse of Barings provides insight into the challenges regulatory authorities must try to handle. Prior to the event, Mr. Eddie George, governor of the Bank of England, wrote in *The Observer* newspaper of July 24, 1994, that

> We now have an expert team monitoring derivatives who are getting even better every time they go in to see a firm. What they are reporting back from the most active players in the market is very reassuring. These people know what they

are doing whether it's at director level or the chaps on the desk.

Just three months later, Barings was destroyed by a rogue derivatives trader. An investigation into the collapse concluded that the Bank of England did not understand the business it was supposed to be regulating:

> We believe the Bank should explore ways of increasing its understanding of the non-banking businesses (particularly financial services businesses) undertaken by those banking groups for which it is responsible . . .

A further element of risk may be introduced by the very mathematical models used to price derivatives. These models, typically derived from the physical sciences, are based on the characteristics of the probability distributions of random movements. Besides relying on a hypothesis of perfect arbitrage (as discussed in chapter 3), the fundamental Black-Scholes model further assumes that price movements follow the same lognormal distribution as the Brownian motion displayed by many physical phenomena. Intellectually, the Black-Sholes formula for pricing option contracts represented a profitable piece of arbitrage—from Einstein's famous 1905 paper on Brownian motion—to financial economics seventy years later.

Unfortunately the model is not in full agreement with the facts. More price changes tend to be concentrated at the extremes than the log-normal distribution would predict. This is because the cumulative effect of a beauty contest may result in massive concentrations of extreme price swings. In these circumstances the mathematical models that drive much of today's programmed trading will tend to price events at the extremes incorrectly. "Multifractal" and other sophisticated approaches to modeling such fluctuations are at today's applied mathematics research frontier. But as discussed below, even they fail to capture the intrinsically historical nature of the financial beauty contest.

Even more important is the problem that may undermine even the best-designed derivatives hedge: liquidity. In 1993, Metallgesellschaft AG, Germany's fourteenth largest industrial company, was almost ruined by losses of over $1 billion suffered in derivatives trading in the oil market by a United States subsidiary and by the refusal of the company's lead banker, Deutsche Bank, to finance the trading strategy further. It was argued by some distinguished economists that the fault lay not with Metallgesellschaft's trading strategy but with Deutsche Bank's refusal to fund the financial strategy over the longer period in which it would bear fruit. But this argument rests too strongly on the proposition that the capital market is "perfect" in the sense that it is possible to borrow virtually unlimited sums today with the prospect of gain far in the future.

In fact, risk aversion is likely to rise with the sheer scale of borrowing, a phenomenon known as the "principle of increasing risk." In the Metallgesellschaft case a lack of liquidity created severe problems for the firm. Aversion to risk is infectious, rises with indebtedness, can provoke a general rush to cash that destroys even the most sophisticated hedging strategies, and can create systemic risk. Liquidity ultimately rests on a diversity of beliefs concerning asset values—when some want to buy, some want to sell. Where a tendency exists for beliefs to be shared and transmitted, the possibility of cumulative liquidity crises rises—everyone wants to sell. In these circumstances "management of financial risk" is an illusion.

The potential systemic risk inherent in highly leveraged markets became all too clear in the autumn of 1998. On August 17 the Russian government defaulted on payments on its short-term bonds. Overnight they became worthless. This was the defining act of the financial panic that had spread from Asia to Russia and was now to spread to US bond markets. Caught in the ensuing storm was Long Term Capital Management (LTCM), a hedge fund. Its specialty was using sophisticated pricing models to design derivative trades that were in effect highly leveraged bets on price movements. The bets placed by

LTCM had been substantially financed with borrowed money. The models were descendants of Black-Scholes, designed to process effectively all the historical information available in order to detect price movements which were "out of phase," and which the market might be expected to reverse. They faithfully led LTCM into a trap.

The historical data the models utilized simply did not embody anything like the scale of financial panic that followed the Russian collapse. On August 21 investors dumped corporate bonds and, seeking safety, switched heavily into US government bonds. But instead of the discrepancy in returns on corporate and government bonds being reversed by the markets, a panic set in and the discrepancy grew. LTCM was caught out by a beauty contest. On September 21, LTCM lost $500 million in a day and itself became the focus of the market's fears. If it were forced to liquidate its investments, worth as much as $1250 billion, the panic sales could undermine markets throughout the world.

In the end the Federal Reserve organized a consortium of banks and finance houses (most of which had lent to LTCM) to take over the firm and rescue the portfolio. The bailout cost $3.6 billion. Losses amounted to $4.4 billion: $1.9 belonged to the partners personally, $700 million to Union Bank of Switzerland, and $1.8 billion to other investors, half of them European banks (including, in a bizarre twist, a central bank, the Bank of Italy).

The potential failure of LTCM terrified the Federal Reserve. Alan Greenspan, the Federal Reserve Chairman, commented that he had never seen anything in his lifetime that compared to the panic of August–September 1998.

The new international financial order had revealed its potential to self-destruct.

ECONOMIC TRENDS

As noted in chapter 1, three issues have dominated the experience of almost all major industrial countries over the past twenty years: *first*, the slowdown in growth to about two-thirds of the growth rate attained in the 1950s and 1960s; *second*, a common fall in the share of GDP devoted to investment; and *third*, a rise in unemployment (only in the US is the unemployment rate at levels comparable to the 1960s, an important exception that will be considered in detail below).

In all industrial countries, long-term trends in growth and employment show a distinct break at some time around 1970 as is shown in Tables 4.1 and 4.2. Up to that time growth rates were at all-time highs and unemployment rates saw historic lows. It was a "Golden Age" as the major capitalist economies grew faster than ever before or since. But after the early 1970s, growth slowed and unemployment levels show a distinct rise. In the last few years, while unemployment has continued to rise in France and Germany, a rise associated with the pursuit of deflationary policies in both those countries, trend unemployment rates have fallen in the US and UK.

The commonality of experience throughout the major industrial countries is especially striking. It suggests that the causes of low growth and higher unemployment in the past twenty-five years are to be found in factors which affect *all* countries in a broadly similar manner, rather than in the individual circumstances of each country.

Four candidates for the role of a common source are: *first*, the impact of the oil crises of the 1970s; *second*, the end of the postwar reconstruction boom in which Europe and Japan were "catching-up" with the US; *third*, structural changes in world trading relationships associated with the increasing mobility of capital and the rapid growth of third world manufactured exports, particularly from China and the Pacific Rim; *fourth*, changes in the international financial environment since 1973.

Oil Crises

The collapse of the Bretton Woods system was not the only economic shock visited on major industrial economies in the 1970s. After several years in which raw material price inflation

Table 4.1

Growth in the G7, 1964–73, 1983–92 and 1993–98 (percent per year)

	1964–73	1983–92	1993–98
Canada	5.6	2.8	2.5
France	5.3	2.2	1.7
Germany	4.5	2.9	1.5
Italy	5.0	2.4	1.3
Japan	9.6	4.0	0.8
UK	3.3	2.3	2.7
US	4.0	2.9	3.0

Note: Figures for Germany up to 1993 are for West Germany; 1993–98 figures are for the reunited Germany.

had accelerated, in 1973 the price of oil quadrupled, followed by another huge hike in 1979. These increases had an enormous impact on international financial markets. A need arose to recycle petrodollars from OPEC surpluses to fund deficits elsewhere. "Elsewhere" was predominantly the third world, as industrial countries facing rising inflation and deteriorating external balances deflated their economies hard.

Together with the contractionary measures taken by governments in reaction to the oil price rise, these major dislocations might be thought to be the source of the deterioration in economic performance after 1970. The OECD secretariat estimated that 20 percent of the loss in real income in major industrial countries in the mid-1970s was due to the high price of oil. The remaining 80 percent was due to concerted deflation policies which characterized the response of western governments. But the oil price rises of the 1970s are not an adequate explanation of the sustained low growth and high unemployment up to the present day. For not only had western economies absorbed similar rises in raw material prices at the time of the Korean War without a similar slowdown, but also oil prices and other commodity prices collapsed in 1986 without stimu-

Table 4.2

Unemployment in the G7, 1964–73, 1983–92, and 1998
(percent of the labor force)

	1964–73	1983–92	mid-1998
Canada	4.23	9.64	8.40
France	2.23	9.70	12.10
Germany	0.79	6.03	11.20
Italy	5.48	10.13	12.00
Japan	1.22	2.71	4.20
UK	2.94	9.79	6.60
US	4.46	6.69	4.60

Notes: Annual standardized unemployment rates as percent of the labor force, averaged for each ten-year period. Figures for Germany are for West Germany, except 1998 which is for reunited Germany.

lating a new round of high growth (although, as the major consumer of energy, the US economy benefited from the price reductions in comparison to its rivals).

The End of "Catching-up"

Post–World War II reconstruction in Europe and Japan resulted in rapid growth during the process of recovery and provided momentum in the form of high rates of investment and invigorated institutions to finance that investment. An enormous advantage was to be gained by introducing new techniques already developed in the US. The technological advantages of "catching-up" were a powerful stimulus to high growth and employment. But this particular stimulus could not outlive its own success. Once Europe and Japan began to approach technological parity there was bound to be a slowdown. But there was not bound to be a slowdown in the US, too.

As can be seen in Table 4.3, recent years have seen a sharp reduction in productivity growth in all the major industrial countries, a slowdown greatest in Japan and least in the US and

Table 4.3

Overall Productivity Growth,
GDP per person employed, percent per year

	1961–70	1979–90	1991–96
France	5.0	2.2	1.2
West Germany	4.3	1.8	1.4
Italy	6.2	1.7	2.0
Japan	9.0	3.0	0.6
UK	3.3	1.7	2.1
US	2.3	0.6	1.1

Note: The last figure for West Germany is for 1991–94.

the UK (in both of which productivity growth was relatively low in the earlier period). Indeed the fall in productivity growth has everywhere been greater than the fall in the overall growth of demand, which means that reduced productivity growth has contributed to the creation, or at least preservation, of jobs.

In each of the G7 countries the slowdown in productivity growth has been less pronounced in manufacturing than in the economy as a whole. There has been a tendency for productivity growth rates to converge in those industries, like manufacturing, which are exposed to international competition. This convergence has coincided with a general reduction in the pace of productivity growth. "Catching-up" explains part of this process, but not all. It does not explain the common, general reduction in productivity growth.[2]

Structural Changes in the World Economy

An issue of considerable importance is whether the rise in competition from the newly industrializing countries, particularly those on the Pacific Rim, has jeopardized growth in the major industrial countries. The large devaluations which followed the recent Asian crisis are undoubtedly placing considerable pressure on major countries' markets. But in many industries these new pressures simply reinforce old ones. The possibility of high growth in developed economies will be significantly diminished if the competitive strengths of the major industrial countries are overcome by the potent combination of low third world wages and ever more mobile capital.

There has been a distinct acceleration of developing country manufactures penetrating G7 markets. In 1968 just 1 percent of G7 domestic demand for manufactures was satisfied by imports from the third world. By 1980 the developing countries' market share had risen to 2 percent; by 1988 to 3.1 percent; by 1993 to 4 percent, and by 1998 to 6 percent.

Competition from the third world certainly leads to a loss of jobs in particular sectors (typically low-skill tradable goods), either directly due to loss of markets or indirectly as innovation in response to third world competition leads to the adoption of less labor-intensive techniques, particularly low skill-intensive techniques. But, up to the recent crisis, exports to the newly industrializing countries had risen faster than imports from them. Leaving aside the impact of the oil price rises, there had tended to be a *surplus* in the balance of trade between the developed economies and the more dynamic of the third world countries—indeed these countries were typically the fastest growing markets in the world.

The phenomenon of low-wage competition from newly industrializing countries is not new to the developed world. The experience of the past twenty years was not dissimilar from the competition that northern European countries faced from southern Europe in the late 1950s. That competition, which resulted in the growth of Italy's share of world manufactured trade from less than 2 percent to over 6 percent in twenty years, did not result in slow growth or unemployment in northern Europe. On the contrary, throughout the period in which competition was most intense, northern Europe suffered from a labor shortage with about 10 percent of the labor force in West Germany and France being immigrants. The structural changes associated with the development of Italy took place in the context of generally high growth rates.

More recent structural adjustments heralded by the rapid growth of manufactured exports from developing countries appear threatening now *because of* persistent slow growth in the developed economies. The threat posed by imports from newly industrializing economies today derives not from the success of their industrialization, but from the desperate measures taken to overcome the financial disaster that has overwhelmed them.

The New International Financial Order

The new international financial order is clearly a "common factor" influencing the economic performance of all countries. The key question is: is there a credible story to be told which links financial market liberalization to the trend deterioration in the economic performance of major industrial countries? If there is a credible argument that links liberalized financial markets to the imposition of deflationary pressures on growth, productivity, and investment, it is likely to involve the pressures exerted on both public and private sectors by the sheer scale of potential capital flows, and the actual and potential volatility of those flows.

The behavior of financial markets suggests there are two ways market liberalization might lead to deterioration in overall economic performance. First, a market that operates as a beauty contest is likely to be highly unstable and prone to occasional severe loss of liquidity when all opinion shifts in the same direction. This will increase the cost of capital and sometimes lead to severe capital shortages — both factors that will tend to discourage investment and reduce levels of activity in the medium term. Second, the operation of the beauty contest in a liberal environment may produce systematic changes in the behavior of both public and private sectors. Although these changes may succeed in reducing instability, they achieve this only at the cost of medium-term worsening in overall economic performance.

THE PERFORMANCE
OF THE PRIVATE SECTOR

Volatile financial markets generate economic inefficiencies, since volatility creates financial risk. Even if facilities exist for hedging that risk, the cost of hedging must be added to the cost of any financial commitment. More generally, volatility may well result in decisions being made on the basis of false information and may induce a general reluctance to take any step that will increase exposure to unpredictable fluctuations in exchange or interest rates. A simple premise might be: the greater the volatility, the greater the reluctance to undertake any exposure to fluctuating variables. The greatest danger of all in open capital markets is of course posed by a general loss of liquidity. The potential costs of liberalization are also raised by the enhanced possibilities for contagion created by the newly integrated markets.

Analyses of financial instability typically focus on short-term volatility, often monthly or even daily price movements. It is not surprising to find that such indicators have risen since the end of Bretton Woods system. On average, the monthly volatility of G7 exchange rates has tripled, with the largest increases being experienced by Japan, the UK, and the US. There has been no tendency for volatility to decrease in the 1980s and early 1990s, but equally, after the sharp increase between the 1960s and early 1980s, there has been no tendency for volatility to increase further despite the fact that currency trading has grown enormously.

Similar increases in volatility are evident in bond yields, although they too have generally eased a little in the 1990s while international bond trading has increased sharply. Volatility of short-term interest rates has also increased.

There is only limited evidence of a significant impact of short-term financial volatility on the real economy. However, studies of the US economy in the 1980s did reveal that for United States manufacturing industries the move to flexible exchange rates was accompanied by significant and widespread increases in uncertainty about real wages, the real price of materials inputs, and real output prices. This greater uncertainty about real output prices seemed to have a negative impact on the investment rate and productivity growth. The key distinction seems to be whether exchange rates are fixed or fluctuating. Short-term volatility in exchange rates is not the relevant measure to show the impact of international capital liberalization on the medium-term performance of the real economy. What does matter are large exchange rate movements over the medium term.

As was noted in chapter 1, capital market liberalization was accompanied in the 1970s and 1980s by huge swings in exchange rates with no obvious relationship to the needs of production. For example, the appreciation of the sterling nominal effective exchange rate by over 20 percent between 1978 and 1981 was accompanied by a doubling of the United Kingdom inflation rate. The stronger real exchange rate resulted in a rapid deterioration in the balance of trade in manufactured goods and a fall in domestic manufacturing output of 20 percent, declines from which British manufacturing has never fully recovered. Similarly, the 40 percent swings in the US effective exchange rate in the 1980s were associated with the growth of the US current account deficit to over $160 billion in 1987 (with a counterpart deterioration in the Federal budget deficit). In the first half of 1999 the dollar strengthened as the US trade balance deteriorated and US jobs were lost.

As well as exchange rate instability, the 1980s and 1990s also experienced both an increase in the volatility of interest rates on bonds and a general increase in the real level of the long-term bond rate. A clear body of evidence links the volatility and high rates of return demanded in deregulated capital markets to bond default and corporate failure. Volatility makes the cost of capital uncertain and limits a firm's ability to borrow, and small firms in particular can be hard hit by the impact of high interest rates on the cost of loans. But the greatest impact is via corporate cash flow. It is well known that retained profits are the key determinant of corporate investment. High and volatile interest rates reduce cash flow and make it less predictable, and hence undermine investment plans. This suggests that high and volatile rates will lead to a significant deterioration in corporate performance, especially for companies with high debt-equity ratios.

Figure 4.1 is a startling illustration of the impact of the creation and demise of the Bretton Woods system on the default rate on US corporate bonds. The Bretton Woods era is characterized by historically low default rates, while default rose sharply as that era ended and climbed steadily throughout the 1980s. The same pattern is observed in corporate failure rates amongst US businesses. The corporate failure rate was peculiarly low in the Bretton Woods era and rose sharply in the 1980s. And the key explanatory factors behind the failure rate are the real interest rate and the corporate debt-equity ratio.

These observations suggest that deregulation of national and international capital markets has raised the cost of capital and introduced instability into the local financial environment of Middle America. The corporate survival rate was sustained in the Bretton Woods era by a combination of macroeconomic steady growth and the microeconomic benefits of low interest rates and financial stability provided by a tightly regulated capital market. Globalization of finance has meant that, whereas international disequilibria may in the past have been manifest in exchange rate movements, today they affect interest rates in domestic money markets. The instability of local interest rates means that international financial pressures are felt by small and medium-size firms operating in local markets, and not only by large companies operating internationally.

THE PERFORMANCE
OF THE PUBLIC SECTOR

It is widely believed that the power of liberal financial markets places a "healthy" discipline on the public sector, encouraging

Historical Default Rates
Percent

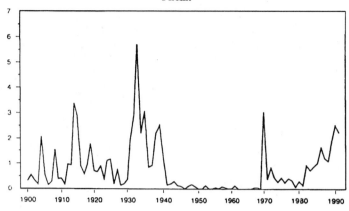

Source: *Keating and Wilmot (1992)*

Figure 4.1:
Default Rate in US Corporate Bonds, 1900–91

the pursuit of "market friendly," anti-inflationary policies which should support investment and growth. For example, it was argued in *The Economist* magazine in October 1995 that:

> . . . a government's loss of powers is reason to cheer, not fear: all that is being lost is the power to pursue damaging policies and practice economic deception by letting inflation rip.

That governments have lost power is undeniable. Open financial markets place government's financial policy at the mercy of market confidence. A general loss of confidence will result in weakening exchange rates, falling bond prices, and higher interest rates.

The tendency for financial markets to move erratically is an important qualification to the alleged "healthy" discipline they are believed to impose. The IMF has, for example, argued that "the discipline exercised by capital markets over policy is neither infallible nor is it applied smoothly and consistently." The rise and fall and rise again of the dollar in the last two decades, the rise and fall of world bond markets in 1993 and 1994; the crisis in the Mexican peso at the end of 1994, are all examples of highly erratic "discipline." The BIS recently concluded that operations of liberal markets often result in significant medium-term price "misalignments" and that, "Such misalignments have great potential costs in terms of a misallocation of resources. They also heighten the risk of abrupt and disorderly corrections and hence of broader financial instability."

It was just such a "disorderly correction" that in early 1995 forced the United States and IMF into the unaccustomed role of lender of last resort to the Mexican money markets and compelled Mexico to increase its already crippling burden of foreign debt. As the BIS commented at the time, the crisis was precipitated by financial factors despite the fact that "external deficits in Mexico have this time coincided with both microeconomic and macroeconomic 'fundamentals' that were healthy by any standards." The Mexican economy, far from staying "healthy," became distinctly "unhealthy" with severe social consequences.

The Mexican example exposes an ambiguity in the use of the term "fundamentals" beyond the examples already presented in chapter 3. In some discussions this term is used to suggest the "true model" of the economy. In others it is used more pragmatically to mean simply a position that is sustainable. Of course if the "true model" is indeed "true," then these two interpretations can amount to the same thing. But if it is not, then the definition of what is sustainable may itself be a function of self-fulfilling behavior of the financial markets.

"TRUE" MODELS

To take this point one step further, the Salter-Swan, portfolio balance, and Mundell-Fleming models reviewed in chapter 3, were for thirty years considered by professional economists to be "true," despite the fact that their predictions about the behavior of exchange rates notoriously failed to fit the data. Salter-Swan is internally consistent but has been bypassed by events. With a remarkably long lag, recent analysis has shown that the other two models simply do not contain enough internal structure to determine exchange rates.

The moral is profound. Ultimately, conventions about the exchange rate are supposed to be driven by fundamentals but the linkage between fundamentals and the spot rate does not exist. Therefore, there is no reason to expect (or not expect) that international financial markets as driven by conventions will promote "healthy" policy. The exchange rate as the key variable regulating any economy's relationships with rest of world is determined by a history of expectations about its own future values. The forces impinging upon a floating rate (or upon the structure of controls supporting a fixed rate) are ever-varying and impossible to predict.

If the model of the economy implicit in market behavior is not "true," then there is no reason to believe that discipline enforced by markets will be healthy. This does not mean that the outcome implied by market behavior will not be forthcoming, only that it will not necessarily correspond to real economic efficiency. There is nothing efficient about zero inflation and 10 percent unemployment, for example. If market behavior is not based on a true model, or if the performance of the real economy is not independent of historically contingent financial market behavior, then erratic and disorderly market movements are not merely "overshooting" or temporary fluctuations around a true mean. They may be the determinants of systemic and long-term inefficiency economy-wide.

Governments in Search of Credibility

Liberalization of financial markets has clearly reduced the power of governments to manipulate the economy. If exchange rates are fixed, governments fear the trilemma or "impossibility problem": the perceived impossibility of sustaining fixed exchange rates, free capital movements, and an independent monetary policy. With flexible exchange rates, control over short-term rates can be recovered to some degree, but long-term rates are still subject to the judgments and whims of the international bond traders. Moreover, control over short rates is only recovered if, like the United States Federal Reserve Bank, the authorities are apparently unconcerned about movements in the exchange rate—a rare luxury and perhaps a costly one.

If the financial markets were simply enforcing the logic of real economic efficiency, strengthening the self-adjusting powers of competitive markets, then the "disciplining" of governments would be benign. But if markets are pursuing the rules of a beauty contest and imposing self-fulfilling prejudices on the workings of the real economy, then the outcome may be very damaging.

Faced with an overwhelming scale of potential capital flows, governments must today as never before attempt to maintain market "credibility." Credibility has become the keystone of policymaking in the nineties. A credible government is a government that pursues a "market friendly" policy, that is, a policy in accordance with what the markets believe to be "sound" and "efficient." Particularly favored are measures designed to meet a "prudent" predetermined monetary target or impose nominal anchors on monetary policy, and balancing the budget (preferably by cutting public expenditure rather than raising taxes). Governments that fail to pursue "sound" and "prudent" policies are forced to pay a premium in higher interest rates. Severe loss of credibility will lead to a financial crisis. The determination of what is credible and how governments lose credibility is a product of the market players' beliefs about what other market practitioners are thinking.

The costs of losing credibility can reverberate over many years, and re-acquiring credibility can be very costly in real terms. So if governments are risk-averse, the demands of credibility will impose broadly deflationary macroeconomic strategies. In the 1960s the managed international financial framework permitted expansionary, full employment policies which were contagious both domestically, encouraging private investment, and internationally, underwriting the growth of world trade. Since the 1970s the deregulated financial framework encouraged policies that elevate financial stability above growth and employment. This ratcheted up real interest rates which have in turn reduced domestic investment, reduced the growth of world trade, and slowed the rate of growth of effective demand.

Markets are just as likely to settle into a low-growth, high unemployment equilibrium as any other. The behavior of financial markets may well be an important factor driving an economy towards such an equilibrium. The markets are neither omniscient nor benign. When their influence is combined with the persistent search for government "credibility" defined in terms of "sound money" and "prudent" deflationary policies, then the low level position is a likely outcome.

This is in sharp contrast with the 1950s and 1960s when public sector objectives were expressed in terms of target levels of growth and employment (usually the target was *full* employment) rather than financial and monetary targets, today's "macroeconomic discipline." It is clearly true that *lack* of macroeconomic discipline is no way to secure sustainable growth. Burgeoning fiscal deficits and high and rising inflation will undermine any growth strategy. But what is most striking about the superior economic performance of the 1960s, when objectives were customarily defined in terms of growth and employment, is that fiscal balances typically displayed lower deficits than has been the case since liberalization, and, indeed, fiscal surpluses were not uncommon. The reason for this was of course the interdependence between public sector balances and private sector activity. High levels of investment by the private sector encouraged by a public sector commitment to growth and employment in turn resulted in healthy tax revenues.

Three elements link international financial liberalization to this change in public sector behavior: the potential threat posed to financial stability and the real economy by large capital flows, the belief that those flows are motivated by a particular view of "sound finance," and the additional fear that contagious financial crises may strike without warning. In this environment, defining public policy in terms of "sound money" is a safety-first strategy.

LIBERALIZATION AND THE PUBLIC, BUSINESS, AND HOUSEHOLD SECTORS

There is thus a clear story linking financial market liberalization to the deterioration in overall economic performance in the major industrial countries. High and volatile interest rates together with other uncertainties have reduced the potential return on investment and cut into the cash flow that finances investment. Public sector policymakers, seeking safety in a volatile financial world, set their objectives in terms of financial stability and hope that some stimulus may be forthcoming from the private sector.

The apparent exception to these generalizations is the United States. Because of the international role of the dollar, only in the US can government policymakers safely take expansionary fiscal and monetary stances (as the Reagan experience amply demonstrated), although by the mid-1990s the push for a "balanced budget" showed that they were beginning to have their doubts. Corporate managers can plan investment programs without nagging international worries, though volatile bond rates cause concern. The contribution of business capital formation to demand growth in the 1990s was less vigorous than in previous upswings. The American household sector was the main source of demand expansion in the latter part of the decade. Consumption-led output growth and falling unemployment were backed by internal financial expansion and external borrowing on a scale that no other economy can dream of. But even in the US, growing financial imbalances may be storing up future problems with the markets. The external position bears a strong family resemblance to that in East Asia in 1997 and Brazil in 1999 as analyzed in chapter 5. There is a risk of destabilizing capital movements as in Asia, and the current account is vulnerable to an interest rate shock as in Brazil. Internally, the household sector's portfolio is increasingly shaky. Stock-stock and stock-flow disequilibria between financial portfolios and the real side of the economy are by no means confined to the developing world.

THE POSITION OF THE UNITED STATES

The basic reason why the US has not encountered external difficulties for many years is that the dollar is the world's key currency in several dimensions. In 1995 it accounted for almost 65 percent of total official holdings of foreign exchange or "international reserves" (this share was down from 80 percent in 1975, but still was four times as large as that of the deutsche mark, at that time the second most important reserve currency). Almost half of international trade payments, foreign holdings of bank deposits, and developing country debt are all denominated in dollars—that is, it is the principal "vehicle currency." It serves as the anchor and reference point for many other countries' exchange rates. Both the public and private sectors in the US borrow abroad almost exclusively in terms of dollars, so that as far as their liabilities are concerned they can ignore swings in the exchange rate (the same is not true of their foreign currency assets, of course).

But how long can the US maintain this freedom from pressures in international markets? The current situation dates from the American policy decision around 1970 to pursue a "passive" approach to the capital account of the balance of payments. The result has been an enormous accumulation of external debt over the past three decades. That debt consists of a range of US monetary assets held by foreigners. If they decided to sell a significant proportion of them, major repercussions would be felt in US financial markets. Moreover, the US economy today can only grow by increasing its foreign borrowing. Who does that borrowing, whether government or corporations or households, is vital to the maintenance of growth and employment in America. Finally, the US borrowing strategy has become an important element in keeping up demand around the world. If the US strategy were forced to change, it would have serious implications for the future stability and growth of the global economy.

In chapter 3 it was shown that from the side of demand, the level of economic activity is determined as a balance between, on the one hand, "injections" such as investment, public spending, and exports, and on the other hand "leakages" such as saving, taxes, and imports. In terms of the standard national income and product accounts, the supply of goods and services that results is equal to the total value of goods and services produced in the US, the gross domestic product (GDP), *plus* imports. The dark, solid line in Figure 4.2 shows the evolution of supply over thirty years for the US economy.[3]

Hypothetically one can ask what "would have been" the level of supply had it been determined exclusively by an injection and leakage from each of the three main sectors—private, government, and the rest of the world. For example, the government curve shows the difference between the injection of government spending, G, and the leakages into taxation, $T = tY$, where t is the tax rate and Y the total value of supply. If injections and leakages derived only from the public sector, then since total injections equal total leakages, $G = tY$, or $Y = G/t$. This is the sectoral demand. Similar calculations may be made for the household sector and the foreign sector.

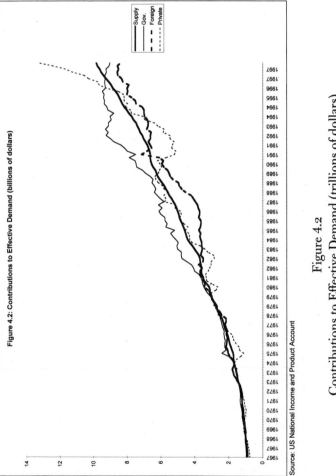

Figure 4.2: Contributions to Effective Demand (billions of dollars)

Source: US National Income and Product Account

Figure 4.2

Contributions to Effective Demand (trillions of dollars)

These sectoral effective demand curves are plotted in Figure 4.2. Three points emerge from the diagram:

First, since 1982 the foreign curve has generally been below the supply line. This means that the external deficit (the excess of imports over exports) has had a contractionary effect on economic activity, with current account leakages (imports) outweighing injections (exports). This drag was briefly lifted in the early 1990s as a consequence of dollar devaluation of about 30 percent between 1985 and 1990 (which stimulated exports and cut back the import share of supply), the Bush recession (which also reduced import penetration), and transfers from the rest of the world of about $100 billion in connection with the Gulf War. All these favorable factors receded after 1992, and the gap between supply and foreign effective demand steadily widened.

Second, governments at all levels—federal, state, and local—combined to stimulate demand through 1997. The federal deficit was responsible for this outcome because state and local governments have chronic budget surpluses. The policy choice to balance the budget led to a steadily declining fiscal stimulus after 1995.

Third, with demand from the rest of the world lagging and fiscal demand in retrenchment, the private sector had to pick up the slack. Its effective demand grew very rapidly after 1992 due to rising investment and a falling saving rate (especially saving from the household sector, which turned negative in mid-1998). At the end of the decade, the *only* factor supporting total effective demand was the exuberance of the private sector.

These demand patterns had financial consequences. If a sector's effective demand lies above total supply, it has to borrow to finance the excess. Quarterly increases in net claims among the three sectors are shown in Figure 4.3. The rest of the world had consistently positive asset accumulation against the other two sectors, except for the transient US surplus in the early

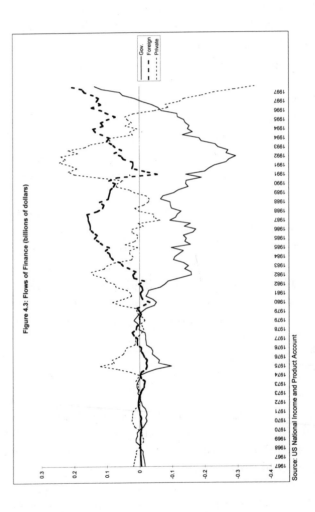

Figure 4.3

Flows of Finance (trillions of dollars)

1990s. The buildup of government debt reached its peak in mid-1992 and then reversed; government began to build up positive net claims—or reduce its net liabilities—in 1997. Net asset accumulation by the private sector was strong early in the decade but then plummeted as the other two sectors rapidly increased their net claims against it. The household sector took the lead in this process. Business saving fell short of investment beginning in 1998. Household flows then were $300 billion in the red, after turning negative in 1993 (at which time business saving exceeded investment by about $200 billion).

Figure 4.3 demonstrates that the private sector tends to swing into deficit at the peak of the business cycle, for example in the late 1990s, 1980s, and 1970s. However, this movement in the late 1990s was extreme. Figure 4.4 shows changes in cross-sectoral claims in prices of 1992. In comparison to the past, the relevant curve shows that *the output "boom" of the 1990s was uniquely stimulated by net increases in private sector liabilities.* The fiscal deficit played a much less important role in supporting demand than in previous upswings. In the first half of the 1990s the public sector did issue liabilities to finance the trade deficit. But in the second half of the decade private debtors took over that function. The world economy has had to finance an enormous amount of American borrowing.

GLOBAL MACROECONOMICS

The patterns shown in Figures 4.2 to 4.4 could not have developed in the absence of capital market liberalization. The US was only able to run current account deficits for so many years because financial markets were open and increasingly dominant institutional investors in all countries initiated a large and sustained flow of foreign capital into the US. But the persistent American deficit has produced a peculiarly unbalanced structure of global financial stocks and flows which may well threaten the future stability of the world economy.

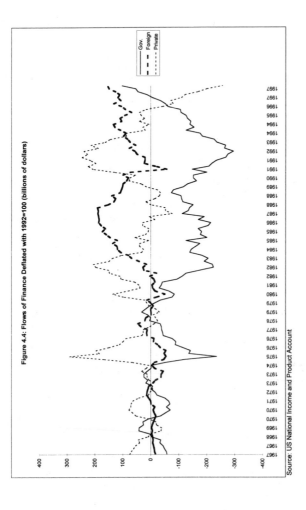

Figure 4.4

Flows of Finance Deflated with 1992=100

At the world level there are three main financial actors—the USA, the fifteen countries in the European Union (EU) functioning as a rather tightly coordinated group, and Japan. At the core of the EU is Euroland, with eleven members that now share a single currency, the euro. China and the other historically rapidly growing economies in East Asia play supporting roles, with the rest of the world (ROW) picking up the slack. Table 4.4 summarizes their current account performances during the 1990s.

The first point to note is that international payments data do not add up as they should. As shown in the last line, the world seems to run a substantial current account deficit with itself—an impossibility because the sum of all nations' current accounts should be zero in another application of Walras's Law from chapter 3. After all, one country's exports are another's imports. The error is comparable in magnitude to the flows of the major players. So the scales, though probably not the directions, of the forces about to be discussed are imprecise.

The two surplus players in the late 1990s were the EU-15 and Japan. Europe ran a current account deficit earlier in the decade but then switched to a surplus partly as a consequence of the contractionary macro policy packages most countries adopted as part of the run-up to the introduction of the euro on January 1, 1999. Aside from the 1991–92 episode, according to the estimates in the table the US has run the major deficit.[4] An American current account gap in the $200 to $300 billion range injects effective demand to the tune of about 1 percent of world GDP into the global macro system. This is a nontrivial amount. The world economy can be very sensitive to a "one percent" shock. That was about the size of the 1973 oil price shock.

There are four key international financial flows:

The US has a structural deficit financed by borrowing from abroad. It has used the resulting capital inflows to support steady if unspectacular GDP growth that began in the early 1990s, based on stable although not low real interest

Table 4.4

Current Accounts in Major Areas (billions of US dollars)

	1990	1991	1992	1993	1994	1995	1996	1997	1998	1999
US	−92	−6	−56	−91	−134	−129	−148	−166	−211	−249
Japan	45	68	112	132	131	110	66	95	125	147
EU-15	−31	−80	−81	9	23	52	91	126	125	137
E. Asia	5	−2	3	6	−3	−22	−31	0	52	33
China	12	13	6	−12	7	2	7	23	12	6
ROW	−196	−249	−228	−200	−177	−137	−148	−150	−205	−206
World Total	−257	−256	−244	−156	−153	−124	−163	−72	−102	−132

Source: OECD (Figures for 1998 and 1999 are estimates from the OECD Economic Outlook No. 64, December 1998)

rates. Calling the decade's results a "boom" is an exaggeration. As is clear from Table 4.1, trend output growth has only been about three-quarters as fast as in the 1960s.

Japan has been stagnant since its "bubble" economy burst around 1990 and runs a secular surplus. As a consequence of the collapse of the bubble its internal credit supply has been limited, leading to slow growth, a weakening yen through 1997, and a strong current account surplus with corresponding capital outflows.

In recent years Europe's growth has been slow and its foreign surplus large. Since the middle of the decade the sum of the European and Japanese surpluses has exceeded the American deficit.

The ROW is the main sink for surpluses originating elsewhere. China/East Asia ran deficits in 1995–96, then switched to a surplus position after the Asian crisis as the countries of the region attempted to export their way out of depression. The region's famous bilateral current account surplus with the US consistently exceeded its overall surplus. The difference is the deficit that the East Asian economies ran with the EU and Japan. In effect they were absorbing some of the excess saving in the EU and Japan and recycling it toward American shores. After all, the US external deficit *had* to be financed from somewhere.

How do the national economies supporting these flows interact? In terms of its output dynamics, the US current account deficit is counter-cyclical. When world activity is low, the US deficit, and hence US borrowing, rises, pumping demand into the rest of the world. Similarly, when world activity is high the US deficit falls, limiting the injection of demand into the rest of the world. America's net borrowing therefore varies against the cycle, just as Britain's did under the high gold standard of the nineteenth century (recall the discussion in chapter 2). Financial flows into the US have behaved in a globally stabilizing fashion.

THE AMERICAN PREDICAMENT

For a nation that borrows, however, capital movements are not a matter of its own volition. A better way to describe the current role of the US is to say that its creditors—Japan directly and the EU once removed—have agreed to lend counter-cyclically to finance the American injection of global effective demand. The inflows illustrated above have built up a huge stock of debt. At the end of 1997 gross US external "liabilities" (in a broad sense, including foreign holdings of corporate equity) were about $4.8 trillion. According to Federal Reserve data, a rough breakdown was government debt at $1.5 trillion; corporate debt, $0.5 trillion; corporate equity, $0.9 trillion; financial sector, $0.7 trillion; and "miscellaneous" (mostly obligations of business and finance), $1 trillion. These sums could lie at the root of at least three potential stock-stock and stock-flow imbalances:

First, the consolidated government sector's foreign debt was 27 percent of its total obligations of $5.5 trillion. But less than 50 percent of the $1.5 trillion it owed externally was owed to foreign governments. Most corporate debt was held privately. Foreign governments' holdings of US debt are at least subject to international negotiation. The same cannot be said of the US debt and equity held by the private sector in the rest of the world. A jump downward of just 6 percent of total foreign holdings of American liabilities (as of 1997) would equal the projected current account deficit in 1999. Just as in East Asia before 1997, there is the potential for huge, rapidly destabilizing capital outflows. The federal government's T-bills in particular could be sold off very rapidly.

A *second* potential source of trouble would be an interest rate increase. If the short-term rate went from its current 5 percent to 10 percent for example, American payments to foreigners on government and corporate debt of $2 trillion would go up by $100 billion. To pay these bills, projected 1999 foreign borrowing would need to increase by one-third. In this sense the external position of the US resembles Brazil's in 1998.

A *third* source of concern is who is actually to do America's borrowing in the future. The main component of *net* US external liabilities (including equity) of $1.3 trillion is government debt built up during the long period of fiscal deficits from 1980 until 1997. Future external borrowing can only take the form of new liabilities issued by the government and/or the three main private sub-sectors: finance, corporate business, and non-corporate business and households. Figure 4.3 shows that the government has been in fiscal surplus since 1997, so reducing both its domestic and foreign liabilities. As noted above, the corporate sector largely finances its capital formation with retained earnings and over the medium term keeps its annual increments of financial assets and liabilities in rough balance (within a range of $200 billion or so). At most, its contribution to the growth in the stock of liabilities available to the rest of the world will be well less than the current account deficit. Similar statements apply to the financial sector's and "miscellaneous" claims, for which foreign assets and liabilities are broadly offsetting. By a process of elimination, households emerge as the *only* major sector in a position to borrow from the rest of the world in the future. But in 1999 households were beginning to demonstrate financial distress just as they were supposed to begin a foreign borrowing spree that would be the fundamental corollary of a reasonable rate of growth in the US.

So a household stock-flow imbalance threatens. Household debt is approaching $6 trillion (roughly 70 percent in the form of mortgages, 25 percent consumer credit, and the balance miscellaneous). At the end of 1997 the ratio of household debt to personal disposable income was 0.98, up from 0.89 in 1993.

Given the structure of global trade and payments, the US will have to borrow $200 to $300 billion externally every year for the foreseeable future. The government sector seems intent on running an annual budgetary surplus in the $100 to $200 billion range. If they follow their traditional borrowing patterns over the cycle, the business and finance sectors will soon start saving more than they invest. It is the spending of households that must offset all these savings. If household income is (optimistically) assumed to grow steadily at 2.5 percent per year, then the household debt/income ratio would rise to about 1.12 by the end of 2002. It is impossible to say how households and their creditors would respond to new borrowing of such magnitude, especially if a fall in the stock market (which must happen some time) results in a serious plunge in personal sector wealth ($33.6 trillion at the end of 1997, up from $19.6 trillion ten years before).[5]

To illustrate the potential American debt trap(s), it makes sense to take a look at how the external position is likely to evolve if business continues as usual. At the end of 1997 the breakdown of US *net* foreign assets by type of instrument was monetary, $0.1 trillion; credit market, -$1.7 trillion; equity, $0.1 trillion; and miscellaneous, $0.2 trillion. Historically the US has received a strong positive return on its equity and similar holdings, with profits on net foreign direct investment (FDI) exceeding interest on America's net debt. However, that surplus vanished in 1997 when portfolio and FDI income were -$82 billion and $68 billion respectively.

Forward projections under fairly conservative assumptions about the trade deficit, volumes of FDI, and investment income flows suggest that net foreign liabilities may rise from $1.3 trillion at the end of 1997 to $2.5 trillion at the end of 2002 *if current levels of macroeconomic activity and hence foreign borrowing are sustained.* Which of the major economic sectors—business, government, or households—will directly or indirectly run up the new foreign debt every year is a key policy question. For reasons already discussed, households may not be able to shoulder the burden. If they do not and deep recession is to be avoided, the federal budget will have to move into substantial deficit. This is not a question of "fine-tuning." It is a question of whether the government will be capable of moving to counter a potentially very deep recession when the private sector's borrowing spree runs out. The popular prejudice against government deficits suggests that it will not.

And, it must be remembered that US growth and employment is today sustained by the inexorable growth of *foreign* debt.

EXTERNAL DANGERS?

The most recent runs on the dollar took place in the 1970s and 1980s. The former helped provoke the Volcker interest rate shock, a significant recession worldwide, the developing country debt crisis, and other major adjustments. As discussed above, doubts about the dollar in the mid-1980s were instrumental in triggering the 1987 stock market crisis. A decade is a long time span in terms of such events; after all, the Bretton Woods system lasted for only about twenty-five years. What scenarios may unfold if the US in particular and the world system more generally get into trouble once again?

So far the US has managed to borrow in a globally stabilizing fashion and faces only potential flow-flow and stock-flow disequilibria. There are risks however on both fronts. With regard to borrowing, the real decisions will be made in Europe and Japan. The latter has been under international pressure for years to restructure its economy so aggregate demand can be driven by domestic spending as opposed to exports. Through early 1999 very little had been achieved, and the Japanese current account surplus continued to be recycled via Wall Street. This situation may very well continue.

Europe on the other hand may now grow more rapidly with the Maastricht process ended and the euro born. In that event, higher activity levels and interest rates in the EU would draw in imports and capital flows. US borrowing could begin to be squeezed as the European trade surplus declines. It is also possible that the introduction of the euro, the only currency with a potential status in international trade and finance similar to that of the dollar, will create a potentially unstable currency duopoly. It is argued below that international arrangements might be put into place to limit fluctuations among the dollar, euro, and yen. But suppose this does not happen, and speculative pressure mounts against the dollar?

A sell-off of the dollar would produce sharp falls in US bond prices and hence a rise in interest rates. Would higher interest rates stop the rot, would they be "credible"? The potential disequilibria—portfolio shifts away from the US, bigger interest obligations on its debt, and growing financial stress on the household sector—could begin to feed on one another and on the views of the markets. At that point, with an expectational run on the dollar fueled and not staunched by higher interest rates, dollar devaluation, austerity, and the other usual policy moves, all hopes for global macro stability could disappear. A massive international rescue campaign would certainly be required, with worldwide implications impossible to foretell.

A medium-term policy mix for the US, then, will require an expansion in government spending to offset the solvency problems that the private sector (especially the household sector) will soon confront. Monetary expansion will not do the trick, since *some* domestic sector has to borrow to offset the current account deficit. But still more is required. The dollar is perhaps not so "overvalued" as it was in the mid-1980s, but a real exchange rate correction could help reduce the external deficit and slow the debt accumulation process just described. Talk of depreciation in the 20 to 30 percent range was in the air in the first part of 1999.[6]

REAL ECONOMIES AND
THE GLOBAL FINANCIAL SYSTEM

The broad characteristics of the relationship between liberalized international financial markets and the performance of the industrial economies are now clear. The downside risks created by volatility and contagion create a deflationary bias in government policy and in the private sector of the real economy. This is reinforced by the very high costs of debt in a situation in which real interest rates typically exceed growth rates by a substantial margin. High real interest rates are themselves the outcome of the attempt to maintain financial stability in a potentially volatile world. So the postwar goal of "a high and stable level of employment" is abandoned and replaced by the goal of "long term price stability"—the path to which is defined according to the rules of the beauty contest.

The easing of bond yield volatility in the 1990s probably reflects widespread adjustments to financial market constraints rather than improvements in the functioning of the markets themselves. Policy has been adjusted to accommodate the pressures of volatile markets. Private sector decision-makers have also adapted to the new low-level situation. With governments no longer committed to maintaining full employment levels of effective demand, the prospective growth of sales is reduced and the attractions of investment curtailed. Falling private sector investment will tend to precipitate some deterioration in the government's fiscal balance, further exacerbating deflationary pressures. Only the household sector in the US has been immune to the general pessimism. But in an overall deflationary environment even American consumers may be riding for a fall.

It is *potential* volatility that creates the pressures on government policy. As governments increasingly accept the new rules of the game and as demands for "international surveillance" and "openness" enforce those rules with increasing ferocity, observed volatility may diminish. A relatively slow growth, high unemployment, monetarily stable system can endure indefinitely. This is the case even in circumstances of rapid technological change. New technologies might be expected to spark off a Schumpeterian wave of new investment, but with macroeconomic balances maintained in a carefully constructed deflationary stance, the impact of new technologies is felt more on the composition of activity than on the rate of growth. The low overall rate of growth ensures that the average rate of productivity growth remains low.

A low rate of growth with low ratios of investment and saving to GDP will not lessen the influence of the bond market. Even though the flow of savings may be diminished, the stock of financial assets remains enormous, and it is the turnover of that stock which determines long-term interest rates. As liquidity increases with the creation of ever more sophisticated financial products, the stock market begins to operate like a bond market. Institutional investors increasingly demand that dividend rates should be maintained irrespective of corporate performance, thereby imposing a further deflationary burden on corporate cash flow.

In sum, a liberalized, sophisticated financial system, with a premium placed on the possibility of exit, is a fragile financial system. The development of new derivative products to manage the risk that the liberal financial system has itself created has in turn produced new systemic risks. Indeed, the complexity of such instruments leaves them vulnerable to a sudden loss of liquidity.

The explanation presented here of the impact of international capital liberalization is consistent with the deterioration of economic performance in the post–Bretton Woods era. It does not of course *prove* causation. It simply comprises a set of hypotheses on the operation of financial markets and the real economy, and the interaction between them, which would suggest that liberal financial markets with very high turnover would tend to impose deflationary pressures on the economy.

If the foregoing hypotheses do indeed capture the essence of the current operation of the international economy, it raises the question of what can be done to improve the relationship between the operation of the international financial system and the overall efficiency of real economies. It is often argued that nothing can be done to change the present system since capital flows can overwhelm a large number of measures decided by any one government. This is certainly true. But it is equally true that the foundation stones of the world financial system are the monetary instruments issued by a small number of major governments. The US dollar, the deutsche mark, the yen, and the pound sterling were on at least one side of the transaction in 80 percent of currency trades in 1989 and 1992, and in 77 percent of trades in 1995. With the advent of the euro, the dominance of the four currencies will have increased.

The power implicit in these foundations will only be made manifest if governments themselves espouse a different theory of economic policy than the orthodox view currently dominating the economic and political debate. In many cases the assumed superiority of a liberal market strategy derives not just from conventional theory but also from a belief in the inherent economic incompetence and even venality of governments — an unflattering picture that some governments seem to have adopted about themselves. Of course, a number of examples exist which justify pessimism. But examples of bad and incompetent policy are not sufficient reasons to hand the future of the economy over to liberalized markets that render systematic policymaking impossible. Rather, they should encourage the creation of an environment in which good and competent policy can be effective.

The challenge is to find a set of policies which will garner the benefits of liberal financial markets while reducing their all too obvious dangers. In national economies that goal has been achieved by the development of wide-ranging structures of financial market regulation underpinned by a powerful lender of last resort. The perils of worldwide capital market liberalization derive substantially from the absence of similar structures in the international economy.

NOTES

1. Such contracts were available in fifteenth-century Venice. *The Merchant* also contains an interesting example of financial contagion. Due to the vagaries of Venetian law as interpreted by Portia, Shylock, a third party holding an unusual OTC contract with Antonio, ends up bearing much of the cost of the latter's unhedged risk.

The insider Antonio's net worth survives, thanks to Portia's disguised lender of last resort intervention in the closing scene.

2. There is an important controversy over what "productivity" actually measures in an era in which there has been rapid change in the types of commodity which the economy produces, notably a rapid increase in the output of the IT industries. These qualitative changes are not captured by broad indices, and hence the fall in productivity growth is said by some analysts to be overstated.

3. To give a feel for the change in nominal borrowing and lending levels over time, Figures 4.2 and 4.3 are set up in terms of current prices. With average prices in 1992 at 100, the GDP deflator (a measure of the average price level) rose from a value of 26 at the beginning of 1967 to 113 in early 1998. The index reached levels of 50 in 1978 and 75 in 1984, reflecting the inflation of the 1970s.

4. Table 4.4 has the US running a small current account deficit in 1991, while Figures 4.2 to 4.4 indicate a small surplus. The discrepancy stems from the different data banks underlying the figures and table respectively. Such statistical problems run rife, making global macro analysis very imprecise.

5. Although it is difficult to trace in the data, household borrowing almost certainly would have been greater without the boom in the stock market. "Capital gains dividends" from mutual funds and many other channels not captured in the national accounts no doubt helped transform stock market gains into ready money.

6. As more than a curiosum, the dollar *must* depreciate over the medium term if the US hopes to keep its trade deficit stable as a share of GDP. Imports into the US respond more strongly to income growth than do imports of its trading partners to their own higher incomes. If US income is to expand as rapidly as the rest of the world's, therefore, the dollar has to weaken steadily to cut back on American import demand.

5—Developing Countries and the New Financial Order

Everyone knows the epigraph to *Anna Karenina*, "Happy families are all alike; every unhappy family is unhappy in its own way." Tolstoy may well have been right about families, but making this same observation about developing economies hit by capital market crises distinctly fails. Their causes and unhappy consequences in Latin America, Asia, and Eastern Europe over the past twenty years have many elements in common.

These include a pegged exchange rate and the government's withdrawal from regulating the real side of the economy, the financial sector, *and especially the international capital market*. This premeditated laxity created strong incentives for destabilizing private sector financial behavior on the part of both domestic and external players. Over time, private actions cumulated through each country's macroeconomic system to a point where exchange rate fundamentals were widely seen to be out of line. In a Keynesian reversal of conventions, the fixed rate became impossible to defend and a crisis followed.

The common elements do *not* include the trilemma, with its implicit exoneration of the private sector from any misdeeds in causing crises. Most recent boom and bust episodes took place in countries that had their fiscal, monetary, and moral hazard houses in order. Even in Russia and Brazil, private speculation rather than public extravagance threw the fiscal accounts out of balance by driving up interest rates on outstanding government debt.

To think about how international finance can be rebuilt in a more stable fashion, we have to understand why the crises happened in the first place. That requires breaking new analytical ground. Standard theories do not adequately explain Latin America's "Southern Cone" crises around 1980, Mexico and the "tequila" crisis in 1994, events in East Asia in 1997–98, the

Russian crisis of summer 1998, and Brazil's in early 1999. The argument of this chapter begins with a review of mainstream explanations and then proceeds to a narrative proposed by people who operate close to macro policy choices and micro financial decisions. Their ideas lead to reasonable policy lines nations can follow in the wake of the latest disasters.

MAINSTREAM CRISIS MODELS

All mainstream models of these events share the premise that the public sector caused them through errors of commission. In a typical scenario as proposed in the late 1970s by MIT economist Paul Krugman, the nominal exchange rate is fixed (or perhaps has a pre-announced percentage rate of devaluation $\triangle e \mathbin{/} e$ under an *active* crawling peg policy). The local interest rate i exceeds the foreign rate i^*. In the case of a "credible" fixed rate regime, the *expected* pace of devaluation $\triangle e^{\mathrm{exp}}$ will equal zero. In line with UIP theory as discussed in chapter 3, we can define an interest rate "spread" as $\Sigma_i = i - [i^* + \triangle e^{\mathrm{exp}} \mathbin{/} e]$. The fact that $\Sigma_i > 0$ under the assumptions we are making will favor investments in the home country.

Now suppose the government pursues an expansionary fiscal policy, increasing the fiscal deficit. If the household and business sectors do not alter their saving levels, along twin deficit lines foreign saving S_{row} or the external current account deficit will have to rise. This diagnosis lies at the heart of traditional IMF stabilization packages that have thrown many countries into recession. The external imbalance can lead to crisis via several channels. Consider these three:

The *first* is pure trilemma. It is based on the recognition that the government has to issue more debt to cover its bigger deficit. If the debt cannot be placed in external markets, the government will have to borrow domestically. To maintain its own balances, the financial system will have to raise new resources from the private sector. Its easiest course is often to "monetize" the fiscal deficit by issuing new short-term liabilities. On the standard assumption that the domestic price level P is driven up by such money creation, then along PPP lines the real value of the currency eP^*/P (where P^* is the foreign price level) will appreciate. Imports are likely to rise and exports to fall, leading to greater external imbalance. With more borrowing ruled out by assumption, foreign reserves will begin to erode.

Falling reserves suggest that the trade deficit cannot be maintained indefinitely. When they are exhausted, presumably there will have to be a discrete "maxi"-devaluation, a regime shift which will inflict a capital loss on external investors holding liabilities of the home country denominated in local currency. At some point it becomes rational to expect the devaluation to occur, making Δe^{exp} strongly positive and reversing the spread. A currency attack follows and the economically untenable fiscal expansion is rapidly erased.

A *second* version of this tale is based on the assumption that the local monetary authorities raise "deposit" interest rates to induce households to hold financial system liabilities created in response to greater public borrowing. To cover their greater costs of raising funds, financial institutions will have to jack up lending rates as well. The spread Σ_i immediately widens. Foreign players begin to shift portfolios toward home assets so that reserves rise. If the monetary authorities allow the reserve increase to feed into faster growth of the money supply, we are back to the previous story. If they "sterilize" reserve inflows by cutting the growth of new household or business debt, then interest rates will go up even further, drawing more foreign investment into the system. Pressures will mount for the current account deficit S_{row} to increase, say via exchange appreciation induced by inflation or else a downward drift of the nominal rate as the authorities allow the currency to gain strength. A foreign crisis looms again.

Third, crises can be fabricated from moral hazard. The standard line of argument is that developing country governments self-insure by accumulating international reserves to back up poorly regulated financial markets. National players feel justified in offering high returns to foreign investors, setting up a spread. Domestic liabilities are acquired by outsiders (or perhaps nationals resident in more pleasant climes or just engaging in offshore manipulations) until such point as the stock of insured claims exceeds the government's reserves. A speculative attack follows.

The leitmotif of an alert private sector chastizing an inept government keeps recurring. By creating moral hazard, the government in the last model encourages reckless investment behavior. All a sensible private sector can be expected to do is make money out of such misguided public action.

A MORE PLAUSIBLE THEORY

A more realistic perspective is that the public and private sectors generate positive financial feedbacks between themselves first at the micro and then at the macro level, ultimately destabilizing the system. This line of analysis has been advanced by Salih Neftci, a market practitioner, and Roberto Frenkel, a macroeconomist. Both focus on an initial situation in which the nominal exchange rate is credibly fixed, or $\Delta e^{\mathrm{exp}} = 0$, and show how an unstable dynamic process can arise.

A Frenkel-Neftci (or FN) cycle begins in financial markets which generate capital inflows. They spill over to the macroeconomy via the financial system and the balance of payments as the upswing gains momentum. At the peak, before a (more or less rapid) downswing, the economy-wide consequences can be overwhelming.

To trace through an example, suppose that a spread on interest rates (e.g. on Mexican government peso-denominated bonds with a high nominal rate but carrying an implicit exchange risk) or asset prices (e.g. capital gains from booming Bangkok real estate) opens. A few local players take positions in the relevant assets, borrowing abroad to do so. Their exposure is risky but *small*. It may well go unnoticed by regulators; indeed for the system as a whole the risk is negligible.

Destabilizing market competition enters at a second stage. The pioneering institutions are exploiting a spread of (say) 10 percent, while others are earning (say) 5 percent on traditional placements. Even if the risks are recognized it is difficult for other players not to jump in. Traders or loan officers holding 5 percent paper will reason that the probability of losing their jobs is close to 100 percent *now* if they do not take the high-risk/high-return position. Such potentially explosive behavior is standard market practice. In one description from an interview study, ". . . the speculative excesses of the international investors in the Asian financial crisis were not an exception, . . . but instead the result of normal business practices and thus to a certain degree inevitable."

After some months or years of this process, the balance sheet of the local financial system will be risky overall. It will feature "short" (indebted) positions in foreign claims and "long" positions in local assets.[1] There may also be problems with maturity structures of claims, especially if local players borrow from abroad short-term. Nervous foreign lenders may then contrast a country's total external payment obligations over the next year (say) with its international reserves. Such comparisons proved disastrous for Mexico in 1995 and several Asian countries in 1997.

But the real problem lies with the currency or locational mismatch of the balance sheet—in light of developing country experience it emerges as a fundamental factor that can lead to exchange rate crises. Potential losses from the long position are finite—they at most amount to what the assets cost in the first place. Losses from short-selling foreign exchange are in principle unbounded—who knows how high the local currency-to-dollar exchange rate may have to climb?

In a typical macroeconomic paradox, individual players' risks have been shifted to the aggregate. Any policy move that threatens the overall position—for example cutting interest rates or pricking the real estate bubble—could cause a collapse of the currency and of local asset prices. The authorities will use reserves and/or regulations to prevent a crash, consciously ratifying the private sector's market decisions. Unfortunately, macroeconomic factors will ultimately force their hand.

In a familiar scenario, suppose that initial capital inflows have boosted domestic output growth. The current account deficit will widen, leading at some point to a fall in reserves as capital inflows level off and total interest payments on outstanding obligations rise. Higher interest rates will be needed to equilibrate portfolios and attract foreign capital. Adverse repercussions will affect both the private and public sectors. Business saving will fall or turn negative as illiquidity and insolvency spread, threatening a systemic crisis. Bankruptcies of banks and firms may further contribute to reducing the credibility of the exchange rate. If the government has debt outstanding, escalating interest payment obligations as rates shoot up can provoke a fiscal crisis—witness events in Russia and Brazil in the late 1990s.

A downturn becomes inevitable since finally no local interest rate will be high enough to induce more external lending in support of what is recognized as a short foreign exchange position at the economy-wide level. Shrewd players will unwind their positions before the downswing begins (as Mexican nationals were said to have done before the December 1994 devaluation). They can even retain positive earnings over the cycle by getting out while the currency weakens visibly. But others—typically including the government's macroeconomic policy team—are likely to go under.

The dynamics of this narrative differs from that of standard crisis models. It does *not* involve a regime shift when a spread switches from positive to negative. Rather, movements in the spread itself feed back into cyclical changes within the economy concerned that finally lead to massive instability. In the jargon of mathematical catastrophe theory, the standard models invoke a "static" instability such as a buckling beam. More relevant to history are "dynamic" or cyclical instabilities that emerge when effective damping of the dynamic system vanishes. A classic engineering example is the Tacoma Narrows suspension bridge. Opened in July 1940, it soon became known as "Galloping Gertie" because of its antics in the wind. Its canter became strong enough to make it disintegrate in a 41-mile-per-hour windstorm in November of that year. Despite their best efforts, economists have yet to design a system that fails so fast.

Finally, a soupçon of moral hazard enters an FN crisis, but more by way of pro-cyclical regulation than through "promised" lender of last resort interventions or government provision of "insurance" in the form of international reserves. After a downswing some players will be bailed out and others will not. But such eventualities will be subject to high discount rates while the cycle is on the way up. In that phase traders and treasurers of finance houses are far more interested in their spreads and regulatory acquiescence in exploiting them than in what sort of safety net they may or may not fall into sometime down the road.

WHAT REALLY HAPPENED IN THE SOUTHERN CONE?

The financial crises around 1980 in the Southern Cone, especially in Argentina and Chile, are important empirical references for both mainstream models and the FN narrative just sketched. As it turns out, the former distort much of relevant history. That is, public and private sector actions clearly interacted to derail the external finances. Capital market upheavals originated in a domestic cycle rather than as the consequence of an overnight change of heart (or the sign of a spread) of market players.

In the mid-1970s, Argentina and Chile were going through similar political and economic phases. *Peronista* and *Unidad Popular* governments had been succeeded by military dictatorships in the midst of domestic economic upheavals. Initially, macroeconomic policy did not deviate significantly from the traditional stabilization recipes that both countries had repeatedly applied since the 1950s (and which the IMF later built into its standard practice). Price controls were lifted, wages were repressed, and the currency was devalued. After that a crawling peg was adopted aimed at holding the real value of the currency stable in the face of ongoing inflation. Fiscal adjustment was mainly based on reduction of the government wage bill. Real wages fell dramatically in both countries and employment dropped in Chile. The fiscal adjustment was deep and permanent in the Chilean case and less significant and less lasting in the Argentine. An innovation in economic policy was domestic financial reform: the interest rate was freed and most regulations on financial intermediaries were removed.

Both economies had been isolated from international financial markets in the first half of the 1970s and did not have sizable external debts. Their external accounts had already been balanced by the stabilization packages. The orthodoxy of the military administrations gained credibility with the IMF and international banks despite the fact that both economies still had high inflation rates (160 percent and 63.5 percent per year in 1977 in Argentina and Chile respectively). High real domestic financial yields which followed market deregulation attracted capital inflows even before controls were relaxed. Confronted with these pressures, the authorities initially gave priority to controlling the domestic monetary supply and attempting to curb inflows with tighter regulations.

In the second half of the decade, first Chile and shortly after Argentina implemented new and similar policy packages. Liberalization of the exchange market and deregulation of capital flows were added to domestic financial reforms. Trade liberalization programs were launched simultaneously. Exchange rate policy was the anti-inflation component of the package. Nominal rates were fixed through pre-announcement of monthly devaluations. In Argentine jargon, this "active" crawling peg was scheduled to arrive at a constant exchange rate with zero inflation after some months. (The rates were posted in the famous *tablitas*.) The stylized facts about the outcomes go as follows:

From the moment the exchange rate regimes were established, the inflation rate fell but was systematically higher than the sum of the programmed rate of devaluation plus the international rate of inflation. PPP violation occurred in the sense that the real exchange rate eP^*/P declined; at the same time the ratio of non-traded to traded goods prices indexes rose.

The launching of the packages was followed by injections of funds from abroad. In each country the monetary base, bank deposits, and credit grew swiftly as did the number of financial intermediaries. There was rapid appreciation of domestic financial and real asset prices. Domestic demand, production, and imports all expanded. The import surge, caused by trade opening, currency appreciation, and expansion in domestic demand steadily widened the trade deficit. The current account deficit showed a more gradual increase because the external debt was small. At the outset, capital inflows were higher than the current account deficit and reserves accumulated. No attempt was made to sterilize the inflows, so the money supply expanded.

The evolution of external accounts and reserves marked a clear cycle. A continuous but gradual increase was seen in the current account deficit, which after a time exceeded the level of inflows. Reserves reached a maximum and then contracted, inducing monetary contraction overall. However, the cycle was not exclusively determined by this mechanical element—the size of capital flows was not an exogenous datum. Portfolio decisions regarding assets denominated in domestic currency and dollars were affected by the evolution of the balance of payments and finance. Both played a crucial role in boom and bust.

The domestic interest rate reflected financial aspects of the cycle. It fell in the first phase and then turned upward. Because the exchange rate rule initially enjoyed high credibility, arbitrage between domestic and external financial assets and credit led at the beginning to reductions in the domestic interest rate and the expected cost of external credit (which became negative in both countries). Lower interest rates helped spur real and financial expansion. It led to increased "financial fragility"—more players took positions in which their interest obligations were not covered by expected income flows in at least some time periods.

In the second phase, rising domestic interest rates and episodes of illiquidity and insolvency appeared, first as isolated cases and then as a systemic crisis. What explained the increase in nominal and real interest rates? Along UIP lines, domestic rates began to be driven by expectations of devaluation, or the spread Σ_i reflecting exchange and financial risks.

Risk rose in Chile and Argentina in conjunction with financial fragility. But more importantly, the widening spread was driven by the evolution of the external accounts. Persistent growth of the current account deficit—and at some point the fall in reserves—reduced the credibility of the exchange rate rule. Higher interest rates were needed to equilibrate portfolios and attract foreign capital. This dynamic proved to be explosive in both countries. Runs on central bank reserves led finally to the collapse of the exchange rate regime, and the resulting devaluations deepened the financial crisis.

Fiscal deficits and moral hazard in the form of public guarantees on bank deposits did not play significant roles. Both were present to some extent in Argentina, but Chile had a fiscal surplus and deposit guarantees had been eliminated with the explicit goal of making the financial system more efficient. Neither balance of payments attack models nor moral hazards had any relevance to these primordial developing country capital market crises. So much for received theory.

Destabilizing factors that *were* important included the rudimentary nature of the financial systems concerned and weaknesses in banking supervisory norms and practices. These are generic background features of capital market liberalization attempts in Latin America and elsewhere. If such packages had been postponed until financial systems were robust, diversified, and well-monitored, then they never would have been implemented, whether in the 1970s or twenty years thereafter.

MEXICO

Mexico in the 1990s was no more financially sound than the Southern Cone economies were two decades earlier, even though it had been an active laboratory for economic policy. The main success was an anti-inflation program anchored by a fixed exchange rate and real wage cuts. It took advantage of favorable initial conditions created by a previously orthodox phase. The great failure of course was the financial crisis of 1994.

The roots of the disaster trace back to well before the debt crisis of 1982. Mexico was then faced with the problems unleashed by loan-pushing on the part of commercial banks and the country's too-ready acceptance of foreign credits to undertake expansionary policies aimed at putting into concrete form the jump in national wealth that the massive oil discoveries in the mid-1970s had brought about. At least during the 1970s growth was rapid, but more disquieting developments included real currency appreciation with inflation rates that rose to 28 percent per year, capital flight, and a massive accumulation of external debt.

After the crisis broke in August 1982, Mexico was forced to transform an external current account deficit of about 5 percent of GDP into a 3 percent surplus within less than a year to compensate for the loss of "fresh money" in the form of new loans that the commercial banks had cut off. The economic team achieved the current account adjustment using the time-tested tools pioneered in the Southern Cone three decades earlier.

They caused a recession by devaluing the peso and cutting the fiscal deficit and monetary emission. Such actions usually cause stagflation, as they certainly did in Mexico—GDP growth averaged out at zero between 1982 and 1988, while by 1987 prices were rising 160 percent per year.

During the 1987–88 presidential transition, stagflation was attacked in two ways. One success was the implementation of an exchange rate–based inflation stabilization program. Despite IMF opposition, in 1987–88 an "Economic Solidarity Pact" aimed at stabilizing prices combined a pegged nominal exchange rate with a wage freeze, trade liberalization, and more austerity. This heterodox package did brake inflation, but at a high cost. Real wages were reduced once again, and $10 billion in foreign reserves built up after 1982 was spent on supporting the fixed exchange rate and bringing in imports. The output growth rate however did not improve.

The authorities tried to stimulate growth by resorting to extreme market friendliness. They privatized state-owned industries, further liberalized foreign trade by dismantling export subsidies and an import quota system built up over decades, and—most importantly for the present discussion—removed restrictions on inflows of direct and portfolio investment. The push to sign the North American Free Trade Agreement was the capstone of all these efforts. The macroeconomic outcomes were disquieting on at least eight counts:

First, foreign capital came in, letting the trade balance shift from a small surplus in 1988 to a deficit of about $20 billion in 1993. The current account deficit was around 6 percent of GDP in 1993 and 9 percent in 1994. Output growth rose to 4.4 percent in 1990, but tailed off thereafter. The foreign credits were largely short-term, in part because of quirks in the BIS or Basel standards discussed below in connection with the Asian crisis.

Second, along the lines suggested by the FN model, capital inflows were enticed by a Mexico/US interest rate spread exceeding 10 percent (and an internal Mexican real interest rate of about 5 percent). Perhaps an even stronger incentive took the form of capital gains on the stock market or *bolsa*. The share price index rose from around 250 in 1988–89 to over 2500 early in 1994, setting up a large capital gains spread. After mid-year the *bolsa* index fluctuated erratically as unnerving political events and interest rate reductions of a few percentage points made Mexico a less attractive place to invest. In effect, there was a three-way beauty contest. The players who determined movements of funds across the border comprised bulls (mainly foreign), bears (mainly Mexican), and "sheep" who wobbled in between to generate a teeter-totter market with multiple equilibria—a boom in the early 1990s, an unstable intermediate balance in 1994, and then a crash.

Third, substantial internal (peso) credit expansion took place as banks accepted inflated securities as collateral for loans. Between 1987 and 1994 commercial bank credit doubled, with loans for consumption and housing increasing by 450 percent and 1000 percent respectively. The ratio of the overall money supply to "base money" or central bank liabilities also doubled due to a reduction in reserve requirements and elimination of quantitative credit controls. Regulation was pro-cyclical, with a vengeance. After the crash, an upward spike in nominal interest rates decimated bank balance sheets—bad debt within the system now amounts to around 15 percent of GDP. Local banks were not aided by Mexico's 1995 "rescue" package, which largely protected foreign creditors. How to refinance bad peso debt remains a flaming political issue to this day.

Fourth, while it lasted the external capital inflow had to enter the economy via the widening trade deficit already noted—there was no other channel. The deficit was engineered partly by a steadily appreciating real currency value and partly by trade liberalization. Under a crawling peg exchange rate regime, the value of the peso in terms of both consumer and producer prices fell by about 45 percent between the mid-1980s and 1994, with most of the drop prior to 1991. One reason for depreciating the nominal exchange rate more slowly than price growth was to restrain inflation, but Mexican authorities were also pushed toward a powerful peso by incoming foreign capital. In the midst of radical trade liberalization, allowing the peso to violate PPP conditions so markedly was a perilous policy to pursue.

Fifth, in contrast to external financial investment, real capital formation within Mexico did not rise much above 20 percent of GDP, despite increases in the early 1990s from the extremely depressed levels of the previous decade. From the side of demand, low domestic absorption was the basic cause of slow growth. Private investment was not robust for several reasons: real interest rates were high; profit margins of companies in the traded goods sector were held down in real terms by the strong peso; and public investment which historically had "crowded in" private projects was cut back as part of the liberalization/ austerity program. For both consumption and investment spending, the import content shot up.

Sixth, investment fell back from historical levels, but private (both household and business) saving dropped even more — from roughly 15 percent to 5 percent of GDP in the 1990s despite high interest rates. The resulting incremental increase in the private sector's financial deficit (or total investment minus total saving) was immediately reflected into a bigger "twin" trade deficit supported by the strong peso/high interest rate/trade liberalization policy mix already discussed. As in Chile before its financial crash early in the 1980s, somehow the allegedly beneficial effects of public sector thrift did not transmit themselves to private firms and households.

Seventh, while the game lasted foreign money kept pouring in, blind to devaluation risk. The foundation for this house of cards was the ever-increasing stock of external debt, much of it short-term. It began to crumble when prices on the *bolsa* stopped rising after the first few months of 1994 while American interest rates continued to increase. The collapse came with Mexico's devaluation the Tuesday before Christmas. It spread rapidly when investors began to compute the volume of short-term obligations due in 1995. The sum was $50 billion, as compared to Mexico's $6 billion in reserves. In terms of its international exposure, the economy was highly illiquid.

Finally, the fundamental problem was the financial system's locational imbalance. But one can argue that other "mistakes" in policy such as reduced interest rates in anticipation of the September 1994 presidential election worsened the situation by deterring capital inflows. A far more important point is that the balance of international financial power strongly influenced the end game. When inflows slowed, the Mexican authorities issued a new instrument—peso-denominated *Tesobonos* which were indexed to the peso/dollar exchange rate. Asset-holders switched en masse from non-indexed government debt to *Tesobonos* apparently in the belief that they could be cashed in for dollars freely. After the crisis hit in December, US Treasury/ IMF bail-out loans were made conditional on *Tesobono* convertibility. An alternative (permitted under Article 6 of the IMF charter) would have been for Mexico to redeem *Tesobonos* in pesos and impose controls to deter dollar flight. But Washington denied that option. The result was that *Tesobono* holders on Wall Street were bailed out, while Mexico incurred tens of billions of dollars of additional debt to pay them off. The widely circulated assertion that *Tesobonos* were *dollar*-denominated was a follow-up public relations move by the US financial community to cover its players who had guessed badly wrong in increasing their Mexican exposure.

Such a public relations "spin" cloaks but does not erase the basic contradiction: By the early 1990s, Mexico had come as close as practical politics permits toward adopting a fully orthodox package of fiscal, monetary, and external adjustments. The fiscal account was in surplus, and barriers to external transactions had been removed. Yet the foreign account was heavily in deficit because private savings had collapsed and hot money was flowing in. The private sector was the principal source of macro imbalance, abetted by the government's insistence on full capital market liberalization, abandonment of reserve requirements and other supply-side restrictions on credit expansion, and the maintenance of an overvalued currency.

EAST ASIAN CRISES

With their importance varying from country to country, the same factors carry over to the pan-East Asian crisis of 1997-98. That Asia's typhoon was not foreseen is not surprising—in the past many if not most such gales have struck without warning. This one has provoked an enormous retrospective literature.

It is important to recognize that there are marked differences in institutional structure between East Asian and Western (especially Anglo-American) capitalism, as numerous scholars have pointed out. In terms of "ideal types," one can point to four major Asian departures, especially prior to a liberalization phase that got underway around 1990:

First, especially in the "Northern tier" of Japan, Korea, and Taiwan, relationships between business and government were historically close and mutually interactive. "Administrative guidance" was the state's chosen means for microeconomic intervention as opposed to legislation and/or judicial proceedings such as American antitrust actions. Decades of near-double digit output growth throughout the region are conclusive evidence that far more than crony capitalism was involved.

Second, corporate finance was largely channeled through banks, especially a "main bank" for each enterprise or conglomerate. Such durable relationships are said to allow business executives to take a long planning view because they are not threatened by hostile stock market takeovers. As discussed later, one implication of reliance on bank finance is that, depending on the specific country concerned, corporations have carried high debt/equity ratios. Representative values clustered around 2.0 in Korea in the 1990s and Japan in the 1960s and 1.0 in Malaysia and Thailand in the 1990s. By way of comparison, the aggregate ratio in the US has fluctuated between about 1.5

during the stock market slump in the late 1970s to about 0.35 in the bull market of the 1990s. In Asia, corporate debt loads depended on industrial policy as banks and the state coordinated the provision of cheap, directed credits to targeted manufacturing sectors. Had cross-border capital movements not been strictly regulated by exchange controls, this sort of intervention would not have been possible.

Third, just as capital markets were far from open, product markets and investment decisions by firms were regulated. "Excess competition" in the sense of over-investment by firms and extreme cost/price cycles in sectors subject to economies of scale were avoided by the planning authorities. One corollary is that besides major investment decisions, import and export trade had to be regulated by the state. The goal was to maintain economies open to trade but with "strategic" as opposed to "close" integration with the world economy.

Finally, social tensions never spilled over into high inflation rates, and growth was relatively stable. Communist transitions in China, Indochina, and North Korea aside, the region did not experience macroeconomic earthquakes after World War II, in sharp contrast to Latin America. This is one reason why the events of 1997–98 were an enormous psychological shock to both economic policymakers and the general public.

Of course not all the economies (not even Japan and Korea) followed the "Asian" model slavishly. Differences between the Northern and Southern tiers were significant. In Thailand and Indonesia, Japanese firms (collaborating closely with the Japanese government) played a big role in steering industrialization after the mid-1980s. Aside from sporadic efforts at industrial intervention in specific sectors, local governments remained passive. The state took a more explicitly developmentalist stance in Malaysia, but again in collaboration with Japanese multinationals. All the Southern countries, nonetheless, retained trade barriers or "distortions" in support of their various versions of industrial policy.

The model changed somewhat over time. Asian intraregional trade as a share of total trade grew from less than 40 percent in the 1960s to over 50 percent in the 1990s with the volume concentrated around the continent's Pacific rim (the corresponding intra-trade share for Latin America is around 20 percent). Trade restrictions were gradually relaxed. Exchange controls and other capital market regulations were removed much more abruptly in the 1990s, more or less simultaneously with decontrol of national financial systems.

The region's macroeconomic environment was also evolving. The Plaza Accord of 1985 marked a big transition when it set off substantial yen appreciation against the dollar. Japanese (along with Korean and Taiwanese) companies began to seek cheaper platforms for manufactured exports. The Southern tier was the natural place to go, especially because its economies pegged their currencies more or less tightly to the weakening dollar.

Credit was relatively cheap in Japan, and after its stock market and real estate bubbles burst in 1990 the trade surplus soared as the real economy stagnated. Much of the resulting Japanese acquisition of foreign claims took place in the Southern tier.

Some of this flow took the form of direct foreign investment from Northern tier companies, in effect turning the Southern countries into subcontractors for third country export markets. By the mid-1990s their economies were running into skilled labor shortages and chronically inadequate infrastructure. Beginning in 1996, export growth dropped substantially from the 10 percent to 20 percent annual rates observed earlier in the decade. Part of this collapse can be attributed to exchange rate changes. The Chinese devalued the yuan by 35 percent in 1994. The dollar rose by 50 percent against the yen after 1996, strengthening Southern tier rates because of their dollar pegs and adding to the pressure. This latter shift was especially damaging because Japan was still the region's major trading partner.

Other capital flows into Southeast Asia were "financial" in nature. North Asian, European, and American players all invested heavily in short-term notes, in part because the Basel capital adequacy standards encouraged banks to lend in that fashion. They also masked transactions by using off-balance sheet accounting and derivatives. (Both this ploy and reasons for short-term lending are discussed in more detail below.) To a degree the Americans may have been animated by moral hazard induced by the bail-out of Wall Street's exposed position in Mexico in 1995, but the same cannot be true of the Asians and Europeans. All were attracted by ample spreads and Southeast Asia's growth cachet.

According to published and presumably perused BIS estimates, consolidated bank claims on South Korea, Thailand, Indonesia, and Malaysia were $202 billion at the end of 1995 and $248 billion a year later—an annual rate of increase of 23 percent! In mid-1996 about 70 percent of claims against Korea and Thailand had maturities of one year or less. The figures for Indonesia and Malaysia were 62 percent and "only" 47 percent respectively. As will be seen, the assets used as collateral for all this short-term borrowing were far from being rock solid. Insofar as their prices were high as a consequence of speculative booms or were linked closely to nominal exchange rates which had been stable for a decade, their valuations were at risk.

Beginning in 1995 there *were* disturbing signs in East Asia—a breakdown of traditional regulatory regimes, a major hiccup in export-led growth, substantial short-term borrowing backed by a shaky asset base, and exchange rates drifting out of line. Not enough bad news to back a strong forecast of crisis perhaps, but in retrospect it is surprising that more people weren't scratching their heads. Market conventions were about to change.

THAILAND

Thailand was the most "Latin" of the rapidly growing Southern tier economies. Its FN cycle beginning in 1993 bears an uncanny resemblance to events in Mexico and the Southern Cone. Early in that year Thai companies were permitted to borrow in international capital markets. Together with lax financial regulation this move led total credit to the private sector to leap from 39 percent of GDP in 1992 to 123 percent in 1996, a bigger increase than even Mexico's. A public sector fiscal error of commission was nowhere to be seen, but the government surely erred in omission by suddenly allowing businesses to borrow as much abroad, and with such a short maturity structure, as they did. The oldest story in the trade is about inexperienced financial players who seek high short-term returns and thereby set off a chain of events leading to a crash.

Over-expansion was most evident in loans for real estate investment, although the property market was beginning to slow down already in 1993. Prices fell drastically beginning in 1995 and the stock market crashed in mid-1996. The busts landed about two-thirds of the country's financial and securities firms into serious trouble, exacerbated by the fact that they had neither hedged their future exchange risks with forward contracts nor attempted to assure future earnings flows in foreign currency. Belief in the immutability of the baht/dollar exchange rate was apparently universal. Zero expected baht depreciation created interest rate and (before the real estate and stock markets crashed) capital gains spreads that were very appealing to foreign lenders. Thai financial intermediaries borrowed from them, mostly short-term. They may have thought they were hedged because much of their re-lending within the country was short-term also. But a portfolio balanced in maturities was no protection against foreign exchange risk.

By 1997 the economy as a whole had around $60 billion in short-term obligations and $40 billion in reserves—not quite up to Mexican or (as will be seen) Korean standards, but still a substantial liquidity imbalance. The current account deficit abruptly widened from just under 6 percent of GDP in 1992–94 to over 8 percent in 1995–96 when exports leveled out. Via the savings-investment balance, the internal reflection of this jump in S_{row} was an increase in the private sector's financial deficit, while the government maintained a small fiscal surplus. The adjustment took the form of a 2 percent increase in the investment share of GDP, although the quality of the underlying projects may not have been high.

The crisis as such was triggered by the conjuncture: Japanese hints at an interest rate increase, the collapse of a leading financial house (Finance One), and growing fears of a maxidevaluation which cut expected spreads. In July the baht was allowed to float and promptly sank as bulls metamorphosed into bears and the sheep stampeded. The IMF arrived with a package in August, which had only temporarily favorable effects (as discussed in more detail later). The East Asian crisis was underway.

INITIAL CONTAGION

Thailand's troubles instantly focused the minds of the international financial community, as had Mexico's thirty months previously. Investors began to look at indicators such as ratios of debt coming due within one year to international reserves, debt/equity ratios in the business sector, and the currency composition of foreign liabilities—all readily available data that had somehow previously been ignored.

Banks—especially Japanese banks—began to call loans. According to BIS data, in 1996 the net flow of capital into the five most affected economies (Indonesia, Korea, Malaysia, the Philippines, and Thailand) was $93 billion. There was a net outflow of $12 billion in 1997 with the most volatile item being commercial bank credit, which shifted from an inflow of over $50 billion in 1996 to an outflow of $21 billion the following year.[2]

The overall turnaround of $105 billion was close to the five countries' total reserves of $127 billion and exceeded 10 percent of their combined GDP (about two percentage points higher than the impact of the 1982 debt crisis on the GDP of Latin

America). It was a supply shock with sharp contractionary effects on the real economy. Taking advantage of the short-term nature of their credits, banks ran from their borrowers before they had a chance to default, making default itself or a massive international bail-out a self-fulfilling prophecy.

KOREA

Why did the Southern tier crisis jump north? Taiwan devalued by 12 percent in October despite its ample stock of international reserves ($83 billion at the end of 1997, or about nine months' imports), and there was a run on the Hong Kong stock market. The exchange rate held however, after short-term interest rates went up by about three percentage points. Both the Taiwan and Hong Kong wobbles were transitory but redirected investors' concerns toward the Northern tier in general and Korea in particular. The main source of its vulnerability appears to have been a badly designed attempt at liberalizing the country's entire economic system, with (misplaced) emphasis on financial markets.

Korea's fundamentals in 1997 were far sounder than those of its neighbors to the south. The won was overly strong, but even so the current account deficit was only about 3 percent of GDP. The fiscal budget was largely in balance and gross public debt amounted to only 3 percent of GDP. There was little significant inflationary pressure. The main substantive change from the past was government emphasis on "deregulation," undertaken in part due to the intellectual convictions of the policy team but also in response to international (especially American) pressure. Korea's desire to join the OECD also contributed to the policy reorientation.

In one key area the government abandoned its traditional role of coordinating investments in large-scale industries to avoid "excess competition." It allowed excess capacity to emerge in sectors such as automobiles, shipbuilding, steel, petrochemicals, and semiconductors, which eventually led to a fall in export prices and a run up of nonperforming loans.

In the name of financial liberalization, the government also failed to monitor foreign borrowing activities, especially by newly licensed "merchant banks." These entities were very loosely regulated, and proceeded to acquire $20 billion in external debt. They operated with a large maturity imbalance, 64 percent of their liabilities were short-term, and 85 percent of assets long.

The activities of the merchant banks and a general bias in the local regulatory system toward short-term international borrowing (administrative controls on long-term loans were more strict) were instrumental in a rapid buildup of $150 billion of external debt, with 60 percent of the obligations having less than one year to maturity and over 25 percent at ninety days. The major similarity with the Mexican and Southeast Asian crises rests here. The government allowed the private sector to act in destabilizing fashion while holding its fiscal house in order.

A third problem was that the authorities were sold on the idea that inflation control was the most important objective of macro policy and that the exchange rate should be the principal anchor. The predictable real appreciation damaged export performance.

Finally, the government committed "mistakes" and suffered a run of bad luck as its economic troubles worsened. It dithered over the fate of the third largest car manufacturer, Kia, unnecessarily undermining confidence. As the crisis deepened, it wasted $10 billion (one-third of foreign reserves) trying to defend an indefensible exchange rate, exacerbating the foreign exchange shortage. External events also came into play. Southeast Asia's slump reduced demand for Korean exports and dealt a blow to financial companies speculating in that region's capital markets (more details later). The entrance of new Taiwanese semiconductor manufacturers drove down the prices of memory chips, which accounted for nearly 20 percent of Korean exports when their prices were high. But the main problem was a failure of oversight by a government priding itself on deregulation.

With panic in the air in late 1996, foreign investors could easily find reasons to worry about Korea. The growth rates of exports and GDP had slowed in 1996, there was industrial overcapacity, and interest on debt obligations was crippling savings of the business sector (the ratios of "operating income" and "financial expenses" to sales in 1996 were 6.5 percent and 5.8 percent respectively, leading to a very low aggregate value of business saving). The country had historically enjoyed stunning export growth and a high credit rating; its authorities (in contrast to those in the other miracle exporters Taiwan and China) had never felt the need to carry a big stock of international reserves. At the end of 1996 the reserves stood at $34 billion, around one-third of the total of short-term external obligations the country had built up. The run against the won got underway in October 1997, and the IMF was called in by the government one month later.

DERIVATIVES, ASSET PRICES, BALANCE SHEETS, AND BANK INCENTIVES

Before discussing how IMF policy and other international interventions transformed the regional bust into a pandemic, it makes sense to take up four issues bearing on how events unfolded—the uses and misuses of derivatives; changes in the quality of national assets remaining (how their prices changed, and whether Asian enterprises are especially vulnerable because of high debt burdens); how bad debt can be dealt with; and incentives for short-term lending by international banks.

As discussed in previous chapters, financial derivative contracts—swaps, forwards, and options in the first instance—have their vices and virtues. Among the latter is the ability they give financial players to reduce risk (from price volatility, at least) on their own positions by diversifying it to the broader market. Had Asian financial houses consistently hedged their exchange risks with forward contracts in currencies for example, the crisis very well may not have happened. Prior to the crisis in fact, American hedge funds were selling Asian currency forwards short and reaped substantial profits as a consequence.

As the Long Term Capital Management episode in the US underlined, the most notable vices of derivatives are that they can be used to build high leverage and to *hide* risk (in a broad sense of the word) in financial transactions. Obscurity is deepened by the recent practice of placing many commitments off– as opposed to on–balance sheets. An example is a "special purpose vehicle" (or SPV). A bank can transfer some of its stock to an SPV, setting up a corresponding counterclaim on its own balance sheet. The SPV can issue short-term paper in international credit markets using the stock as collateral (if the SPV defaults, the creditor will get the underlying stock). The SPV then uses the foreign exchange to take a position the bank desires. Fundamentally, the bank itself has assumed the foreign liability. Yet it will never show up on its balance sheet.

"Total return swaps" (or TRS) added derivative complications to such maneuvers, helping accelerate the Asian contagion. This is not the first time that new financial vehicles have worsened downswings (remember the margin calls in the 1929 Great Crash), but how the present crop can be dealt with is a contemporary regulatory problem. Consider the following example:

During 1995–97 interest costs of long-term floating rate liabilities of Korean banks went up due to tighter credit conditions in Japan, various scandals, and the weakening of historically close relationships between the state and the *chaebol*. At the same time Indonesian companies were seeking funding but lacked South Korea's credit standing.

Double swaps were thereby set up between the Indonesians and international investment banks on the one hand, and between those banks and the Koreans on the other. The Indonesians paid the international banks the international reference interest rate plus 3.4 percent.[3] They in turn swapped the underlying paper to the Koreans at LIBOR+280bp (both differentials narrowed over time as more players entered). The counter-swap took the form of Korean liabilities at LIBOR+75bp. Payments on these obligations were made regularly, every six months or one year. As part of the package, Korean banks committed themselves to compensate the international banks for the loss if the Indonesian companies went bankrupt.

The upshot apparently was that the Indonesians acquired credit market access while the Korean banks made a high return. All went well until the companies defaulted and the Koreans could not get credit in international markets to compensate the international banks for their bankruptcy loss; indeed they themselves began to default, mainly to their Japanese backers. In this way part of the Indonesian crisis was transmitted to Korea and then to Japan. Meanwhile the international banks had to absorb their Indonesian losses.

What the swaps did finally was create highly opaque loan books. The TRS also failed to diversify Indonesian risk, which is what derivatives are supposed to do in the first place. Just "how much" of the Asian crisis can be attributed to off-balance sheet transactions and improper use of derivatives is a question that cannot properly be answered, in part because "appropriate" accounting procedures are still being developed. What *is* known is that total transactions of this sort were large, in the tens of billions of dollars.

Turning to internal asset markets, two issues deserve discussion: changes in asset prices (and returns) and their effects on balance sheets. The history in Asia was broadly in line with Keynes's notions about how asset prices move in unison to equalize (approximately) own-rates of return. When the currency in each country started to depreciate, the local share price index dropped in percentage terms just about in proportion. Short-term interest rates rose universally (sometimes to dramatic double or even triple digit levels), but were obviously unable to stem the depreciation of real currency values caused by departing capital.

What were the implications for business balance sheets? As noted above, corporations in some Asian economies have debt/equity (gearing or leverage) ratios that are high by Western standards. A "representative" ratio in the West might be in the range of 0.5 to 1.5; banks and their regulators become dubious about loans to firms when their ratios significantly exceed unity. The ratios in Asia have gone up since the crisis because of falling asset prices and depreciating currencies. The interest rate increases also cut into corporate cash flow.

Standard economics suggests that such problems are of second order — finance is a veil and the performance of business enterprises is independent of their liability structure. This assertion is not completely true, as Minsky's work discussed in chapter 2 demonstrates. But it is not completely false either. The distinction between debt and equity is in part a matter of convention, and conventions can change.

In Anglo-American finance for example, equity is beginning to look more like debt as rebelling stockholders call for assured dividend pay-outs. Similarly, debt can be made to look like equity if obligations to pay interest are relaxed. One common method is to sell public debt to the nonbank private sector and use the money raised to pay for restructuring of weak balance sheets in the financial sector. The US dealt with its S&L crisis in this fashion (putting the public debt off-balance sheet for the federal government, incidentally). To clean up its banking system's nonperforming assets to the tune of a third of GDP after the crisis in the early 1980s, Chile did the same thing via the central bank, which refinanced with the government which then re-refinanced abroad with the help of international institutions. For debt denominated in the local currency, how to set up such a package (a task which inevitably has to be undertaken by the government) is a political question. The Chileans and Americans apparently had no problems. The Japanese government is encountering political difficulty in cleaning up the remnants of the bubble economy and the Mexican government faces a similar problem with its post-1995 banking system bad debt—the obligations amount roughly to 10 percent and 15 percent of GDP respectively. In both countries the public does not want to pay off the financiers. Both took steps in that direction in 1998, but much remains to be done.

Another way to deal with a debt overhang is for the government to step in and organize moratoria on domestic repayments and enforce rollovers of short-term loans. This route was taken by the Korean government in 1972 to deal with a domestic debt crisis.

Finally there is the option of running a "controlled" inflation to shrink the real value of debtors' obligations and force real interest rates below zero. On the financial side, banks have to "monetize" growth in some asset, e.g. credits to the private sector, to cover the bad debt. On the cost side there would have to be some agreement about margins vs. nominal wage growth. Inflation and forced rollover strategies would almost certainly have to be accompanied by a reimposition of tough controls to restrain capital flight.

For the Asian economies the harder question is what to do about foreign currency debt. Here international support is needed. Initiatives to reduce the debt burden have been strikingly unsuccessful to date.

A final financial point worth mentioning has to do with incentives for short-term lending by international banks. At present the Basel capital adequacy provisions for *all* foreign bank loans of less than one year's maturity require only 20 percent backing, as opposed to 100 percent for loans to non-OECD members with more than one year's maturity[4]. This provision was apparently introduced to protect the inter-bank market, but for this purpose a low backing ratio for loans of three-month (or even one-month) maturity would probably be enough. As it stands the provision offers considerable encouragement to OECD bankers to lend to developing economies short-term. This regulatory bias has certainly been as important as some sort of generalized moral hazard in affecting the volume and profile of international bank loans.

THE IMF IN ACTION

So far we have been describing an international financial crisis perpetrated by the private sector operating under lax and ultimately complicit public supervision. The remaining actor on the stage is a "public" institution, the International Monetary Fund. Its interventions during the Asian crisis made a bad situation far worse. Amazingly enough it went on to repeat the same errors in the Russian and Brazilian crises of 1998–99.

With regard to the substance of the stabilization policies it convinced countries to adopt, the Fund's behavior was completely predictable from its past record. With regard to economic restructuring, it went well beyond its traditional mandate. We will briefly review the first topic and go on to raise questions about the second.

The Fund's specialty is running a recession to improve the trade account of the balance of payments by cutting imports. Its procedures were originally devised to deal with more or less chronic current account problems in developing countries as opposed to sudden reversals of capital inflows, as in the 1982 debt crisis and the exchange rate crises more recently. The well-known twin deficits rationale for its "financial programming" exercises was sketched briefly above and can be developed fully in terms of flow of funds and national income and product accounts. A familiar policy package always materializes: currency devaluation; reduction of the fiscal deficit by expenditure reductions or tax increases; tight monetary policy; closing down ailing banks and other financial institutions; financial liberalization including removal of restrictions on entry of foreign banks; and trade liberalization. In exchange the Fund disburses credits from time to time as the specific "conditionality" requirements attached to its package are satisfied.

Beyond trade balance improvement, such interventions are supposed to restore the confidence of foreign investors so they will start lending again to crisis-afflicted countries. In East Asia the Fund's moves failed resoundingly in this regard. In the words of Indian economist Mihir Rakshit, ". . . following the announcement of the IMF bail-out, for the country concerned there was an immediate improvement in stock and currency markets which generally pulled up markets in neighboring nations as well. However, the upswing did not last for more than a few days and soon currencies and share prices tended to resume their downslide. Quite clearly, after a more serious scrutiny the market recorded disappointment with the IMF package."

Why were results so dismal? Several factors can be mentioned. One is that, as observed previously, East Asian economies are tightly linked in terms of trade and asset ownership. Contractionary effects in one area spread readily to all others. Moreover, the trade-improving impacts of devaluation in one country will be dampened by its import dependence on its neighbors.

Finally, because of conditionality restrictions the bulk of the credit attached to the bail-out packages was not in fact disbursed. As Canadian economist G. K. Helleiner noted in mid-1998, "It is striking that the amounts quickly supplied to Mexico during its crisis far exceeded the amounts slowly being made available to the East Asian countries . . . Only about 20 percent of the financial package put together for East Asia has so far been disbursed." According to estimates from the Institute for International Finance, his prognosis was correct. Private capital flows to the five most affected countries in the three years between 1996 and 1998 were $103 billion, -1 billion, and -28 billion respectively. Official flows for the same years were -3 billion, 30 billion, and 28 billion. In other words, in 1997–98 the five economies "lost" a total of $235 billion ($104 billion + $131 billion) in comparison to the private inflows they that received in 1996. They "gained" $64 billion from official sources.

The net loss per year was about $85 billion. Given the contractionary impact of such a reversal of capital flows it is no surprise that GDP growth rates dropped in tandem all over the region and were strongly negative in 1998.

Fund interventions may even have worsened the contagion. In the words of Harvard's Jeffrey Sachs, ". . . instead of dousing the fire the IMF in effect screamed fire in the theater." Investor confidence plummeted instead of being bolstered by the Fund's orthodox shows of force. Outsiders can recognize a depressed economy and social unrest when they see them. The ultimate outcome may have been to transform a short-term "liquidity" crisis into one of "solvency" in which an economy can never stabilize its external debt to GDP ratio because its output growth rate has been driven below the real rate of interest.

All of this is depressing, but no surprise. The contractionary and distributionally perverse effects of IMF programs are achingly familiar in Africa and Latin America. A novelty in East Asia is how much worse the impacts can be when the package is applied jointly to a set of closely linked economies. The even more disquieting issue however is that the Fund is doing its very best to dismantle the Asian economic model discussed above by insisting on wholesale restructuring of economic systems (witness the exceptionally heavy-handed interventions in Korea and Indonesia). Why? And what will be the outcomes?

To answer the first question requires walking a fine line between explanations based on interests and a conspiracy theory. On the side of the interests, there has been some agreement among the OECD (or rich) countries that steps should be taken to liberalize the world economy in several dimensions: revision of the IMF articles to *require* member nations to remove all controls on capital markets, liberalization of trade in financial services and suppression of industrial policy interventions, by the World Trade Organization (WTO), and the OECD's own multilateral investment accord (recently blocked for the moment when the US representative objected to other countries' attempts to incorporate environmental and labor standards into the document). These initiatives all respond to a felt need on the part of international banks and transnational corporations to have relatively unfettered market access worldwide.

How the Asian story will end is completely unclear. The Asians had been successful for decades prior to 1997. A complete remake along Anglo-American lines will certainly not happen. Well-entrenched institutions are not readily removed.

THE RUSSIAN CRISIS

Economic historians will need many years to sort out the tumultuous changes in Russia during the 1990s. It is far too early to disentangle all the causes of the summer 1998 currency crisis. But its economic aspects do share striking similarities with the boom-bust episodes already discussed. As was true elsewhere, Russia had minimal restrictions on international financial transactions; a pegged exchange rate at a "strong" level; wide spreads between returns available domestically and costs of raising funds abroad; and an unregulated financial system long on ruble assets and short on dollars. All these factors went together with a highly orthodox effort to stabilize the inflation rate and led to the collapse of the ruble in August. An IMF "rescue" package put into place in July failed to stem the reserve losses that ultimately forced the Russian authorities to allow the ruble to float, in an almost exact parallel to developments in Brazil a few months later.

Russia's previously tightly controlled capital account had been thrown open when economic restructuring began in 1992, facilitating capital flight (funded by a consistent trade surplus and foreign capital inflows) to the tune of $20 to $30 billion per year. The nominal exchange rate was roughly stabilized as an anti-inflation anchor. The result was that throughout the mid-1990s, depending on which price indexes are used in the calculation, the real exchange rate appreciated by a factor of between three and five. Because there was virtually no financial regulation, balance sheet mismatches were unconstrained.

Money emission had been cut back sharply in the fight against inflation so that ratios of money and bank credit to GDP were very low by international standards. Many economic transactions were conducted through barter—by most estimates at least 50 percent by May 1998. Demonetization *increased* simultaneously with the decrease in the inflation rate. Barter trade was not a reaction to fears of a loss of the ruble's value. Rather it was generated by difficulties in making transactions and desires on the part of all players to maintain liquidity.

Besides demonetization there was a self-induced fiscal crisis. The strategy for fighting inflation entailed reduction or abrogation of previously budgeted expenditures. This practice led the state to default on its fiscal obligations to regions, firms, and civil servants, which became a continuing practice. As expenditures shrank so did tax collections. That the two processes were closely connected to each other is nicely illustrated by the case of Gazprom, the energy conglomerate, which in early 1999 owed the state some thirteen billion rubles in taxes, but which had not been paid by federal and local budgets for deliveries of oil and gas to the tune of fourteen billion. In a shrinking economy receipts fell more rapidly than expenditures could be cut, leading to a fiscal deficit that was financed by issuing government bonds (as opposed to borrowing from the banking system).

The government was forced by its creditors to pay high interest rates. By the end of 1997 the interest burden of the internal debt was more than 55 percent of tax receipts in the federal budget. Equity prices rose sharply beginning in 1996. Both interest rate and capital gains spreads were large, and foreign investors poured in. As the relevant intermediaries, Russian financial institutions took on unbalanced positions. In particular, banks borrowed heavily abroad to speculate on the government's short-term liabilities. They did not hedge their positions, although some foreign investors are rumored to have hedged with *Russian* banks, which presumably plowed the resulting dollar assets back into rubles. The Russian players were effectively bankrupted by the devaluation in August. The collapse of the banking system resulted in the virtual disappearance of the already under-monetized domestic payments mechanism.

The main contrast with Mexico and East Asia was the large fiscal deficit. However, it is overly simplistic to call Russia's situation a trilemma. With its self-induced revenue collapse the government had no choice but to borrow more and more just to keep up its interest payments, along perfect Ponzi lines. The strict monetary policy was the other side of the Ponzi coin, in a Muscovite rerun of early Reaganomics. High interest rates and the strong ruble were part and parcel of the debacle, stimulating the acceleration and then speculative reversal of capital inflows.

As of early 1999 the fiscal problem appeared to be intractable. For the public sector (central government, local governments, off-budget sheet funds) to be at least in balance, it would have had to run a "primary" surplus (before interest payments) of 4 to 5 percent of GDP. Even such stringency would leave unresolved the government's arrears in public sector wages, pensions, and debts to firms. Fiscal balance may be desirable, but it seems most unlikely that any Russian government will be able to attain it given the depression, difficulties in raising revenue, and pressures to boost expenditures.

More generally, "free market" nostrums applied by the first generation of Russian "reformers" and their foreign advisers have brought the country to the brink of ruin. Future governments there will have to resolve economic problems by their own means. One step could be to impose controls on trade and international payments. A significant tariff surcharge on imports, say 20 percent, might be introduced. Together with a depreciated exchange rate this would generate substantial ruble revenues quickly. On the export side the main problem is that throughout the 1990s hard currency earnings were usually not repatriated, contributing to Russia's enormous capital flight. Exchange controls emerged as the only plausible solution. In late 1998, the authorities imposed a requirement that 75 percent of export earnings should be paid directly to the Central Bank. More generally, wide capital controls like those used by the UK and France in the immediate post–World War II period were under consideration. Such moves might possibly short-circuit the "hot money" flows that were the proximate cause of the crisis. In mid-1999 they were under serious consideration at the Central Bank, in the face of vigorous opposition by the IMF.

In many ways the situation in Russia in 1998 was worse than in Western Europe in the late 1940s — purely physical destruction was less but social and institutional dislocations were far greater. The country was in an advanced process of state collapse, economic life suffered from criminal activities, and corrupt links grew between business and political elites. In a society that long valued economic equality, the personal income distribution jumped from being one of the least to one of the most inegalitarian in the world (income concentration now rivals the levels in South Africa and Brazil). In such a desperate situation, desperation measures of the sort just outlined should be judged by just two criteria — the preservation of democracy and the pursuit of long-run economic goals. How well the measures may fare in satisfying these ends only the future can tell.

BRAZIL 1999

Although the real side of its economy is far more robust and its financial institutions more developed, Brazil joined Russia in running a Ponzi scheme in the wake of the Asian crisis. Along the way it followed the familiar policy path associated with liberalized capital markets made familiar in the Southern Cone and Mexico. Briefly, events went as follows:

Brazil enjoyed a highly successful inflation rate stabilization in 1994. Based on a new currency, the Real, it combined the usual elements of capital market liberalization with a big current account deficit (it jumped from near zero in 1994 to 3 percent of GDP in 1995). A nearly fixed exchange rate supported spreads large enough to bring capital inflows exceeding the current account gap. Reserves consequently grew from around $50 billion in 1995 to $80 billion in 1997 in a scenario paralleling the Southern Cone's twenty years before.

The Ponzi game began when Brazil's creditors started withdrawing their funds in October 1997. Interest rates were raised to 50 percent per year to keep reserve losses down and support the exchange rate. In a peculiar international income transfer, Brazil began to borrow at around 8 percent from official sources like the IMF to pay 50 percent interest on its debts to the private sector. In line with the UIP formula, the implied expected depreciation was steep.

The fiscal deficit doubled from 4 percent of GDP in 1997 to 8 percent in 1998 for exactly the same reasons as in Russia. Interest obligations were huge and tax receipts contracted as the high rates forced the economy to slow down. In another parallel with Russia, an IMF rescue package was announced with great fanfare in October. Three months later the exchange rate collapsed. The reasons were the same. The Fund did not provide nearly enough resources to cover reserve losses, even in the presence of astronomical interest rates. By February 1999 reserves had fallen to $25 billion and the exchange rate was close to 2.0 Reals per dollar as opposed to 1.2 in October. No one has any idea how Brazil might pick up the pieces, especially if the world economy turns down.

The irony is that policymakers in Brazil were fully aware of all the history recounted in this chapter. They were among the chief contributors to the theory of exchange rate–based stabilizations in the first place. In contrast to their Russian counterparts it is impossible to accuse them of excessive dependence on foreign advisers or irrational optimism combined with profound naïveté about the true workings of a semi-industrialized capitalist economy. They walked into the Ponzi trap with eyes open, presumably confident it would not snap shut. Even Keynes might marvel at the rigidity with which they clung to their macroeconomic conventions in the wake of the past few years' events.

POLICY ALTERNATIVES

The principal message of this chapter is that financial crises are not made by an alert private sector pouncing upon the public sector's fiscal or moral hazard foolishness. They are better described as private sectors (both domestic and foreign) acting to make high short-term profits when policy and history provide the preconditions and the public sector acquiesces. Mutual feedbacks between the financial sector and the real side of the economy then lead to a crisis. By global standards the financial flows involved in a Frenkel-Neftci conflagration are not large — $10 to $20 billion of capital flows annually (less than 10 percent of the inflow the US routinely absorbs) for a few years are more than enough to destabilize a middle income economy. The outcomes are now visible worldwide.

A number of policy issues are posed by these experiences. This chapter concludes by considering the steps countries can take to reduce the likelihood of future conflagrations. Topics covered in chapter 7 include actions that both an afflicted country and the international community can take to cope with future crises if and when they happen, and how the international regulatory system might be modified to enhance developing economies' stability and growth.

MACRO FUNDAMENTALS

Regardless of whether its exchange rate is fixed, floating, or some mongrel, if a country chooses to liberalize its capital market, its macroeconomic situation will be begin to be judged by potential or actual lenders in terms of fundamentals. In line with the discussion in chapter 3 however, the market's perception of their significance will be shaped by an ever-changing—

yet possibly rather stable — set of conventions. Favorable conventions can offset adverse fundamentals (at least for a time) and vice-versa. Unless they are adepts of Keynes's ". . . fourth, fifth, and higher degrees of perception of others' conventions" in the international financial beauty contest, all national policymakers are unavoidably at the mercy of foreign investors' own conventions and whims.

Nevertheless, it *is* possible to try to keep fundamentals under control. Consider the list set out in chapter 3, which includes:

They should avoid wide violation of relative price norms, in particular PPP and a big ratio of non-traded to traded goods prices (often adequately approximated by the ratio of the consumer to the wholesale price index). Exchange rate "overvaluation" in either the traded/non-traded goods price ratio or PPP sense of the word can invite lenders' wrath. On the other hand a strong exchange rate usually leads to high real income flows and real wealth stocks in the home country and can be politically difficult to reverse.

UIP violation — or a wide spread between domestic and international financial returns — can also be perilous, especially if it is driven by mistaken faith in the stability of the local exchange rate.

Fiscal and/or current account deficits are often seen by the market as unwelcome, even though they may be out of the country's control (as in the Russian and Brazilian cases just discussed). Questions can be asked about other forms of "flow" disequilibrium. Are rising interest obligations likely to cut into savings and investment? Are flows cumulating to produce locational or maturity mismatches in balance sheets? Another precursor of crisis is the relationship between the volume of capital inflows and the current account deficit. If the former exceeds the latter, reserves will rise, perhaps lulling the authorities into a false sense of security. As in the Southern Cone and recently in Brazil, they will be rudely awakened as reserves vanish when interest payments on accumulating foreign debt begin to exceed the amount of capital flowing in.

Of greater import, "flow" imbalances of the sort just mentioned may simply be symptoms of more fundamental "stock-flow" or "stock-stock" problems in the national balance sheet. Chapter 4 presented some examples for the US, and many others were seen in developing countries:

Stock-flow imbalances: Have some asset or liability stocks become "large" in relation to local flows? East Asia's short-term debt exceeding 10 percent of GDP was a typical example. It was a stock with a level that could change rapidly, with sharply destabilizing repercussions. Rapid expansion of bank credit to the private sector as a share of GDP while booms got underway in the Southern Cone, Mexico, and Thailand might have served as an early warning indicator had the authorities been looking. The causes included monetization of reserve increases and growth of loans against collateral assets such as securities and real estate with rapidly inflating values.

Stock-stock relationships: Besides locational or currency mismatches in balance sheets in the financial sector, indicators such as debt/equity ratios and the currency composition of portfolios (including their "dollarization" in Latin America recently) become relevant here. They can signal future problems with financing investment-saving differentials.

Quality of debt: Finally, there is a question about the quality of collateral assets that borrowers hold. Much of the credit expansion in Thailand and Russia went to players holding assets with rapidly rising prices such as real estate and shares. With an asset price collapse in a crisis, such loans suddenly became "non-performing." In early 1999, China was in a similar situation. Although its capital controls and massive reserves kept that country out of the first Asian crisis, its internal financial imbalances may yet change investors' conventions enough to provoke an external crisis.

When seen as "excessive," any of these factors can feed rapidly into capital outflows. But in recent developing country experience, more than a simple reversal of conventions has been involved. In these cases, clear cyclical patterns led to collapses. How can they be avoided or dampened?

The key control variables for external accounts in any economy are its exchange rate, quality of financial regulation, and capital and exchange controls. Especially for a middle income country that is "small" in terms of the global macro system, all have substantial international implications. They are taken up in chapter 7 in the context of the potential role of a World Financial Authority.

NOTES

1. In the parlance of forward markets, traders who sign a contract to sell the underlying asset at some future date are said to have a "short" position if they in fact do not own the asset in question; selling short is a way of speculating that the price will decline. Buying "long" is the opposite position. Note that these descriptions of market positions are *not* the same as "short-term" and "long-term" maturities for deposits or loans.

2. Indeed, banks played a central role in triggering crises worldwide. According to data from the Institute for International Finance (a Washington-based "global association of financial institutions"), capital flows from banks to twenty-nine major emerging markets were 1995, $99.5 billion; 1996, $120.4 billion; 1997, $30.9 billion; 1998, -$29.1 billion.

3. The reference is the "London interbank offered rate" or LIBOR. The extra 3.4 percent is often expressed as 340bp, where one bp is a "basis point" or 0.01 percent.

4. In June 1999 the Basel Committee on Banking Supervision announced a review of the capital adequacy framework which will include replacing current fixed risk weights with "external credit assessments."

6—Regulation on a Global Scale

The development of a modern banking system is a fundamental reason for the success of market economies over the past two hundred years. Without a banking system it would have been impossible to mobilize the huge volumes of capital which, from the beginnings of the industrial revolution, have transformed the world. Nor would it have been possible to manage the multi-dimensional payments systems that reflect the division of labor that in turn has been the counterpart of technical progress. An efficient financial system is necessary to maintain and enhance real living standards.

The success of the banking system has been built on two foundations of its operation, foundations that are paradoxically also major sources of weakness: intermediation and leverage.

Intermediation is the process whereby banks collect deposits and lend them on. The deposits are highly liquid. Many of the loans are not. In principle, deposits are short-term while the maturity or payoff period of a loan may be rather long. Intermediation thus involves a "maturity transformation" at which banks have become adept.

But while deposits are highly liquid and short-term, depositors do not typically demand the return of their deposits as cash. Instead they are content to use their bank deposits to pay debts through the issuance of checks or by direct electronic transfer. Banks are therefore able to lend a substantial proportion of deposits, retaining only a relatively small proportion as liquid assets to meet any demands for cash that may arise. Suppose $100 is deposited in the banking system. The bank retains $10 to ensure it can meet anticipated demands of depositors for cash, and makes (it hopes) profitable loans of $90. The recipients of the loans typically deposit the $90 back in the banking system. On the basis of the new deposit the banks retain $9 as cash and lend out $81, which in turn is redeposited, and so on. By this process of lending the initial deposit of $100 grows into total deposits of $1000, $100 of which the banking system holds as cash and $900 of which are income-earning loans. On the basis of an initial cash deposit, banks are able to make loans that are a substantial multiple of that amount—this is leverage. This process both creates liquidity for the economy and is hugely profitable for the banking system.

The downside of intermediation and leverage is the financial risk they create. The collection of many deposits and their dispersion as loans clearly poses a risk to the bank, as loans may fail or be insufficiently liquid in relation to the needs of depositors. This intermediation risk is greatly heightened by leverage. If depositors demand the immediate return of their $1000 as cash, which they have every right to do—it's their money—the banking system has only $100 in cash to meet that demand. Banks would be forced to default on their obligations and the banking system would collapse, taking the rest of the economy with it.

That is why, alongside the development of banking systems, central banks were also developed with the responsibility of maintaining confidence in the banking system by acting as lenders of last resort. Then if a run on the banks occurs, the lender of last resort must stand willing to provide cash to banks to the value of their assets prior to the loss of confidence. Since the argument was put forward over a century ago by Walter Bagehot, founding editor of *The Economist* magazine, it has been generally accepted that this assistance should be provided at a penal rate of interest to discourage unnecessary borrowing from the lender of last resort. It is also commonly argued that the central bank should only provide liquidity to solvent, but temporarily illiquid, institutions. However, the distinction between liquidity and solvency is not so clear-cut. A general loss of confidence in the market, perhaps from some macroeconomic shock such as a change in the exchange rate or in interest rates, will result in previously solvent banks becoming insolvent. A refusal to lend to such insolvent institutions will simply exacerbate the crisis.

Other procedures which perform a similar role to lender of

last resort function are deposit insurance and open market operations, whereby when the money markets lack liquidity the central bank purchases financial assets, so providing the needed cash.

Leverage is risky, and highly profitable. Ignoring any adjustment for risk, the greater the leverage the greater the return. If in the numerical example the banks retained $5 of every $100 deposited as cash, then the initial $100 deposit would leverage $1,900 worth of income-earning loans. There is thus a powerful incentive to increase leverage, and simultaneously increase risk. But while the risk may be increased for the bank, the risk to society of the contagion spreading from the losses of an individual bank is typically far greater than the loss to the bank's managers and shareholders. Hence the need for a lender of last resort safety net. As Alan Greenspan has argued:

> With leveraging there will always exist a remote possibility of a chain reaction, a cascading sequence of defaults that will culminate in financial implosion if it proceeds unchecked. Only a modern central bank, with its unlimited power to create money, can with a high probability thwart such a process before it becomes destructive. Hence, central banks will of necessity be drawn into becoming lenders of last resort. But implicit in the existence of such a role is that there will be some form of allocation between the public and private sectors of the burden of risk of extreme outcomes.

How is that burden to be allocated? The provision of this safety net by the central bank is a form of free insurance for the banks. While attempting to protect society against the risk posed by intermediation and leverage, the central bank is at the same time creating new risks. Part of the risk that would be carried by the banks is transferred to the public sector, with the consequence that banks are induced to take excessive risks. This is the problem of moral hazard. It can result in the market allocation of financial assets being highly inefficient. Risky decisions are taken by those who do not bear even the personal risk of failure let alone the risk to society as a whole. This is why it is necessary to develop a structure of financial supervision and regulation. Without regulation the lender of last resort function leads to an increase in the inefficiency it is designed to prevent.

This failure has made necessary a degree of supervision and regulation that would not be needed without the safety net. Regulators act as a surrogate for market discipline when the market's assessment of risk has been substantially muted by the safety net. Even in the case of deposit insurance, the cost of insurance or of access to the safety net does not provide an accurate surrogate for the market pricing of risk.

The intermediation risks carried by banks are also present in securities firms, asset management companies, mutual funds, and pension funds. These forms of enterprise have grown rapidly over the past thirty years, bringing with them an increasingly "professional" management of savings. Whereas in the past individual investors would buy and hold shares or bonds, building up relatively small portfolios, today institutional investors aggregate individual portfolios into enormous funds with a worldwide investment perspective. This is particularly evident in the changing pattern of assets held by institutional investors. In the United States and Japan, the proportion of pension funds' assets invested in foreign securities was negligible in 1980, but by the mid-1990s had risen to over 7 and 12 percent respectively. Over the same period the commitment to foreign assets by British pension funds rose from 10 to over 20 percent of total assets.

Institutional investors have been a main force behind the growth of the global capital market. They have also driven associated changes in technology. Expanding institutional investment and widening financial innovation have stimulated one another. The competition between institutional investors manifests itself as an ongoing race to demonstrate superior returns in order to attract more funds. Successive high short-term gains are more effective in this respect than longer-term returns. This is so even if over a number of years the overall return on successive short-term investments is no greater, and perhaps even somewhat smaller, than a long-term investment. An institutional investor pursuing a short-term strategy that tops the performance tables in nine years out of ten will tend to attract more funds than the long-term investor who performs extremely well once in ten years. The average holding period for institutional investors is less than two years, compared to almost five years for individuals. The enormous flow of funds into institutional hands requires a persistent search for new high-return investment opportunities that can be exited easily. Innovation is geared toward this goal.

Shareholder capital backs 100 percent of assets held by institutional investors. There is therefore no need to require deposit insurance against the risks of leverage. Indeed, mutual funds have used the absence of such charges as a competitive device, enabling them to offer lower-cost services to investors than can the banks. Nonetheless, institutional investors require liquidity to cover shareholder withdrawals. Demands for withdrawals can precipitate severe market disruption. In an attempt to reduce such disruptions the US Federal Reserve was authorized in 1991 to act as a lender of last resort to the securities markets. The provision of this liquid safety net to securities firms in turn demands the same sort of regulatory oversight applied to the banks. In particular, securities houses may be required to keep a proportion of their assets in cash in order to meet normal market fluctuations.

Institutional investors also typically indulge in proprietary trading on their own behalf. It is a standard regulatory requirement that such funds should be rigorously separated from customers' funds.

A further institutional development in international financial markets has been the appearance of highly leveraged institutions that deal primarily in derivatives markets. By dealing on the margin in futures and other derivatives such institutions (often called hedge funds) make huge nominal investments on a relatively small capital base. The investments are so large that substantial profits can be made on very small variations in asset prices. As with all leveraged investment the greater the leverage the greater the profitability, and the greater the risk, too. While the development of derivatives markets has been a vital way to hedge risk, the leverage characteristics of these markets gravely threaten the market as a whole. As outlined above, if, facing imminent failure, the management of Long Term Capital Management had been forced to liquidate its entire portfolio, the fire sale could have undermined the value of financial contracts worth as much as $1250 billion. The decision of the US Federal Reserve to orchestrate the refinancing of LTCM extended central bank responsibility into entirely new areas. No public money was involved. The rescue fund of $3.65 billion was provided by fourteen major securities firms. But it is clear that the Federal Reserve brought its formidable persuasive powers to bear, severely twisting a number of arms to provide the liquidity LTCM needed to work out its investments.

The actions of the Federal Reserve (and the supportive action taken by securities regulators in London) were motivated by fears of severe disruption, even collapse. By these actions the Federal Reserve extended the role of the central bank into management of the systemic risk created by highly leveraged institutions, even institutions such as LTCM which are highly secretive and which, as private partnerships, are not required to disclose their trading strategies.

The LTCM case is a striking example of the fact that the integration of financial markets, and of financial institutions, demands that central banks and regulators integrate their activities, too. Financial markets have become "seamless" domestically and internationally. Risks encountered in one area of the financial system may originate in a quite different piece of terrain. The LTCM crisis created serious risks for banks, securities houses, and even for a central bank—the Bank of Italy had invested $350 million of its assets in LTCM! Systemic risk is now an aspect of the entire international financial system and must be managed as such.

SYSTEMIC RISK

In chapter 1 the presence of systemic risk was likened to that of dirty smoke. It is an "externality," a cost imposed on society by the actions of an individual over and above the costs that that individual incurs. Risk is a cost because the presence of risk reduces the return on an investment. Suppose for example that a hypothetical investment which bears no risk costs $100 and over a year yields a return of $110, resulting in $10 profit, or a rate of return of 10 percent. Compare this with a risky investment for which the return is uncertain, perhaps even the final cost is uncertain. The riskier the investment, the less valuable it will be. If the risks are very small (for example, that the US government will default on a Treasury Bill)[1] then the return is only a little less than 10 percent. If however there is a fifty-fifty chance the return will not be paid at all, then the expected value of the return is only $55 and the expected rate of profit minus 45 percent. Of course the assessment of risk is far more complicated than a simple fifty-fifty split. Typically risks may be expressed as a probability distribution that defines the likelihood of particular outcomes, some quite likely, some very unlikely. Information about past price movements is used to construct probability distributions for the prices of particular financial assets. And the distribution is then used to evaluate the range of risks associated with a particular investment. The calculations involved are often very sophisticated indeed—the "rocket science" of the financial markets.

Risk may be assessed as a spread of prices around the price level deemed most likely. The investor must decide what the likely volatility of prices might be, and hence what is the value at risk in any particular investment for any given range of movement. The investor may be willing to assume the risk over a relatively narrow range of movement or may believe that a wide range of movement should be allowed for. The greater the range of price movement taken into the calculation, the greater the value at risk will be. In many cases large swings in prices may be regarded as unlikely. But two characteristics of financial markets make them particularly risky:

First, because financial markets operate as a beauty contest in which average opinion tends to follow average opinion, large swings in prices are distinctly possible and when they occur may acquire a cumulative momentum.

Second, a defining characteristic of financial markets in the modern era is that unforeseen events keep happening that have never happened before, or at least never happened before to quite the same degree. So history is a misleading guide to future performance, and the probability distribution based on past outcomes is a misleading guide to risk. Asset valuations of the rocket scientists may prove highly inaccurate. Real rockets are far more predictable.[2]

In the management of systemic risk the task of regulation is to "internalize the externality," that is to ensure that, as far as possible, individual decision makers take into account not only their risk but also the risk which society as a whole faces as a result of the contemplated action.

The difference between the private evaluation of risk (private cost) and the social evaluation of risk (social cost) is the "social spread." This is the extra cost imposed on society by the individual investor's actions. The sum of the private evaluation of risk and the social spread is equal to the total value of the risk to society.

To ensure that each investor in reaching an investment decision takes into account the full cost his or her actions impose on society, the regulator must take steps to have the social spread included in the investor's calculations. This may be achieved either by imposing conditions such as capital adequacy requirements, which ensure that some of the social spread's cost falls on the individual investor. Or, if such measures are not feasible, the regulator may attempt to reduce the social spread by directly limiting the actions the investor may legally make. For example, as outlined in chapter 3, the authorities in Chile imposed a charge on short-term capital inflows. That charge narrowed the difference between the value of private risk and the value of the risk which short-term flows posed for the Chilean economy. If such measures were ineffective then the authorities might, in pursuit of the same objective, decide to place direct controls on certain capital flows as is done for example in Malaysia, China, and India.

In chapter 1 it was noted that the total risk involved in a particular financial placement arises either from risks peculiar to the activities of the firm itself, such as counter-party risk, or from market fluctuations in general such as changes in interest or exchange rates. Or risk may originate in a combination of both these factors. In particular, an increase in market risk is likely to precipitate unforeseen changes in the risks associated with counter-parties. That is why the neat distinction between "firm specific" and "market" risks does not survive any significant shift in the markets.

The privatization of foreign exchange risk in the early 1970s increased the scale and incidence of market risk enormously. It also led to a significant widening of the social spread between the private evaluation of risk and the social evaluation of risk. This was the result of the introduction of a major new market risk into the risk calculus. The new market linkages (domestic and international) created by the liberalization widened the potential impact of failure by any one investor or firm. Contagion became possible on an international scale.

The scale of market risk is greatly increased in an open international capital market spanning many financial authorities and currencies. The open market will permit financial innovations in a particular currency outside the supervision and control of the monetary authority to which the currency "belongs." In London, banks operating in the Eurodollar market create credit in US dollars outside the supervisory powers of US authorities. Over time the major financial centers have cooperated in an attempt to bring such activities under supervisory control, but their efforts have been limited by the growth of "offshore" havens such as the Cayman Islands, were investors are attracted by low taxes and "light" regulatory regimes. A "light" regime reduces the cost to the firm by permitting it to operate without taking account of the systemic risk it creates. A low cost, low regulation regime leads to firms taking excessive risks, and so threatens the economic stability and efficient operation of financial markets far beyond the "offshore" center.

The variety of different currencies also creates an entirely new set of risks. Changes in exchange rates can lead to a dramatic redistribution of the values of assets and liabilities. As experience in developing countries throughout the 1990s clearly showed, currency mismatch can create severe mismatches on balance sheets. The rate of return implicit in exchange rate changes can completely disrupt the structure of interest rates throughout the economy. And the lender of last resort function is severely compromised for the pragmatic reason that printing another country's money is just not allowed!

Foreign exchange risk is of course a market risk. But it readily translates into the counter-party and credit risk faced by the individual firm as the redistribution of wealth that accompanies a change in the exchange rate transforms the circumstances of individual debtors and creditors. And the causation can flow in the opposite direction, too. The failure of an individual institution can lead to a general loss of confidence in a currency, transforming individual risk into market risk.

THE MECHANICS OF REGULATION

The objective of the regulator, management of systemic risk, is easy enough to define. Domestically it is difficult to achieve. Internationally it is *very* difficult to achieve.

First, there is the fundamental problem of discovering the exact financial position of a bank, securities firm, hedge fund, savings and loan, or insurance company. Regulatory authorities need timely, accurate information. Despite attempts to improve accounting conventions and standards of disclosure, it remains true that the opaqueness of financial data is the Achilles' heel not only of effective regulation but also of market discipline. Even in the banking sector the accounting standards developed by the International Accounting Standards Committee have not yet received widespread official recognition. This poses a significant risk to the international financial system. Differences in accounting conventions and standards, and in requirements for disclosure, are exploited by investors. The introduction of internationally recognized and enforced accounting standards should be a major objective of the public authorities. Absence of such standards makes a mockery of attempts to manage systemic risk in international markets.

But the problem of discovering exactly what is going on is not simply a question of accounting standards. It is also important that firms keep accurate records on an ongoing basis. The value of a firm's assets and liabilities may change from moment to moment with profound consequences for its viability. If those financial instruments are traded then this is a matter of "marking to market" the stocks of assets, liabilities, and (most importantly) derivative contracts. In the case of over the counter (OTC) instruments the valuation of a firm's position is more problematic, relying on probabilistic modeling procedures for the pricing of cover and exposure. These modeling procedures must be a matter of considerable interest to the authorities given the potential risk to which inaccurate valuation can expose the firm and the system as a whole.

Second, the entry of firms into financial markets must be controlled by a system of licensing. Firms and individuals should be licensed to operate only after demonstrating that they are fit and proper, that they have effective operation and control procedures, and that they meet prudential financial criteria. And of course authorities must be able to rescind the license when firms and/or individuals do not meet appropriate criteria.

Third, there must be effective surveillance to ensure that firms adhere to regulatory principles and rules. However, surveillance does not only involve the policing of firms' operations, it is also an essential intelligence operation. The authorities need to know what developments are taking place in financial markets in order to assess the changing structure of risk to which the system is exposed. Moreover, authorities should be better informed than market participants by virtue of their statutory access to confidential information. The knowledge that the authorities have broader and more accurate information increases market acceptance and legitimacy of regulators' activities.

Fourth, the authorities should be in constant dialogue with the firms they supervise, providing guidance and building a compliance culture. A good relationship with supervised firms, with a continuous flow of information and mutual advice, will be far more efficient than adversarial policing.

Fifth, when supervisory dialogue fails, authorities must be able to enforce regulatory principles and rules. Enforcement could take a wide variety of forms from discreet admonition to criminal proceedings. Given the speed with which financial circumstances change, it is highly desirable that disciplinary procedures be clear, flexible, and speedy, thereby earning the (perhaps grudging) support of the industry. Enforcement should also include the power to restructure delinquent or failing financial institutions. Systemic risk is often best managed by restructuring an institution and changing its management rather than forcing it to close. If liquidation is the only viable option, then the regulator should have the power to implement a credible exit strategy, managing the wind-up in an orderly manner.

Sixth, regulating authorities should have at the very center of their organization an energetic, integrated policy function, an ongoing program of research that determines and drives all other activities. The fundamental characteristic of financial markets is their remorseless dynamism. Since the 1970s liberalization the pace of change has been breathtaking. No one can predict what the structure of financial institutions will look like in five years, nor what risks will be packaged, priced, and traded tomorrow. All that can be predicted with confidence is that they will be different from today. As the structure and activities of the markets change, so do the risks. It is inevitable that, given this rapid change, the regulator should always be running several paces behind the market. What is important is that the gap not widen. In particular the gap should not be allowed to grow due to arbitrary rules of demarcation. In national economies such arbitrary and damaging demarcation takes the form of boundaries that designate which financial institutions are assigned to which regulators: banks, securities firms, savings and loans, insurance, and so on.[3] Today these artificial boundaries are an irrelevant danger to the markets and the public.

These then are the requirements needed to effectively regulate systemic risk: information, authorization, surveillance, guidance, enforcement, and policy. And the most important of these is policy.

POLICY DEVELOPMENT

The continuous reassessment and reformulation of policy is at the very heart of regulation. The policy function should lead. It should be cutting edge, flexible and inquisitive, and command the respect of the industry. It is what financial regulation is about in the modern world. If the policy function does not meet these goals, meaningful regulation will be seriously weakened.

Effective risk management demands a clear identification of the scale, structure, and origins of risk, and the introduction of controls and standards to manage exposure to risk. The principal defenses against risk are controls and capital.

By the very nature of modern financial markets, capital is no substitute for effective risk management. Capital requirements are inevitably based on some readily quantifiable aspects of a firm's portfolio. Yet typically it is inattention to the less quantifiable risks which leads to failure. Moreover it is entirely appropriate that a firm which manages risk well should enjoy lower capital requirements. But if risk is managed badly, responding by imposing higher capital requirements is neither appropriate nor adequate. Capital can never be "enough." When discussing new product development, there is a tendency for firms and regulators to focus on the implications for capitalization. This can be misleading. The issue should be approached through the risk management function, with any implications for capitalization being the result of such deliberations rather than the starting point of the exercise.

It is particularly important to ensure that both regulators and firms identify the structure and origins of risk as accurately as possible. Regulatory approaches that fail to do so can lead to perverse incentives and other outcomes desirable neither to the regulator nor to the regulated. For example, credit derivatives have highlighted some of the shortcomings of the trading book/ banking book split, itself largely a consequence of a distinction between market risk and credit risk which is becoming increasingly untenable. The key task of the regulator is to understand the character of the risk being bought and sold—market innovation continuously bundles risk into new packages—and to take all possible steps to ensure that risk is managed competently.

In a rapidly changing world, fixed rules and principles can equally become rapidly outdated. Risk is most effectively managed (though, from society's perspective not most accurately priced) by those who are exposed to it, and consequently exposed to failure. This releases regulatory resources to focus on the core problem of systemic risk and policy development. The development of an efficient risk management function requires that firms take responsibility for their own failure. Hence, risk management must be supplemented by rules on advance provision for orderly wind-down, should the necessity arise. It should also lay down rules to protect customers' assets.

In addition, it is the regulator's responsibility to ensure that appropriate information is available so firms can accurately assess risk, and that fair and honest dealing underpins commitments and transactions.

It is vital that regulation of financial markets be "at the cutting edge" of market developments, where the pace of innovation is high and, if anything, accelerating. The necessity of understanding contemporary developments arises both from the core activity of systemic protection and from the need to be sensitive to the needs of firms while encouraging innovation and entrepreneurship, and understanding the incentives and pressures under which firms operate.

In today's fast-changing financial markets it is essential that the regulator be "close to the market" with a profound understanding of the need to balance regulatory prudence and regulatory cost. The regulator should be flexible and open to considering new solutions offered by firms. That is why it is important for the policy function to design a framework for regulation based on risk-management principles, not on a set of rules. Not only is it obvious that rules cannot address every eventuality, but also prescriptive rules and a product-based regime are too inflexible and cannot accommodate new products. Rapid response on the basis of clear principles is essential to maintain healthy and innovative markets.

This is why policy development must be the leading function for a financial regulator.

REGULATORY BALANCE AND EXPERTISE

Within national economies, regulatory techniques have developed considerably over the past thirty years in an attempt to keep pace with the whirlwind of change produced by market liberalization. It has not been easy. At one and the same time regulation requires legal authority and flexibility. Legal authority is therefore typically conferred in terms of overarching Principles which participants in the financial markets are required to obey. These Principles are translated by the regulator into "codes" or "rules" which seek to apply the Principles in an ever-changing financial environment. Complex legal issues can and do arise.

But the problem is not only legal. The objective of managing systemic risk is to make the market economically and socially efficient. But it is quite possible for regulation to achieve exactly the opposite. Not only is regulation itself costly, absorbing the time of many talented people working for the regulator and the regulated, but excessively restrictive regulation could also stifle innovation and reduce efficiency. There is a need for balance and there will undoubtedly be strong and divergent views on exactly where that balance should lie.

To attain the regulators' goals demands significant expertise. This is not easy to obtain. Those who understand the markets best are likely to be employed in the markets in positions that pay far more than those funded by the public purse. There is also considerable danger that the regulator will convey the impression that risks are being effectively managed when in fact the authorities do not have the expertise to do the job. Alan Greenspan has posed this dilemma:

> Another question is whether supervisory authorities have the expertise and resources to provide meaningful oversight and develop accurate assessments of the risk-taking activities of large, diversified, globally active financial institutions. If the answer is no, as might well be the case, should we nevertheless convey to market participants the sense that we are in fact adequately supervising such activities? Wouldn't that reduce the incentives for market participants themselves to provide discipline? Would a statement that all major financial firms, even the most diversified ones, are subject to coordinated supervision suggest a degree of support that effectively extends, to an unwarranted extent, the subsidy associated with national safety nets? Would it generate a de-

gree of moral hazard that could itself be the source of systemic risk?

Greenspan did not answer his own questions, other than to express confidence in present structures. Nonetheless he highlighted a very important issue. It is no good proposing elaborate structures of regulation to manage risk if the people are not available to actually do the job. Yet it is not only in the interests of public authorities to ensure that systemic risk is effectively managed, it is also in the interests of market participants. The authorities should not overlook the fact that private sector practitioners have an incentive to lend their expertise to the design and implementation of public regulation.

In the past few years the complexity and speed of market developments have led to the proposition that the market participants themselves should be responsible for regulating the markets in which they operate — after all, they are likely to know more about what is happening than the authorities. The shift toward reliance on firms' own risk modeling to determine capital adequacy is a reflection of this view. However, while it is clearly true that the practitioners are the repository of cutting-edge technique and have an interest in systemic stability, their own risk-management cannot substitute for the role of the public authorities. First, the public authorities will always have access to a wide range of commercially sensitive information not available to competing firms. Second, the authorities will tend to take a longer-term view of the relationship between the developments in financial markets and the well-being of the national economy. Third, market participants will not internalize the externality of systemic risk and hence tend to mis-price risk from the perspective of society as a whole. While more responsibility for the measurement of risk will undoubtedly fall on participants in future, it will be the public authorities, national and international, who must decide how that responsibility is structured.

THE DEVELOPMENT
OF INTERNATIONAL REGULATION

Getting regulation right at national level is hard enough. But the national level is not what matters most anymore. Barings Bank was brought down by events in Singapore, not London. The failure of LTCM would have hit markets all round the world. In a recent important case a major Japanese financial institution was prosecuted when some its staff, licensed in London operating from Hong Kong, attempted to manipulate the Australian futures exchange. About half of all derivatives traded involve non-home country counter-parties. Today the financial systems of most developed and many developing economies are part of a seamless international financial system. Most markets and many firms and products are defined on an international scale. Within those markets, national firms and products are subject to international market disciplines and buffeted by international storms. Market liberalization transformed systemic risk from a primarily national into a primarily international phenomenon. If markets are to operate efficiently and the greatest social benefit is to be attained, then systemic risk must be regulated on an international scale.

The privatization of foreign exchange risk in the fall of 1973 and subsequent drive toward liberalization of capital markets at home and abroad rapidly exposed the new competitive strains and systemic risks inherent in the new international financial order. It was under pressure from major private banks, that central bankers of the Group of Ten countries agreed in 1974 to establish the Committee on Banking Regulation and Supervisory Practices based at the Bank for International Settlements in Basel.

One of the most urgent tasks of the new committee was to establish the division of responsibilities between national supervisors in the open international environment. In the "Basel Concordat" it was agreed that supervision of banks' solvency is the responsibility of the home authority in the case of foreign branches, and the host authority in the case of foreign subsidiaries. The collapse of the Banco Ambrosiano in 1982 led to a significant revision of the concordat in which each national authority was required to satisfy itself that its home banks' foreign operations are conducted in jurisdictions with effective supervision, and that foreign banks to which it is host are adequately supervised in their home environment.

In 1988 the Basel Committee took an entirely new initiative in international regulation, going beyond cooperation to coordination. The new accord embodied a commitment to establish minimum capital adequacy standards for the banking industry. All banks falling within the jurisdiction of parties to the accord were to maintain a minimum ratio of 8 percent capital to weighted credit exposures. The weighting system ranged from a 0 percent weighting for lending to governments in developed economies to a 100 percent weighting for long-term commercial lending to developing economies. The objective was both to strengthen the international banking system and avoid foreign banks obtaining a competitive advantage by operating on a low capital base.

The weighting system is excessively crude. No distinction is made between the risk profiles of different borrowers within broad national categories, and the criterion is therefore biased against effective portfolio diversification, contradicting a standard approach of many regulators to the reduction of risk. Another fundamental problem is that capital adequacy ratios focus on only one aspect of a bank's activities, its counter-party risk, and ignore other factors influencing its risk management. Finally, as noted in chapter 5, the form of risk-weighting adopted pushed banks in the direction of excessive short-term lending to the developing world.

Nonetheless, despite these and other detailed criticisms leveled at the 1988 standards, acceptance of the standards as the international criterion of prudent banking established the principle of the coordination of international regulatory standards which has been built on by the Basel Committee ever since. Other developments include the incorporation of measures of market risk and the use by some banks of value at risk modeling to determine their capital requirements.

Another aspect of increasing coordination has been the attempt to standardize the quality of supervision. Following the collapse of the Bank of Credit and Commerce International in 1991, the committee issued minimum standards for the supervision of international banking groups and their cross-border establishments requiring, among others, that a home-country authority should "capably perform consolidated supervision" of its international banks. The authorities should monitor banks' worldwide operations based on verifiable consolidated data. They should forbid the creation of corporate structures that impede consolidated supervision. And most importantly they should be able to prevent banks from establishing a presence in jurisdictions that are not properly regulated. It is difficult to see how this requirement can be met. Countries are not likely to take kindly to detailed critiques of their regulatory procedures on a bilateral basis, and there is no mechanism available for the multilateral evaluation necessary. The Basel Committee has attempted to address this international deficiency by formulating twenty-five Core Principles for Effective Banking Supervision. Principle 23 states:

> Banking supervisors must practice global consolidated supervision, adequately monitoring and applying appropriate prudential norms to all aspects of the business conducted by banking organizations worldwide, primarily at their foreign branches, joint ventures and subsidiaries.

Principle 24 states:

> A key component of consolidated supervision is establishing contact and information exchange with the various other supervisors involved, primarily host country supervisory authorities.

The Core Principles are an important step in developing the policy function in international regulation. The problem now is how they are to be implemented and enforced.

The Committee on Banking Supervision is primarily responsible for considering the management of systemic risk arising from the activities of institutions. The recently renamed Committee on the Global Financial System (formerly the Eurocurrency Standing Committee) is responsible for considering the risks inherent in the operation of markets. This Committee was established after the early 1980s debt crisis to examine the risks that arise from the expansion of bank lending. One of its most important acts has been to instruct the BIS to collect detailed information on the development of markets and products, and to highlight potential strains in the international system. For example in 1996 the committee drew attention to the large short-term foreign exchange exposures of Thai and Korean banks, and to the sharp reductions in premiums on risky investments. These warnings were ignored. The committee has recently considered the impact of derivatives on market stability, and the BIS has begun publishing statistics on derivatives markets.

A third BIS-based committee is the Committee on Payments and Settlements Systems. This committee is devoted to considering the implications of market changes for so-called "Herstatt risk," the risk of disjuncture or event failure of payments systems producing not only the failure of an individual firm but also contagious failure. In recent years it has turned its attention to settlement procedures for securities and foreign exchange.

As well as attempting to create regulatory structures that can confront the risks created by the international banking system, the BIS has also been host to attempts to cross the increasingly artificial boundaries between banks, securities houses, insurance companies, and other financial institutions. In 1987 the technical committee of IOSCO (the International Organization of Securities Commissions) began to consider minimum standards for securities firms akin to those set for banks. Agreement has proved difficult to achieve. However in 1991, IOSCO set out its *Principles* for use by securities and futures regulatory authorities in developing memoranda of understanding with their foreign counterparts. In 1996, IOSCO and the Basel Committee issued a *Joint Statement* setting out eight major principles of supervision which should apply both to banks and to securities firms. There is now a Joint Forum on Financial Conglomerates established in Basel for concerted investigation by the Committee on Banking Supervision, IOSCO, and the IAIS. The committee has just issued a collection of papers entitled *Supervision of Financial Conglomerates* outlining schemes for the application of capital adequacy principles, fit and proper principles, and for a framework of supervisory information sharing to regulate diversified financial conglomerates.

These developments have in their various ways been a response to the new regulatory challenges posed by the new international financial order. Inevitably they have often followed upon crises and shocks, but in that respect they do not differ from the development of national regulation. What is particularly striking about these increasingly sophisticated international arrangements is their informality. They are not the outcome of treaties between sovereign states. Instead they are built on voluntary agreements between national regulatory authorities which are then incorporated into national principles and codes. This informality has been a great strength. It has allowed the committees to act quickly to changing circumstances and permitted a similarly informal exchange of information. This informality also created a climate for the successful progress from cooperation to coordination and standardization.

The virtues of the "club" atmosphere have been seen as a barrier to the expansion of the BIS committee's membership beyond the G-10. William White, head of research at the BIS has argued that:

The fact that the size of the committees is relatively small facilitates the decision making process, so does the tradition of making decisions by consensus. The recognition that a failure to reach international agreement would open the door to both unfair competition and regulatory arbitrage also drives the process forward. . . . The issue is how to reconcile an expansion with the maintenance of the intimate club-like atmosphere (also involving shared values and shared conceptual frameworks) that facilitates agreement and decision making on the basis of consensus.

But informality has not been enough. National governments have become increasingly concerned over the instability and contagion characteristic of the new financial order. They are no longer willing to leave matters on an informal basis. At successive G7 meetings beginning at Halifax, Nova Scotia, in 1995, heads of government and finance ministers have expressed anxiety about the stability of the international financial system. They have urged the international financial institutions, i.e. the IMF, World Bank, and Basel committees, to take action to manage what were perceived to be increasing risks.

Their worries were overtaken by events. The East Asian financial crisis in 1997 and the subsequent contagion, including the shock of the Russia default on August 17, 1998, demanded action. After a succession of meetings, on October 30, 1998, the G7 finance ministers declared:

We agree that better processes are needed for monitoring and promoting stability in the international financial system and for the International Financial Institutions, working closely with the international regulatory and supervisory bodies, to conduct surveillance of national financial sectors and their regulatory and supervisory regimes with all relevant information accessible to them.

We agree therefore that we will:

(i) support the establishment of a process for strengthening financial sector surveillance using national and international regulatory and supervisory expertise, including through a process of peer review, and the IMF's regular surveillance of its member countries under Article IV;

(ii) to this end bring together the key international institutions and key national authorities involved in financial sector stability better to cooperate and coordinate their activities in the management and development of policies to foster stability and reduce systemic risk in the international financial system and to exchange information more systematically on risk in the international financial system. . . . we asked Dr. Tietmeyer to consult the relevant international bodies on these reforms.

Hans Tietmeyer, governor of the Bundesbank, presented his report to the Bonn meeting of the G7 finance ministers in February 1999. In the report, Dr. Tietmeyer argued that

Recent events in international financial markets have highlighted three areas in which improvement is needed.

First, strengthened efforts are necessary to help identify incipient vulnerabilities in national and international financial systems and concerted procedures are needed for a better understanding of the sources of systemic risk and to formulate effective financial regulatory and supervisory policies to mitigate them.

Secondly, more effective procedures are required to ensure that international rules and standards of best practice are developed and implemented, and that gaps in such standards are effectively identified and filled.

Thirdly, improved arrangements are necessary to ensure that consistent international rules and arrangements apply across all types of significant financial institutions, and that procedures exist for the continuous flow of information among authorities having responsibility for financial stability . . .

> Sweeping institutional changes are not necessary to realize these improvements. Instead, a process . . . should be set in motion to ensure that national and international authorities and groupings can coordinate efforts to promote the stability of the international financial system and to improve the functioning of the markets in order to reduce systemic risk . . .
>
> The G7 should take the initiative in convening a Financial Stability Forum. Such a Forum should meet regularly to assess issues and vulnerabilities affecting the global financial system and to identify and oversee the actions needed to address them.

The Financial Stability Forum (or FSF), which met for the first time in April 1999, represents a major step forward in international regulation. Its failure to incorporate countries outside the G7 is an obvious weakness, but this was recognized by G7 finance ministers in their launch communiqué, which included the promise to extend membership.

The strength of the FSF is that it builds on the proven achievements of the BIS committees. In the BIS tradition, the main powers exercised by the FSF are to be club consensus and peer pressure. The size of the Forum was deliberately restricted in order to maintain an informal approach. It is also notable that the G7 mandate to Tietmeyer's committee referred to the need "better to co-operate and co-ordinate activities . . . and to exchange information." Similarly, Tietmeyer's report refers to the need to "coordinate efforts" to achieve "consistent international rules and arrangements." The power to act lies as it always has with the national authorities, and has been in no way invested in the FSF. Just like the BIS committees, the FSF is there to facilitate cooperation and coordination.

But here lies a contradiction. The intervention of the G7 governments derives from perceived inadequacies in the regulation of international financial markets. In part this is a reflection of the concerns finance ministers feel over a pace of change that imposes ever more complex demands on their domestic regulatory structures, let alone the framework of international consensus. Yet it is the framework of consensus which is being preserved, albeit in a more concerted form. But if the FSF is indeed to "ensure" that action takes place and is to "oversee" the development and implementation of policy, a different format may be required.

THE LIMITS OF REGULATION

The management of systemic risk by regulation should be sufficient to deal with normal risks. For abnormal risks a lender of last resort is needed. The IMF has steadily assumed a role more nearly akin to a lender of last resort, most notably in the Mexican bond crisis of 1994 and in the organization of funding in the East Asian crisis. The resources available to the IMF derive primarily from national quotas to a value of $300 billion. These have been supplemented by the General Arrangements to Borrow in 1962 and were further augmented by the New Arrangements to Borrow of 1997. The latter arrangements effectively doubled to $46 billion the total amount of credit available to the IMF.

Despite these developments, a number of fundamental weaknesses hamper the way the IMF deals with financial crises:

First, liquidity with conditions is not liquidity. The whole approach of the IMF is geared to satisfying lending conditions. Not only does this put the brakes on a process that should be conducted very quickly (the slower the lender of last resort acts, the greater the volume of lending is likely to be), but also the IMF has encountered some difficulty in assessing the cloudy boundary between liquidity and solvency. Indeed, in the circumstances the IMF is likely to encounter, the distinction will be virtually meaningless.

Second, a lender of last resort should be able to lend without limit. The IMF simply does not have the resources to do this. Unless the markets can be confident that a lender of the last resort is willing and able to intervene when required, losses of confidence are likely to be cumulative.

An alternative approach is to develop mechanisms for concerted action by the major central banks. When the BIS has become involved in crisis management it has typically coordinated central bank lending to provide bridging finance prior to the arrival of IMF funds. Central banks have the ability to create liquidity on an unlimited scale, and so concerted action by central banks is likely to lead to a rapid restoration of confidence. However, central banks are likely to be reluctant lenders of last resort to entities outside their jurisdiction—at the very least national taxpayers are likely to demand a clear explanation of what their central banks are up to!

An important change in the character of international financial crises became evident in the 1998 East Asian crisis. While the crisis led to a collapse of national currencies and severe financial embarrassment for national governments, its origins were to be found in the private sector, even in the nonbanking sector. Market risk, in the form of excessive foreign exchange exposure in the balance sheets of banking and nonbanking corporations, resulted in a general loss of confidence in national financial systems. Neither the IMF nor central bank consortia lend to the private sector. In the case of a private sector crisis, their lending to national authorities in turn has to be lent by the authorities to their private sector.

Whether extended lender of last resort facilities are to be provided via the IMF or orchestrated actions of the central banks, a vital prerequisite will be the development of more potent international financial regulatory mechanisms. Without powerful regulation, including the ability to require restructuring of firms along pre-announced lines, not only will enhanced lending facilities create significant moral hazard but also the arrangements will be unacceptable to home legislatures. So while regulation can only assist in the management of normal systemic risk, the presence of a credible regulatory structure is necessary for the management of abnormal systemic risk by the lender of last resort. A credible structure will involve not only agreed regulatory standards and procedures. It will also require confidence that its standards are indeed being enforced, and procedures followed, by a regulatory staff that has the necessary skill and authority to implement them.

The development of regulation on a global scale would involve the adoption of higher standards of financial risk management in financial and nonfinancial firms. While risk management will not save even the most prudent firm in the face of a general loss of confidence, neither will the capital mandated by capital adequacy standards or value at risk criteria. The superiority of the risk management approach derives from its emphasis on good management and awareness and monitoring of risk. No amount of capital is a substitute for bad management. Good management may enable firms to navigate very rough waters. The regulatory horizon must be the same as the risk horizon which the firm faces. For most firms today, whether they operate internationally or not, that horizon is the global financial market.

NOTES

1. Indeed, in practice the return on US Treasury Bills is usually treated as "riskless" even if the assertion is not completely correct. The rate of return earned on short-term Treasury Bills varies as the investment in bills is rolled over (there is "income risk"), and there is always the possibility you might require your money back late on a Saturday night ("liquidity risk").

2. John Maynard Keynes believed that because of the "dark forces of time and ignorance," precise calculation of expected future returns (let alone probability distributions upon them) to assets has no meaning. Imagine the disdain he would have for financial rocket science!

3. In the US the division of regulatory responsibility is further complicated by the segmentation of authority between federal authorities and the states.

7—A World Financial Authority

A liquid, highly innovative financial system is necessary for the growth of modern economies. It is not only the lubricant that smooths the frictions of exchange from the neighborhood shop to global money markets, it is also, when mixed with entrepreneurship, skills, and innovation, the fuel in the engine of economic growth. Flows of finance determine the allocation of resources in economies at home and abroad. Availability of finance sets production in motion.

But finance is a highly volatile material, liable to explode and destroy the very engine it oils and fuels. It must be managed with care.

In the early 1970s the international financial system which had served the world well since the Second World War collapsed under the strains imposed on the fixed exchange rates which were a vital component of the Bretton Woods "management system." That collapse and the privatization of risk it precipitated led in turn to the dismantling of barriers to the movement of capital in domestic and international markets. Floating exchange rates were incompatible with capital controls—they had to go. With rates floating and controls dismantled, it was vital for the successful operation of the world economy that investors be able to spread their risks by diversifying the contents of their portfolios among different assets, currencies, and contingent contracts, and that they be able to change the composition of those portfolios at will.

So was born the modern open financial system, a system of massive, highly liquid flows and complex hedging instruments, of widespread speculation and extensive arbitrage. The scale of financial flows today dwarfs both the real economy and the financial resources of international agencies and nation-states.

Financial flows are propelled by the shifting patterns of convention. Prices in financial markets are determined by what average opinion believes average opinion believes those prices should be. In the attempt to ascertain average opinion, participants in the marketplace rely on convention, otherwise known as the fundamentals. This can be a fragile foundation. The result is volatility and, given the worldwide interconnection of financial markets, contagion.

In recent years the volatility and contagion associated with the new international financial order produced major financial crises in both developed and developing countries. Many though not all of these crises took the form of currency crises. Most resulted in sharp reductions in levels of output and employment, with growth being retarded for years. These reductions were particularly severe in developing countries.

But the new international financial order has not only been characterized by recurring crises, it has also been associated with declines in rates of growth and investment throughout the world. These declines may well be attributable to changed behavior in both the private and public sectors in the face of volatility and contagion. The private sector has become more risk averse, attempting to maintain high levels of liquidity and reluctant to commit resources to longer term real investments. The public sector has redefined the objectives of economic policy in terms of monetary and financial stability rather than, as was the case previously, of employment and growth.

Regulation can be macroeconomic in the form of capital controls and other direct interventions, or microeconomic in the form of prudential regulation of banks, securities firms, insurance companies, and financial markets in general. The new international financial order embodies greatly reduced regulation of financial markets. That reduction derives both from the conscious removal of controls that was a necessary part of the privatization of foreign exchange risk, and from the process of internationalization itself. Liberalization has created a seamless financial world, with regulators confined inside increasingly irrelevant national boundaries.

Of course the positive aspects of the new international financial order have been welcome. And there is no doubt that the main thrust of international economic policy, emanating both from governments of the developed economies and from international organizations, has been to hasten deregulation and liberalization. Developing country governments have been more circumspect. But through the 1990s the tendency toward deregulation and liberalization became more and more firmly established in the Third World. At the same time, from the very beginnings of the drive toward liberalization in the early 1970s, measures have been taken to attempt to recover some of the regulatory control previously lost. A fundamental locus of this effort has been in the banking committees based at the BIS in Basel.

As the negative aspects of liberalization became more pronounced, so did the attempt to recover some of the regulatory power once deployed by national economies in the Bretton Woods era. Within countries following the Asian crisis, there has been a growing acceptance of the proposition that capital controls, especially controls over short-term capital inflows, might be an efficient policy response in certain circumstances. Between developed countries there has been a move toward more concerted regulatory coordination exemplified by the establishment of the Financial Stability Forum (FSF).

The coordination of the regulation of international financial markets via the Basel committees has from its beginning been consensual and informal. Increasing governmental anxiety, evident in G7 communiqués, has now reached a position in which these informal procedures have been placed on a more formal basis—while attempting to maintain the flexibility of the consensual approach. The history of national economies suggests that this tentative extension of the authorities' role will in due course become more closely coordinated. The FSF or successor agencies may one day acquire decision-making powers. Despite the obvious difficulties in the exercise of supranational authority, the regulator will need to operate over the same terrain as the markets. The public domain will attempt to insert itself into the operations of the international market economy to ensure that the market economy survives.

If, as has been argued throughout this book, the floating of exchange rates precipitated many of the economic difficulties of the past three decades, then why not return foreign exchange risk to the public sector by restoring fixed rates? In fact, that is exactly what is happening in various regions of the world.

The Euro

The drive to develop a single currency in Europe acquires its momentum from many sources: from political enthusiasm for European unification, from the search for efficient allocation of capital in a single market, from the wish to reduce transactions costs in a multi-currency area, and so on. An important item in the list is the desire to eliminate foreign exchange risk in Europe. The European Union was made keenly aware of the potential scale of speculative disruption by the 1992 crisis in the exchange rate mechanism. This event compelled those member states that were not unceremoniously ejected from the mechanism to widen the bands within which their currencies might fluctuate around parity from 2.25 to 15 percent. Despite the uncertainties created by the potential 30 percent range of fluctuation, ten currencies[1] ended up having their parities fixed "forever" to create the euro on January 1, 1999.

The new currency is managed by a European central bank that has total authority over monetary policy within Euroland (the euro zone). However, the other economic institutions of Euroland are far from fully developed. The location of the lender of last resort function is unclear. There is no Euroland financial services regulator despite the declared intention of creating a single capital market, with banks and other financial firms operating without heed to national boundaries. However, the European Union does issue capital adequacy directives that typically reflect (though sometimes weakly) the capital adequacy conditions formulated by the Basel banking committee. Finally, there is no effective mechanism for achieving macroeconomic balance between monetary and fiscal policy. The development of the so-called Euro-XI Committee of finance ministers is intended to address this question. But the proposition that it is to be the political counterpart to the European central bank is not universally accepted.

These deficiencies will probably be remedied in future years as their significance is tested by economic shocks. But the difficulties which a close-knit, committed political grouping such as the EU has faced in creating supranational economic institutions to manage the supranational currency are a warning of the difficulties which lie ahead in the regulation of global markets.[2]

Exchange Rates in Developing Economies

In developing countries there are often very good reasons why the exchange rate should be fixed (or limited to fluctuations within a narrow band). A pegged rate is anti-inflationary, a factor crucially important to Latin American stabilization packages beginning with Mexico's in the late 1980s. It can also enhance export competitiveness, as happened when countries in Southeast Asia pegged to the falling dollar after the Plaza Accord in 1985.

However, a fixed rate can create severe problems. Obviously it can be an easy target for speculation. Another problem stems from the fact that it is often convenient for a country to peg its rate to just one of the major global currencies (rather than a "basket"), if only to give clear signals and simplify calculations for its importers and exporters. The risk is that the "anchor" currency can drift out of line. Although the Asian economies benefited from their dollar peg in the late 1980s, they were badly hurt by the strengthening dollar after 1990. Such problems can be reduced if the dollar, euro, and yen maintain relatively stable exchange rates among themselves. Then pegging to a single one of the trio will not be destabilizing.

The benefits and costs of floating rates for developing countries remain to be assessed, although several important economies adopted such regimes after the wave of financial crises in the late 1990s. The main difficulty for developing countries is that markets in their currencies tend to be rather "thin," making the currency prone to large, destabilizing fluctuations. Middle income economies often lack deep futures markets to generate forward values of the exchange rate against which the spot rate can float. Mexico, which after its 1994 crisis adopted a managed float with some degree of capital market regulation, provides an example. An index of the real exchange rate was 71 in 1993, 107 in 1995 just after the crisis, and back down to 85 in 1998. Were currency markets truly self-stabilizing, such worrisome fluctuations would be less likely to occur.

Moreover, any exchange rate regime has to be consistent with fiscal and monetary policies. The required linkages will vary according to the regime chosen and may require complementary measures. In the absence of widespread capital and exchange controls, fixed rates demand large international reserves to be viable (note how even Brazil's billions did not save its pegged rate after serious capital outflows got underway in late 1998). Intermediate regimes require more active intervention in the management of the capital account. Flexible rates can be highly unstable. Certainly all regimes can be aided by some control over capital movements.

Currency Boards

A few countries have moved as far as they possibly can to eliminate exchange risk by adopting the currency of a major country, either directly or indirectly through the mechanism of a currency board.[3] In one very visible case the Hong Kong dollar is tied directly to the US dollar. This did not prevent the link from being severely tested during the Asian crisis, with increases in the Hong Kong interest rate precipitating a collapse in property prices and growing unemployment. Nonetheless, the parity of the Hong Kong dollar survived, no doubt considerably aided by Hong Kong's (not to mention China's) enormous US dollar reserves. In fact, the goal of the Hong Kong policy of maintaining a fixed parity is not to eliminate foreign exchange risk for the economy as a whole, but expressly to sustain confidence in the Hong Kong financial services industry.

The experience of Hong Kong over the past two years illustrates both the strengths and weaknesses of the pegged currency strategy. Hong Kong companies did not suffer the severe balance sheet embarrassment observed in Korea despite their considerable foreign exchange exposure. However, as well as the burden of high interest rates, Hong Kong companies also suffered from an enormous revaluation against the currencies of their major trading partners and competitors. Unless a country conducts the overwhelming majority of its trade with the nation to which its currency is pegged, it will still be vulnerable to major exchange rate swings. Moreover, other than in nations which adopt the currency of another country for all purposes (hence abandoning all monetary independence), pegged rates backed by currency boards are still liable to disruptive speculation. Indeed, given their financial openness, economies with pegged rates are likely to have potentially damaging exposures which speculators may exploit.

Such problems are clearly present in Argentina, the other main exemplar of a currency board. In 1991 its peso was pegged to the US dollar to provide an anti-inflationary "nominal anchor" for the national price system. The experiment has received ample support from international agencies. Fortunately so, because the real exchange rate strengthened notably due to residual inflation after the nominal rate was "irrevocably" fixed. Apart from a period of recession due to the "tequila" effect of the Mexican crisis, the strong peso was associated with a trade deficit in the 1990s in the range of $6 billion per year. About 50 percent of this gap has been covered by official capital inflows. Since the domestic money supply is tied to inflows of foreign currency, when private inflows arrive in high volume the currency board mechanism amplifies them into a boom; when they flow out there is a crash. Over the medium term the economy might prove more manageable if a degree of domestic monetary control were reintroduced via capital controls and modification of the current central bank practice of tying the money supply directly to its holdings of international reserves. With all price relationships to the dollar locked in by currency board rules, it is not surprising that the quantity side of the economy is subject to violent fluctuations.

Bands

The mixed records of both fixed and floating exchange rates reflect a fundamental problem. In a world in which stocks of international debt are so large and potential capital flows so overwhelming, something needs to be done to lessen the foreign exchange risk which undermines confidence and reduces growth and employment. In a completely liberal financial world a return to fixed exchange rates is just not possible. Fixed rates need to be buttressed by exchange controls. What might be feasible would be to raise market confidence by establishing broad bands in the 5 to 10 percent range above and below agreed midpoint bilateral exchange rates of the major currencies (the dollar, euro, and yen). Rates would be subject to "dirty floats" within the bands, but the authorities would make clear to the markets their official intention to maintain the limits by joint interventions.

Management of markets would be unavoidable because (to repeat) exchange rates have no clear and direct linkages to fundamentals such as trade and fiscal deficits or relative price levels. They are the outcome of a beauty contest. Linkages that do exist are in the minds of market players, subject to the moving expectations and possibilities for rapid jumps in conventions that are the hallmarks of the financial beauty game. Managing the bands would therefore be a management of conventions, with all the potential fragility that implies. To move rates up and down within their permitted ranges, policy coordination (including coordination among central banks jealous of their "independence") would be required. To steer rates away from the limits, international collaboration would be essential.

A system of bands would require close monitoring of markets, but it could yield considerable benefits. Private capital flows would be stabilized because the authorities would have explicitly stated their degree of tolerance of fluctuations. The entire history of liberal capital markets clearly indicates that a lack of government guidance encourages contagion when a currency is subject to speculative attack. Third countries would gain because they could peg their currencies to one of the big three without running the risk of major misalignment such as occurred in East Asia in the 1990s.

If the public sector were to readopt some of the foreign exchange risk privatized in 1973, then the authorities would need to create a system to manage that risk. In the absence of capital controls this would require a commitment to defend the limits of the bands by supporting to an indefinite degree any currency which is speculated against. This in turn would require international collaboration in the conduct of monetary policy. Absorption of risk by the public sector would also encourage the private sector to take excessive currency risks. So the bands would need to be complemented by a regulatory regime which would diminish the moral hazard implicit in the public sector guarantee. The interrelationship of greater exchange rate stability and regulatory control will be considered further in the context of the responsibilities of a World Financial Authority.

CAPITAL CONTROLS

The fixed exchange rate regime of the Bretton Woods era was buttressed by capital controls. It is difficult to imagine such extraordinary stability without them. In the new international financial order controls have a somewhat different role—they help manage risk. The volatility and contagion of uncontrolled markets is highly inefficient. Capital controls are simply part of the regulatory framework to manage risk at both the macroeconomic and microeconomic levels. This is why so much attention has been focused of late on the control of capital *inflows* rather than the traditional concern with outflows.

It is important to recognize the significant difference between limiting short-term capital flows into a country on the one hand, and closing markets to foreign goods on the other. In the latter case a country may attempt to acquire a beggar-my-neighbor advantage. The same argument does not apply in the case of limitations on short-term inflows of capital.

Controls in Developing Countries

The demand for across-the-board abolition of capital and exchange controls has been pursued insistently by the US and a few other developed countries in recent years in a number of forums including the OECD, WTO, and IMF. What they urge on others is contrary to their own history of successful economic development experience, which in fact featured long periods of capital controls and only gradual liberalization of capital accounts (recall the discussions in chapters 2–4). The experiences of developing countries outlined in chapter 5 clearly show that abrupt or premature liberalization of the capital account is inappropriate for developing and transition economies, a fact now generally recognized. Strong domestic financial systems, regulation, and supervision are essential elements to guarantee successful liberalization. However, even with strong performance in these areas, it has proved difficult for developing and transition economies to adapt to the volatile international flows that followed liberalization of their capital accounts. Boom-bust cycles are frequently associated with portfolio and short-term capital flows. The composition and not just the magnitude of flows plays an essential role in generating external vulnerability.

Under these conditions, developing and transition econo-

mies should retain the right to impose disincentives or controls
on inflows, particularly in times of capital surges, and on outflows during severe crises. A flexible approach in this regard is
certainly superior to mandatory capital account convertibility.
Best practices in these areas may include reserve requirements
on short-term inflows, various taxes on capital inflows intended
to discourage them, appropriate put and call provisions in borrowing agreements, and minimum stay or liquidity requirements for investment banks and mutual funds that wish to
invest in a country. These measures will tend to increase the
cost of capital to the developing country. But that is exactly in
the interest of economic efficiency. The higher cost of capital is
a measure of the externality of risk being internalized.

Controlling measures taken by developing countries could
also include complementary prudential regulations on domestic financial institutions, such as higher reserve or liquidity requirements on short-term deposits into the financial system
managed in anti-cyclical fashion, and upper limits on the prices
of assets used as collateral during periods of economic expansion. Mechanisms to guarantee a healthy maturity structure for
both external and domestic public sector indebtedness are crucial complementary tools. Such instruments should be regarded as permanent rather than temporary devices as long as
international financial markets remain volatile and domestic
economic structures are weak. Parallel reforms should be oriented towards developing long-term segments of domestic
capital markets.

REGULATION

Macroeconomic regulation deployed to manage exchange rates
and capital flows must be supplemented by microeconomic
regulation of banks, securities houses, insurance companies,
highly leveraged institutions such as hedge funds, and other financial firms. Regulation will never be able to protect firms and

markets against abnormal risk. Then even the best risk management practices will be overwhelmed. But effective regulation can make a significant contribution in managing normal systemic risk. By building confidence in the ability to maintain market stability in normal times, it will make abnormality all the more rare.

The key to effectively managing systemic risk is having regulatory authorities who operate in the same domain as the institutions they regulate, whether that domain is defined in terms of products or currencies or legal jurisdictions. That is why the development of the new international financial order poses such a difficult challenge to the financial authorities of nation-states. Supranational jurisdiction is a very uncomfortable idea. Yet if liberal markets are to survive, the challenge must be met in one way or another.

In the attempt to meet that challenge, the development of international regulation since the early 1970s has gone through two phases, first cooperation, then coordination, and may in the next few years enter a third phase of control. In the cooperation phase, national authorities exchanged information and established division of responsibilities in an attempt to regulate international markets. In the coordination phase they sought to install common standards and procedures. In the control phase, an international authority would acquire policymaking, surveillance, and enforcement responsibilities.

The Financial Stability Forum is a bold step forward in the international structure of regulatory authorities. But the very boldness of the structure exposes the limitations of the consensual approach as currently conceived. Any international authority will need to work with and through national regulators. This relationship between the national regulator and the international organization will determine whether the organization does indeed exercise effective authority over the domain of the international market. Up until now the BIS committees have steadily increased their harmonizing role, moving from cooperation to coordination. Their powers have not been extended to actual control mediated by treaty or through similar statutory powers. Indeed their informality is one of their strengths. Informal structures do facilitate speedy decision-making and prompt action (clearly demonstrated in the ability of BIS to arrange bridging finance while the IMF takes time to organize appropriate "packages"). But experience suggests that the development of international financial markets has now reached such a level of sophistication and fragility that informal cooperation has reached the limits of effectiveness. The FSF does not (at present) possess surveillance or enforcement powers. More importantly it does not possess the power to make and implement policy. Without this latter power the ability of the FSF to adapt its principles and codes to rapid change in the marketplace is severely limited. It lacks the power to act, to impose its authority in managing systemic risk. In sum, the FSF is probably as far as the coordination phase can go.

The concept of a World Financial Authority provides a template for an examination of the scale of the challenges posed by the control phase. Whether a supranational organization would actually take the institutional form of a WFA as proposed here does not matter very much. The objective in considering the economic advantages of a WFA and the economic and legal challenges it would face is to clarify the problems to be solved by any institution or set of institutions charged with meeting the goal of efficiently regulating the new international financial order.

THE WORLD FINANCIAL AUTHORITY

If the WFA is indeed to be an effective regulator in the same domain as the markets it regulates, then it will need to perform the same tasks performed today by efficient national regulators,[4] namely information, authorization, surveillance, guidance, enforcement, and policy. Most of these functions would in reality be performed by national authorities acting in conjunction with and as agents for the WFA. The importance of the WFA is in its harmonizing of standards and procedures and developing the global scope and relevance of decision-making.

Authorization and Guidance

While authorization may be conducted under current home/host arrangements, it would be the responsibility of the WFA to ensure that common authorization procedures are followed and information is fully shared. The WFA would also be an important clearinghouse for the ongoing guidance which is such an important part of efficient regulation. Since guidance requires large numbers of staff members "close to the industry," it can only be conducted by national authorities. Nonetheless, in international businesses there is a need for both full information and harmonization in guidance, and for advice from the WFA for those who dispense national guidance.

Information

The information role will be central to WFA operations. Today the Bank for International Settlements and its committees are sources of a wealth of information on the development and performance of international financial markets. The WFA should establish best international practice for disclosing financial information. This needs to be complemented by developing a way to share appropriate confidential information about the activities of firms.

A vital element in any market is its accounting system, which provides the market and the regulator with information. The quality of that information is a foundation for both market and regulatory efficiency. Despite the obvious need for standard accounting procedures in the new international financial order, progress so far toward anything other than lowest common denominator standards has been painfully slow. A single set of accounting standards could provide early warning of the kind of financial crises that hit both developed Japan and developing East Asia and Latin America. Accounting standards need to meet the needs of international markets and incorporate the characteristics of modern markets including intangible assets, environmental liabilities, and ethical and social risks. The internet, by revolutionizing the speed of financial reporting, provides another challenge demanding international standards of accounting and disclosure.

Clear, comprehensive, and consistent accounting is vital to protect investors. In 1991, US residents had nearly $300 billion worth of holdings in non-US equities. By 1997 the figure was $1200 billion and rising rapidly. An international perspective is necessary if US regulators are to protect their own citizens. This is true of every other national regulator. Effective global accounting standards are a *necessary* condition for an efficient open international financial system. Without accurate information provided by consistent accounting standards, neither market discipline nor regulatory oversight can operate effectively. Without consistency, financial markets will suffer from "accounting arbitrage." The WFA should be charged with overseeing the accounting standards process and working closely with the International Accounting Standards Committee. With the WFA as the ISAC's single customer, problems of accounting arbitrage and the tendency toward lowest common denominator standards will be overcome.

Surveillance

The information system is part of the wider problem of surveillance. The IMF has responsibility under its Articles of Association to produce surveillance reports on the economic performance of member states. The WFA should be given similar responsibility for surveillance of the regulatory performance of states that have signed up to its regulatory regime. Instead of peer pressure (which has not worked very well), the WFA should have the power to check the surveillance systems of participating countries. In doing so it will be able to both offer advice on maintaining better standards and learn of new developments and so disseminate the latest information. This will require a level of frank openness not yet achieved even between G10 regulators. But it is necessary to sustain best practice throughout international financial markets.

Enforcement

But the sensitivities associated with surveillance are nothing compared to the sensitivities associated with enforcement. Of course the vast majority of enforcement cases will be dealt with by national authorities. The task of the WFA will not be to establish its own enforcement department as some form of extraterritorial financial police. Rather it will be to take the lead in coordinating the enforcement activities of national regulators involved in international cases. It is not unusual for enforcement cases today to straddle many jurisdictions. Despite the best will in the world such cases are likely to take excessive lengths of time and involve complex issues of legal responsibility, lead enforcement, multiple jeopardy, and so on. The new international financial order needs a simpler, quicker, and clearer enforcement procedure for the small but increasingly important number of multi-jurisdiction cases. The WFA should be the agency which leads the enforcement effort, bringing to it consistency and coherence.

Policy

The WFA's most important function will be the policy function. BIS committees have already shown considerable expertise in the development of policy, and there can be no doubt that their consensual approach has been very important in bestowing legitimacy on their proposals. But in an important sense the committees have followed national regulators, adapting their best practice to an international domain. What is needed now is a policy function that leads, that continuously adapts the scope and content of regulation to the changing structure of international markets and the changing character of firms. The policy function should determine the character of the WFA and of national regulators.

The primary task of the World Financial Authority will be to manage systemic risk, and hence enhance the stability and efficiency of international financial markets. A WFA could also play an important role in the battle against international financial crime and money laundering. However, the consideration below is devoted to the management of risk. This requires policies at both the macroeconomic level where much market risk is created, and the microeconomic level where market risk and counter-party risk reinforce one another to the detriment of the real economy.

Macroeconomic Regulation and Risk Management

The management of market risk created by swings in exchange rates, interest rates, and other macro variables requires international cooperation. Many goals of an efficient international financial policy can be achieved by effectively coordinating the activities of national monetary authorities. The problem is that the means of achieving that coordination are at the moment very limited. The WFA should be a forum within which the rules of international financial cooperation are developed and implemented. Mutual support is the key to success.

Perhaps the most important area of macroeconomic regulation for the WFA will be managing the restrictions imposed on capital markets by national authorities. Nation-states, after appropriate consultations with the WFA, should have the power to impose restrictions on external capital movements as they see fit. Effective controls, particularly on short-term capital inflows, may well be necessary not only to manage systemic risk efficiently but also to sustain free trade in goods and services since trade controls may well be imposed in the wake of financial crises. If microeconomic regulation of firms is to be effective, it may need to be supplemented with quantitative or tax-based obstacles to cross-border flows of funds. While there should be a presumption in favor of national policies, the form, scale, and duration of such restrictions (which may, if necessary, be deemed permanent) should however be determined in consultations with the WFA. Those consultations and the monitoring that accompanies them would ensure that risk management does not stifle enterprise.

In today's international financial environment, attempts by relatively small countries to manage market risk may be overwhelmed by the scale and speed of capital movements. So once particular conditions for managing capital movement have been agreed to, member states of the WFA should be required to provide assistance to fellow members in their operation.

A second crucial arena for macroeconomic coordination is in establishing and maintaining stable exchange rates among the three key currencies as discussed above. As a regulatory agency, the WFA would not play the central role in setting up such arrangements, but its supportive contributions could be substantial.

Finally, a macroeconomic "vision" within WFA policymaking would provide an important complement to microeconomic regulation. This macro "vision" fundamental to managing market risk is currently not prominent in the work of the BIS committees. For example, the BIS risk weighting of capital adequacy requirements for banks *encourages* short-term flows to developing countries. Loans of less than a year maturity are weighted at 20 percent, while maturities in excess of a year are weighted at 100 percent. The differential is entirely understandable in terms of microeconomic risk to the banks in lending countries, but tends to increase macroeconomic risk in recipient countries by providing an incentive for banks to concentrate their lending to developing countries on the short term.

A macroeconomic vision may also provide a safeguard against the imposition of excessively pro-cyclical microeconomic regulation. Most capital adequacy requirements induce strongly pro-cyclical behavior. Most risk management techniques do, too, with the added difficulty of promoting contagion as negative risk assessment spreads throughout financial markets. The difficulties facing the regulator are obvious: to enforce pro-cyclical behavior in the interests of managing counter-party risk, or to relax risk management standards in the face of adverse macroeconomic developments. A goal of the development of a new financial framework should be to reduce these dilemmas by limiting imbalances in which national financial systems have long internal and short external net positions or blatant stock-flow disequilibrium positions.

Microeconomic Regulation and Risk Management

It will be the WFA's responsibility to provide the lead in the creation, operation, and continuous modernization of a comprehensive regulatory framework for all financial services. There is a great need for a comprehensive view, encouraging the design of efficient risk management techniques for *all* major institutions, banks, mutual funds, highly leveraged institutions (e.g. hedge funds), insurance and pension funds, and covering all onshore and offshore and on–balance sheet and off–balance sheet operations (recognizing how difficult the identification of some of these operations may be). Traditional notions of capital adequacy monitoring are inadequate in today's capital markets. Capital is no substitute for effective management. Risk management should be central to regulatory activity, internalizing risk externalities as far as possible.

By establishing harmonious standards of regulation throughout international financial markets the WFA will establish and spread best practice, limit regulatory arbitrage, and hence limit market distortions.

Thorough microeconomic regulation will help stabilize macro-markets. This is particularly true of foreign exchange markets. The micro regulation which limits the foreign exchange exposure of domestic institutions (by regulating both borrowers and lenders) will enhance the stability of foreign exchange markets by increasing confidence in the economy's ability to weather foreign exchange shocks. This will substantially ease the task of managing exchange rates among the key currencies as discussed above.

Regulation in Emerging Markets

Nowhere will the WFA confront greater problems than in dealing with the financial regulatory problems of developing and transition economies. Their own regulatory capacities are underdeveloped, they lack a suitable number of qualified personnel, and, given their small size relative to the volume of international financial transactions, the risks they confront are proportionately far greater than those of the US, Europe, or Japan.

Much of the instability in capital flows in and out of developing and transition economies can be traced to wide spreads between foreign costs and national returns to assets. Under a fixed exchange rate regime, it is easy to see a 10 percent differential between local and foreign short-term interest rates or a similarly sized gap between the growth rate of the local stock market index or real estate prices and a foreign borrowing rate. Such yields are an open invitation to capital inflows that can be extremely destabilizing. Whether policymakers feel they are able to reduce interest rates or deflate an asset market boom is another question, one that merits real concern.

Another source of potential spreads is through off–balance sheet and derivative operations. Here local regulators can be at a major disadvantage. It is difficult to keep up with the latest devices, and most (but one hopes not all) of any nation's skilled financial operators will be on the other side, inventing still newer devices to make more money. Staying up-to-date as far as possible and inculcating a culture of probity in the local financial system are the best defenses here.

There is thus a serious question as to whether many developing country macro-policies and regulatory systems can meet such goals, especially in the wake of capital market liberalization. Another difficulty arises with timing. It is very difficult to put a stop to capital flows *after* convention has decreed that fundamentals have become adverse. At such a point interest rate increases or a discreet devaluation can easily provoke a crash. The authorities have to stifle a potentially explosive cycle early in its upswing; otherwise, they may be powerless to act. The problem with all indicators of a threatening crisis is that they often lag behind an unstable dynamic process. By the time they are visibly out of line it may be too late to prevent the crisis. Its management becomes the urgent task of the day.

Given all these problems, what sorts of support can an agency such as the WFA effectively provide to developing countries? One contribution would be up-to-date information on the country's international position with appropriate interpretations and warnings. The Asian and Russian crises exploded in part because of inadequate international early warning systems on short-term debt (especially debt owed to international banks).

Second, technical assistance can be crucial. The WFA could organize technical assistance programs for the regulatory authorities. It would have been possible to build up Russia's financial regulatory capability, for example, had Russia been willing to take the politically difficult step of accepting and implementing such aid. Similar observations apply to East Asia as well.

Finally, by setting best practice standards, a WFA could provide an incentive for countries to upgrade their own capabilities and standards. After all, *not* satisfying best practice would mean that a country would have to pay significantly higher costs for access to funds and might have limited access to IMF funding.

The Role of the Banks

Much of the argument of this book has focused on the "seamless" character of financial markets today between products, firms, and countries. Nonetheless, it is the banks that have been primarily responsible for most of the volatility which has hit emerging markets. Between 1993 and 1996 net lending by banks accounted for 71 percent of the increase in total net capital flows to the twenty-nine most important emerging markets. What came in, rushed out. Net lending by banks accounted for

110 percent of the decline in total net flows.[5] Without the banks there would have been no Asian crisis. Three-quarters of the net swing in private external finance between 1996 and 1998 was accounted for by commercial banks alone. Short-term lending by banks is an intrinsically risky form of finance and a return to large-scale short-term bank lending to emerging markets is undesirable. In domestic markets the risks of short-term finance are contained by the presence of a lender of last resort, tough regulation, and effective bankruptcy procedures. In the international context, short-term flows should be managed by the WFA with a combination of macroeconomic measures (agreed-to controls on short-term inflows) and microeconomic regulation. The WFA can form a global view in microeconomic regulation by regulating not only the borrower but also the lender. The WFA can take into account the systemic risks being incurred by the mis-pricing of risk by the lending bank, and take steps to ensure that the full cost is internalized by imposing stringent capital adequacy requirements and other regulatory measures.

THE WFA'S ROLE IN COPING WITH CRISES WHEN THEY STRIKE

A central goal of financial regulation is to reduce the likelihood of crisis. But when a crisis, and especially a currency crisis, strikes, a regulator, even a WFA, cannot cope on its own. International financial assistance, essentially an international lender of last resort, is required. Each crisis follows its own rules, but the recent crises in developing countries point to a few general lessons about steps that should and should not be taken.

Steps to Take

On the "do" side, the contrast between the Mexican and Asian "rescues" is striking: the first happened (at least as far as foreign creditors were concerned) and the second did not. Very slow disbursement of funds by the IMF may well have crippled the Asian effort permanently, pushing fundamentally healthy economies from illiquidity into insolvency. The first and most obvious recommendation that emerges from crisis experience is to disburse rescue money quickly. Finance supplied only on the basis of negotiated conditions and released only after compliance with them is *not* liquidity. East Asian economies became highly illiquid in 1997. By 1999 their position seemed to have stopped deteriorating. But their economic performance had not significantly improved.

The need to inject liquidity naturally brings to the fore the question of an international lender of last resort, which would enhance the confidence and stability of the international financial system and deal with abnormal risk. The natural candidate is the IMF. The IMF can only fulfill this role efficiently if there exists a complementary regulatory agency *operating over the same domain.* That is the task of the World Financial Authority. To meet the demands of the lender of last resort role the IMF's resources should be enlarged (though it must be remembered that the very existence of ample resources for the lender of last resort makes it less likely that those resources will actually be used). Three channels can be considered:

First, effective and swift mechanisms should be devised to increase the Fund's access to official monies in times of crisis. Essentially this would be access to the money-creating powers of national central banks.

Second, it could be granted authorization to borrow directly from financial markets under those circumstances.

Third, and perhaps most importantly, the Special Drawing Rights (SDR) mechanism set up in the mid-1960s could be reactivated. SDRs could be created when Fund member countries face financial difficulties (as indeed the United States advocated before it adopted its "passive" balance of payments strategy in the early 1970s). These advances would be eliminated as borrowings were repaid.

Mechanisms such as these would facilitate the creation of ad-

ditional liquidity at times of crises without the painstaking negotiations of quota increases or arrangements to borrow.
Current measures such as the General Arrangement to Borrow
can only be activated after getting the approval of the suppliers
of funds, with corresponding delays in making new funds available to the Fund and the countries in distress. The anti-cyclical
use of SDRs to manage financial cycles should be part of a
broader process aimed at enhancing their use as an appropriate
international currency for a globalized world.

But as is well known, a lender of last resort increases efficiency only if there is also an effective regulator to diminish
moral hazard. The WFA should provide the necessary regulatory framework within which the IMF can develop as a lender
of last resort. In many countries the WFA would simply certify
that domestic regulatory procedures are effective. In those
countries in which financial regulation is unsatisfactory and
which would therefore not have access to the IMF in a financial
crisis, the WFA would assist with regulatory reform. Many financial crises today derive from unbalanced foreign exchange
exposures of private financial and nonfinancial institutions.
The IMF lends only to sovereign borrowers. Sovereign borrowers use the foreign exchange acquired from the IMF to pursue their domestic lender of last resort activities. In these
circumstances not only will the WFA's surveillance and enforcement of regulatory standards be necessary to reduce moral
hazard and aid financial reconstruction, it will also be necessary
to give confidence to backers of the IMF operation.

The presence of the WFA permits the development of new
financial vehicles not subject to standard IMF conditionality.
Conditionality may be legitimate for drawings that a country
makes when it is experiencing balance of payments problems
originating from inappropriate macro policies, i.e. self-created
adverse fundamentals. But the usual forms of conditionality
are worse than useless when a country faces an externally
induced current or capital account crisis. WFA approval of
national regulatory structures could be deemed a form of pre-

conditionality, allowing a country threatened by financial volatility rapid access to the lender of last resort.[6] This would both increase confidence in the stability of a nation's financial system and act as an important "carrot" to induce the acceptance of WFA best practice regulation. However, when a country's domestic financial regulation and supervision are deemed inadequate, it would be obligated to enter into an agreement with the WFA specifying reforms it should undertake.

Recent experience suggests that lender of last resort interventions can be minimized or even avoided if the rescue team "bails-in" an afflicted country's creditors in the sense of forcing them not to call outstanding loans, instead of bailing them out. Coining another term, the United Nations has proposed debtor-creditor "standstills" at times of crisis. Such a package would include an initial freeze on an afflicted country's external obligations and capital account convertibility. It would then bring borrowers and lenders together to reschedule debt while providing financial assistance to support normal functioning of the economy. These operations would give players in the distressed country a better chance of surmounting their problems. If the crisis involves, as it often does, simultaneous international illiquidity and domestic bank insolvency, creditors would also be more likely to recover the value of their assets. The costs of adjustment would also be more equitably distributed. Again, this would probably make the cost of capital to borrowers slightly higher, and so it should. The extra cost is a measure of the now internalized risk.

To avoid moral hazard on the part of borrowers, it may be advisable to have standstills sanctioned by an agency such as the WFA. They could be combined with (probably modest) lender of last resort outlays to provide the liquidity needed by the economy to function during renegotiation of its debt. An alternative would be for the standstill to be declared unilaterally by the debtor country, but then submitted for approval within a specified period to an independent WFA panel, whose sanction would give it legitimacy. This would be the equivalent in international finance to safeguard provisions in the realm of trade.

To ensure that a standstill mechanism operates properly two rules are essential. First, there should be internationally agreed "collective action clauses" in international lending (as advocated by the G7 in late 1998). Their generalized introduction is crucial to avoid "free riding." Secondly, renegotiations should take place within a specified time limit, beyond which either the WFA or an independent panel would have the authority to determine the conditions of debt rescheduling. Repeated debt renegotiations have been one of the most troublesome features of the international financial landscape in recent decades and an underlying cause of prolonged periods of crisis or slow growth in some developing and transition economies.

After a crisis, countries often have a weighty overhang of "bad debt," typically nonperforming assets of the banking sector. Domestic refinancing via a bond issue to the nonbank private sector, an administratively enforced credit rollover, and price inflation are three ways to deal with the problem. The latter two would almost certainly require reimposition of tight controls on outward capital movements, for which the WFA would need to secure the cooperation of the international community.

Within all afflicted countries, income generation and employment problems are critical. The authorities can repress their peoples up to a point, but ultimately will have to offer them a degree of social and economic support. Such an effort goes diametrically against the emphasis in recent IMF rescue packages. As Cambridge economist Ajit Singh puts it, "To provide such assistance effectively and on an adequate scale will require not only considerable imagination but also a large expansion in government activity and often direct intervention in the market processes. Such emergency safety net programs may include wider subsidies, food for work schemes, and public works projects. How to pay for these measures within the limits of fiscal prudence, let alone within IMF fiscal austerity programs, will be a major issue of political economy for these countries."

Steps Not to Take

The most obvious "don't" is *not* to liberalize the capital accounts of affected countries further. If the single most apparent cause of crisis was a door three-quarters open, the last thing to do is open it fully. As already noted, many rich countries agree that deregulated external financial markets are desirable and should be extended to poor countries as rapidly as possible. This recommendation looks ill-timed at best. The experience of the past twenty years has demonstrated that complete liberalization is inefficient. Unmanaged financial markets are too prone to volatility and contagion to provide the stable financial framework necessary for high rates of growth and employment. Instead, a regulated international system, operating through a WFA will create the possibility of securing the benefits of capital mobility while diminishing the costs. Indeed, such management is necessary to prevent a swing back to widespread protectionism. Campaigns to rewrite IMF articles to require full capital market liberalization by all nations, and the OECD proposal to write full capital liberalization requirements into a multilateral agreement on investment, are without sound intellectual foundation, damaging to the development of an open world economy, and should be abandoned.

THE WFA'S ROLE IN MANAGING CRISES IN DEVELOPED ECONOMIES

The devastating impact of volatility and contagion on developing economies has tended to shift the focus away from the impact of the new international financial order on developed economies. But there is no reason for complacency. It is in the OECD economies that the slowdown in growth has been most evident in the liberalization era. Only the US has managed to grow in the 1990s at rates comparable to its performance in the 1960s, and this is due to the massive accumulation of foreign debt and growing financial fragility of the American consumer. Moreover the failure (and rescue) of LTCM is a reminder of the huge new risks international finance is introducing into national financial systems. That time, developed countries' banks were threatened.

The decline in economic performance in developed countries was characterized in chapter 4 as the outcome of increasing risk aversion in both private and public sectors. In the private sector increased financial volatility reduces the certainty of the flow of funds for corporate investment. In the public sector, elevating the goal of monetary stability above the objective of growth and employment has achieved neither.

The need is for both liquidity and stability, for a financial regime that supports enterprise and risk-taking, but within which risks (including market risks) are properly priced. This requires thorough regulatory overview of the relevant domain, i.e. of the integrated international financial marketplace. Only such an overview will provide the firm foundation upon which national lenders of last resort and national regulators can operate. They are otherwise flying with at best very foggy vision and with their arms tied behind their backs. A World Financial Authority would provide that firm regulatory foundation, clearer vision and strong arms.

GOVERNANCE

This formative picture of the WFA describes the tasks to be done to sustain an efficient liberal international economy. There remains the question of who should perform these tasks and to whom should they be responsible.

There is certainly no appetite today (especially in Washington) to create a new international bureaucracy. Fortunately the infrastructure for the WFA already exists in the form of BIS committees and the cooperative cross-border regulatory framework already developed within IOSCO and the IAIS. These institutions have the experience to do the job and enjoy the confidence of governments and of the financial community. The Financial Stability Forum, while it brings together all G7 and international institutions with an interest in regulatory matters, derives its current character from its BIS origins. This is simply a recognition of the BIS committees' success within their remit.

An alternative to developing BIS committees into a WFA would be to place the WFA function within the IMF. Given that the IMF is an international organization accountable in principle to its membership rather than a cozy central bankers' club, this has some attractions. Moreover the IMF already has statutory responsibility for surveillance of international economies and has the power and responsibility of an international lender. To locate the WFA function within the IMF would be to combine the international roles of a quasi-central bank and a quasi-regulator. In these circumstances the grant of regulatory preconditionality would be a natural extension of the IMF's lending responsibilities.

However, a number of arguments suggests that locating the WFA function within the IMF would be less successful than developing the BIS system. *First*, the BIS committees clearly have the expertise and experience to develop international regulations. It is a system that works. *Second*, it is increasingly recognized that a strong case exists for separating the roles of the regulator and the lender of last resort, even though they must collaborate in managing systemic risk. The task of dealing with normal risk over the entire financial services industry is quite different from dealing with a liquidity crisis generated by abnormal risk. *Third*, the IMF's expertise is in dealing with current fiscal and trade balances, not with the capital account. Confusion between the needs of an insolvent economy and an illiquid capital market was clearly an element in the IMF's mishandling of the Asian crisis. *Fourth*, an important part of the

WFA's role will be to develop and enforce regulatory standards in prosperous developed economies. This is familiar territory for BIS committees, but unfamiliar ground for the IMF. If the WFA function were located in the IMF there would be an understandable tendency to see regulatory problems as an issue relating to borrowing countries. They are not. They are as much a problem of the prosperous lenders as the poorer borrowers. *Fifth*, BIS committees command the confidence of the financial services industry and governments. In financial regulation that is a priceless resource.

There is however an important problem in extending the role of the BIS and its committees. Their success has been based on informality and consensus, and it will be difficult to extend that effective process to fulfill the WFA function. The G7 countries acknowledged as much in the communiqué establishing the FSF, in which they declared their intention of widening FSF membership to include developing economies. A powerful WFA will certainly attract more scrutiny.

The key problem will be to balance real accountability and political legitimacy with the successful informality of the BIS club. An effective regulator needs to be flexible, act quickly, and maintain a close relationship with the industry (though regulators will never be loved). This will be difficult to attain if the regulator is itself closely confined within a tight code of legal practice. It will also be difficult to maintain transparency and accountability while working with confidential information, offering guidance, and reacting decisively on knowledge gleaned in some of the industry's darker recesses. The solution must surely be to build on the achievements of the BIS committees, extend their authority and their remit, expand their role, and widen their membership. The club will undoubtedly become less club-like. But if the achievements of the past twenty years are anything to go by, operating procedures successful in the past will be adapted to the new, proactive WFA function. This is a major reason for building the WFA function on the secure foundations of the BIS and BIS committees.

THE WAY FORWARD

Most likely coordination has been taken to its limit in the functions of the Financial Stability Forum. In the next few years, probably spurred by another financial crisis, international financial regulation will enter the third phase of control. WFA functions will be performed by someone somewhere.

But it is important to record that developed countries need the WFA almost as much as developing countries. Of course financial shocks to developing countries are more severe, but the long-term impact of volatility and contagion on developed countries has been no less costly. Moreover, the rising scale of exposures in highly leveraged markets is jacking up systemic risk throughout international financial markets, developed and developing alike.

Efficient management of that risk will require in the first instance a clear analysis of the operation of financial markets and their relationship with the real economy. Too much of that relationship is obscured by irrelevant and erroneous theorizing. That is why the argument for the WFA outlined in this book has been grounded on a framework of analysis. Some may reject that framework, but in doing so they must clarify their own analytical position and confront the facts of the relationship between finance and economic performance.

The institutional framework of the WFA and the role it would perform in the international economy derive both from the analysis of this book and historical experience. History's experience has confirmed the need for regulation and a lender of last resort in domestic markets. The same sorts of measures are now required internationally if a broadly liberal world financial order is to survive.

NOTES

1. Ten currencies, because the Belgian and Luxembourg francs were already linked in a monetary union.
2. The EU has successfully developed supranational institutions for the conduct of

microeconomic policy, most notably in competition policy, the regulation of take-overs and mergers, and so on.

3. The term emerged in the nineteenth century to describe the monetary arrangements Britain imposed on many of its colonies. The local money had to be 100 percent backed by sterling, with its supply fluctuating in response to flows of sterling into or out of the colony.

4. Implicit in this approach is the question of whether national regulators should be combined to form a single regulatory authority for all financial services, now that the financial services industry is becoming "seamless" between the activities of banks, securities firms, insurance companies, and so on. This approach is being pursued in the UK, where all regulators are being amalgamated into a new universal Financial Services Authority. Whether such amalgamation is appropriate in other countries is an issue beyond the scope of this book.

5. The number exceeds 100 percent because the rush by banks to withdraw their lending was balanced in part by inflows, notably of foreign direct investment.

6. In April 1999 the IMF introduced Contingent Credit Lines "for countries with strong economic policies as a precautionary line of defense readily available against future balance of payments problems that might arise from international financial contagion." The CCL is "a preventative measure intended solely for members that are concerned with potential vulnerability to contagion, but are not facing a crisis at the time of commitment." The CCL is heavily buttressed by "criteria for access," a significant step toward "pre-conditionality."

Further Reading

There are many additional sources on the broad themes pursued in this book. In this section we suggest several lines of exploration.

WEB SITES

A great deal of material on international finance is available on the following web sites from international and national agencies:

Bank for International Settlements	www.bis.org
International Monetary Fund	www.imf.org/external/index.htm
Bank of England	www.bankofengland.co.uk
UK Financial Services Authority	www.fsa.gov.uk
UK Treasury	www.hm-treasury.gov.uk
US Federal Reserve	www.federalreserve.gov
US Securities and Exchange Commission	www.sec.gov
US Treasury Department	www.ustreas.gov

Professor Nouriel Roubini of New York University maintains a comprehensive bibliography at

www.stern.nyu.edu/~nroubini/asia/AsiaHomepage.htm#intro

Research papers supporting much of the analysis in this book are available on the site maintained by the Center for Economic Policy Analysis (or CEPA), New School:

www.newschool.edu/cepa

FINANCIAL THEORY AND EXCHANGE RATES

The classic text is John Maynard Keynes, *The General Theory of Employment, Interest, and Money* (London, Macmillan, 1936). The beauty contest and own-rates of interest are discussed in Chapters 12 and 17 respectively. On the latter topic, see also Nicholas Kaldor, "Speculation and Economic Stability" and "Keynes' Theory of Own Rates of Interest," in his *Collected Economic Essays*, Vol. 2 (London, Duckworth, 1960). Hyman Minsky's particular interpretation of Keynes is accessible in his book, *John Maynard Keynes* (New York, Columbia University Press, 1975). Interest rate parity relationships were first presented by Keynes in *A Tract on Monetary Reform* (London, Macmillan, 1923).

A clear, historically oriented textbook on open economy macroeconomics (including extensive discussion of the exchange rate) is John Williamson and Chris Milner, *The World Economy* (New York, New York University Press, 1991). More analysis of the exchange rate along the lines of Chapter 3 appears in Lance Taylor, "Neither the Portfolio Balance nor the Mundell-Fleming Model Can Determine the Exchange Rate— Each Has One Fewer Independent Equation Than People Usually Think," available on the CEPA web site mentioned above.

FINANCIAL MARKETS

There are two fascinating reviews by Charles P. Kindleberger, *A Financial History of Western Europe* (New York, Oxford University Press, 1993) and *Manias, Panics, and Crashes* (New York, John Wiley and Sons, 1996). A complementary text focusing on the 25 years after World War II in the United States is Fred L. Block, *The Origins of International Economic Disorder* (Berkeley, University of California Press, 1977). The rise and decline of the "Golden Age" is chronicled in Stephen Marglin and Juliet Schor, *The Golden Age of Capitalism: Reinterpreting the Postwar Experience* (Oxford, Clarendon Press, 1991).

Several monographs on international financial issues have recently appeared. The one by John Eatwell, *International Financial Liberalisation: The Impact on World Development*

(New York, Office of Development Studies Discussion Paper Series, no. 12., United Nations Development Programme, 1996) gives more detail on material covered in chapters 2 and 4. See also Robert A. Blecker, *Taming Global Finance* (Washington DC, Economic Policy Institute, 1999), Barry Eichengreen, *Toward a New International Economic Architecture: A Practical Post-Asia Agenda* (Washington, DC, Institute for International Economics, 1998), Stephany Griffith-Jones, *Global Capital Flows: Should They be Regulated?* (London, Macmillan, 1998), and Eric Helleiner, *States and the Reemergence of Global Finance: From Bretton Woods to the 1990s*, (Ithaca, NY, Cornell University Press, 1994). The discussion of the US economy in chapter 4 draws on Blecker, "International Capital Mobility, Macroeconomic Imbalances, and the Risk of Global Contraction," available on the CEPA web site.

For political background on the liberalization experience, see John Gray, *False Dawn: The Delusions of Global Capitalism* (New York, The New Press, 1998). The roles played by the IMF and World Bank in developing countries are reviewed by Ute Pieper and Lance Taylor, "The Revival of the Liberal Creed: The IMF, the World Bank, and Inequality in a Globalized Economy" in Dean Baker, Gerald Epstein, and Robert Pollin (eds.) *Globalization and Progressive Economic Policy: What Are the Real Constraints and Options?* (New York, Cambridge University Press, 1998).

The literature on crises in developing economies is by now enormous. Reference material is available on the web sites maintained by Nouriel Roubini and CEPA mentioned above. See also the "Special Issue on the Asian Crisis," *Cambridge Journal of Economics*, vol. 22, no. 6 (November 1998). The Frenkel-Neftci cycle outlined in chapter 5 is based on Roberto Frenkel "Mercado Financiero, Expectativas Cambiales, y Movimientos de Capital," *El Trimestre Economica*, vol. 50, pp. 2041–2076 (1983) and Salih N. Neftci, "FX Short Positions, Balance Sheets, and Financial Turbulence: An Interpretation of the Asian Financial Crisis," available on the CEPA web site.

Finally, two articles in *Scientific American* comprise a useful primer on the analysis of derivatives (pre- and post-LTCM, respectively): Gary Stix, "A Calculus of Risk," vol. 278, no. 5 (May 1998) and Benoit B. Mandelbrot, "A Multifractal Walk Down Wall Street," vol. 280, no. 2 (February 1999).

REGULATION

The theory of regulation is a branch of the analysis of externalities, i.e. goods or services that are used (perhaps unwillingly) by firms or consumers and for which no payment is made. A good general introduction to externalities is the second edition of William Baumol's *Welfare Economics and the Theory of the State* (Cambridge MA, Harvard University Press, 1967). See also the essay by Peter Bohm, "External Economies," in *The New Palgrave, A Dictionary of Economics*, edited by John Eatwell, Murray Milgate, and Peter Newman (London, Macmillan, 1987), and *Global Public Goods*, edited by Inge Kaul, Isabelle Grunberg and Marc Stern (New York, Oxford University Press, 1999).

On financial externalities a good introduction is provided by the essay by Charles Wyplosz, "International Financial Instability" in *Global Public Goods*. See also *The Economic Rationale for Financial Regulation* by David Llewellyn (London, Financial Services Authority, Occasional Paper Series, number 1, 1999).

For an introduction to what is happening in the fast-moving world of international financial regulation the BIS web site is the best source. The IMF has published a good guide to international regulation, prepared by David Folkerts-Landau and Carl-Johan Londgren, entitled *Toward a Framework for Financial Stability* (Washington DC, IMF, 1998). Recent debates on the role of regulators are surveyed in *Regulatory and Supervisory Challenges in the New Era of Global Finance*, edited by Jan Joost Teunissen, (The Hague, Forum on Debt and Development, 1998).

On the lender of last resort the classic reference is *Lombard Street*, by Walter Bagehot (first published in 1873). For a modern discussion see Thomas Humphrey, "Lender of Last Resort" in *The New Palgrave Dictionary of Money and Finance*, edited by Peter Newman, Murray Milgate and John Eatwell, (London, Macmillan, 1992).

Abbreviations

BIS	Bank for International Settlements
ECB	European Central Bank
EMS	European Monetary System
ERM	Exchange rate mechanism (of the European Monetary System)
EU	European Union
FIRE	Finance, insurance and real estate
FDI	Foreign direct investment
FN	Frenkel-Neftci (cycle)
FSF	Financial Stability Forum
G7	Group of Seven
G10	Group of Ten
GAB	General Arrangements to Borrow
GDP	Gross domestic product
IMF	International Monetary Fund
IOSCO	International Organization of Securities Commissions
IAIS	International Association of Insurance Supervisors
LTCM	Long Term Capital Management
LIBOR	London inter-bank offer rate
NAFTA	North American Free Trade Agreement
NGO	Non-governmental organization
OECD	Organization for Economic Cooperation and Development
OPEC	Organization of Petroleum Exporting Countries
OTC	Over-the-counter
PPP	Purchasing-power parity
QRs	Quantitative restrictions
ROW	Rest of the world
S&L	Savings and Loan
SDRs	Special drawing rights
SPV	Special-purpose vehicle

TRS	Total return swaps
UIP	Uncovered interest-rate parity
VaR	Value at risk
WFA	World Financial Authority
WTO	World Trade Organization

Index